Chelsea School Research Centre Edition
Volume 3

Gender, Sport and Leisure

Chelsea School Research Centre Edition
Volume 3

Alan Tomlinson (ed.)

Gender, Sport and Leisure

Continuities and Challenges

Meyer & Meyer Verlag

First published in 1995 by
CSRC
Chelsea School Research Centre
Chelsea School of Physical Education,
Sports Science, Dance and Leisure
University of Brighton
CSRC Topic Report 4
Gender, Sport and Leisure: Continuities and Challenges

British Library Cataloguing in Publication Data
A catalogue record for this book is available from the British Library

Gender, Sport and Leisure :
Continuities and Challenges / Alan Tomlinson (ed.).
2nd Ed. – Oxford : Meyer & Meyer (UK) Ltd., 2006
(Chelsea School Research Centre Edition ; Vol. 3)
ISBN-10: 1-84126-062-2
ISBN13: 978-1-84126-062-4

© 1997 by Meyer & Meyer Sport (UK) Ltd.
2nd Edition 2006
Aachen, Adelaide, Auckland, Budapest, Graz, Johannesburg,
New York, Olten (CH), Oxford, Singapore, Toronto
Member of the World
Sportpublishers' Association (WSPA)
Typesetting: Myrene L. McFee
Printed and bound in Germany by
Digitaldruck AixPress GmbH, Aachen
ISBN-10: 1-84126-062-2
ISBN13: 978-1-84126-062-4
e-mail: verlag@m-m-sports.com
www.m-m-sports.com

Preface

This collection of articles originated in a day-long symposium held in the Chelsea School Research Centre (CSRC) in June 1993, when six of the contributors to the volume (from England, Australia and Germany) made presentations on their work. The day was planned to complement the interests of CSRC/University of Brighton researchers, seven of whom number among the contributors to the collection.

Two further research seminars held in 1993–94 provided the opportunity to include contributions by other scholars from Australia and Canada. The research presented here, from ten women and eight men, thus reflects widespread international concern with the persisting theme of gender inequities in sport and leisure.

The CSRC symposium and this publication were supported by funds from the University of Brighton's PCFC research initiative, 1992–93, and from HEFCE research income in succeeding years.

Professor Alan Tomlinson
Chelsea School Research Centre (CSRC)
Winter 1994/1995

I am pleased to be able to write an extension to the above, two years on from the publication of this volume. The collection has been consistently in demand, and its re-issue is the second publication in the CSRC Editions launched by Meyer & Meyer in partnership with the Chelsea School Research Centre, The University of Brighton.

Professor Alan Tomlinson
CSRC
January 1997

Contents

INTRODUCTION

Alan Tomlinson* with Sue Mason-Cox
Chelsea School Research Centre
University of Brighton, UK

There has been a welcome expansion of gender-informed and gender-aware work and research on women's relatively low levels of participation in sport, and on the influences which affect these participation levels. There have also been some important interventionist initiatives geared towards removing the barriers to women's increased involvement. Taken together, this theoretical and practical consciousness of the importance of understanding and questioning gender relations in sport and leisure cultures suggests an increasingly raised profile for sportswomen and female participants in sport. But on-the-ground studies might well identify a mismatch between the continuities evident in empirical evidence on persisting gender inequality in sport and leisure practices, and the rise in critical awareness which represents a challenge to the established order of sport and leisure cultures.

So although some commentators might argue that we know enough about women in sport and the circumstances of their involvement, it is important to continue to marshal bodies of evidence on the theme, and to ensure that change and continuities in the gender profile of sport are identified. We have, of course, the general trend-data from national surveys. But it is likely too that many modestly scaled and local studies do not get disseminated widely, and that basic, straightforward but revealing information remains unintegrated into the current corpus of knowledge. In this chapter therefore, data-bases generated by research projects conducted at the University of Brighton's Chelsea School Research Centre are reviewed after a discussion of some national data from Great Britain and the USA and prior to a discussion of fundamental conceptual and theoretical issues, which itself precedes an overview of the pieces contained in this volume.

Sport and leisure practices for women: the evidence

Historical analyses of the role of leisure in women's lives in advanced Western societies have consistently argued that leisure cannot be compartmentalised as separate to and distinct from work. Both domains intersect in women's lives in complexly variant ways. In the majority of cases, these ways differ from the more familiar male-oriented dichotomous work-leisure relationship on which past analyses have been predominantly based (Deem, 1986; Henderson *et al.*, 1989; Green *et al.*, 1990). As these authors argue, such an analysis consistently excludes women's work in the home as well as forms of leisure inextricably tied up with women's work.

Leisure for women, as Deem notes, "frequently has to be slotted into spaces and locations determined by the leisure, work, needs and demands made by others (partners, dependent relatives or children)" (1986: p. 6). Leisure for women is often indistinguishable from work (e.g. child care) or simultaneous with it (e.g. ironing and watching television). Such outcomes differ markedly from the majority of men's leisure experiences. But the male idea and experience of leisure has been dominant.

Definitions of leisure are continually being shaped through ideologies of femininity and masculinity, and the appropriateness and respectability of the different gender roles and behaviours (Green *et al.*, 1990: p. 37). Additional influences on the social definitions of leisure for many women are class and race factors which impact variably on those concerned. Nevertheless, the resultant outcomes of lack of acceptance, alienation and marginalisation in sports and leisure experiences remain the same for most women.

The health and fitness boom of the early 1980s was followed by calls for policy changes in the provision of sports and leisure facilities, management and services (Deem, 1986; Wimbush and Talbot, 1988; Green *et al.*, 1990). The aim was to encourage a greater participation rate of women in physical activity. To ascertain whether such changes have been achieved, regular reviews of national and regional leisure participation surveys need to be conducted. Such reviews can demonstrate the types of changes that have taken place and provide a basis for a consideration of the benefits these have generated for the population at large and, in particular, for women.

The following review of a number of surveys in the South of England has been undertaken with the aim of informing such discussion. However, before that review, a brief overview of trends and patterns of women's sport and leisure (including the constraints and barriers to women's participation during recent years) is useful, for these factors remain crucial in any analysis of provision for women, and of women's participation in sport and leisure.

In studies carried out during the early 1980s (Deem, 1986; Talbot, 1988; and Green *et al.*, 1990) it was shown that fewer women participated in sport and active leisure pursuits than men. Exacerbating this situation was the narrower range of activities women had to choose from. The emergent picture at this time was of home-based, domestic leisure for women, especially for those of the lower socio-economic groups.

These early studies found that a major constraining factor consistently impeding the participation of women in sports and leisure was male or patriarchal control and influence. Women's leisure was largely determined by men through all spheres of the social system. Regulation and policy practices, male disapproval of women's participation, and the control by men of space and location have all restricted women's sporting and leisure activities. For example, men's aggressive actions in hedging-out women spatially during active participation in lane-swimming, and the regular sidelining of women at team sports such as football, basketball and hockey, are indicative of the persistence of male dominance in sport and leisure cultures.

These studies also found that women were consistently excluded from a variety of male domains such as clubs and pubs, and have suffered indirect exclusion through the lack of provision of child care facilities at venues. The traditional expectation that women not only service the home but also their partner's and children's sporting participation, has frequently constrained women's own activities. In these ways, as Deem noted, the major barrier to women's sporting participation, and one which is often overlooked, is the "stranglehold which men have over sport (its image, its management and participation)" (1986: p. 75). Male control thus becomes a normal feature of everyday life (Green *et al.*, 1990).

Media images regularly depicted what were appropriate and respectable gender roles and behaviours. Deem (1986) argues that these conform to conventional patriarchal ideologies which determine what a woman should or should not do, and they certainly depict how a woman 'should' look according to "a male eye" (Mason-Cox and Fullager, ud: p. 23). Such images only strengthen and reproduce conventional male attitudes which convey unflattering messages concerning, for example, the development of muscles in women. At the same time, there has been a prevalent display of media images upholding the values of 'real' sport. These values reinforce the traditional male sporting norms of speed, strength and power while inferiorising and trivialising women's sporting achievements (Mason-Cox, 1992).

Nonetheless, as Green *et al.* (1990: p. 138) point out, male control over women's behaviour, rather than being control by coercion, relies on norms of respectability and appropriateness, and can be regarded as control by 'consent'. However, these authors also stress that there is a range of other more coercive methods for men to use in the control of 'their' women if necessary: these can be emotional, financial or physical.

A further factor found to have frequently restricted women's participation in physical activity was the difficulties many women experienced with transport. Women have generally had less money and fewer driver's licences than men (Deem, 1986). They therefore have had less access to private vehicles. In addition, public transport has regularly been cited as a problem: inappropriate or difficult to use with small children; irregular, particularly out of peak travel time, and at night; or inconvenient or unsuitable for access from home to sporting/ leisure facilities (Deem, 1986; Wimbush and Talbot, 1988; Green *et al.*, 1990).

Women often depended on the availability of friends for transport of themselves and their children. Friendships were also found to enhance women's confidence and motivation to participate in sports and leisure activities (Deem, 1986; Green *et al.*, 1990). More importantly, however, the companionship of these friends alleviated many women's fears of travelling alone to facilities especially at night. However, contrary to the belief that these women actually participated themselves in active physical activities, these earlier studies found that instead, many of these women attended these centres to accompany their participating children. Women who did participate generally did so in "the newer and non-competitive forms of activities — aerobics, yoga, jogging" (Deem, 1986: p. 66). However, the marked inequalities in the choices and opportunities offered for women in sports and leisure activities when compared to those available for men (Deem, 1986; Green *et al.*, 1990), may also provide some explanation for women's lower level and different intensity of participation.

Constraining factors were less prevalent among women in employment. These women were able to benefit from the social and economic advantages which employment ensures. They were found to be more confident in themselves and better able to find the time and space for themselves to participate in sports and active leisure pursuits (Deem, 1986: p. 36).

So, has women's sporting and active leisure participation changed in more recent years? Are policy practices and facilities now better able to incorporate the needs and demands of women, so enabling their greater participation levels? Have women at the end of the 1980s and in the early 1990s had more play and less work than in the early 1980s?

On the national level, the General Household Survey (GHS) and the Henley Centre for Forecasting have regularly monitored trends. The GHS trend data indicate very significant rises in the involvement of women in physical activity, though when closely scrutinised such figures show what a low base women's participation started at, and that the activities in which women have participated more are individual-based and far from time-intensive (Philips and Tomlinson, 1992). Only 3% of women were reported as participating in Keep-fit/yoga in 1977, and 2% in 1980. This had risen to 5% by 1983 (HMSO, 1986). By 1987 Keep-fit/yoga attracted 12% of women (HMSO, 1991), though this comprised 18% of 'professional' women and a mere 4% of 'unskilled manual' women. By 1990 the percentage of women participating in Keep-fit/aerobics in the GHS survey was 16% (Sports Council and Women's Sports Foundation, 1992). After walking, this was the most popular women's sports activity in Great Britain in 1990.

Caution must be taken in reading dramatic changes into these trend data, for the GHS introduced methodological changes in 1987, moving away from "an open-ended question about leisure to a prompt list of specific activities of interest" (HMSO, 1991: p. 1). This resulted in "the mean number of sports activities in the four weeks before interview mentioned by informants" rising from "0.82 in 1986 to 1.35 in 1987", and "particularly large increases in the proportions reporting … Keep fit and yoga (3% to 9%)" (*ibid.*). But whatever the scale of the rise in participation, type of activity or mode and intensity of involvement certainly continued to be gender-specific, as the Henley Centre's *Leisure Futures* (Henley Centre, 1993) has reported. Women's frequency of participation — across individual sports, team sports, sports centre visits, spectating, and swimming — was consistently lower than that of their male counterparts.

The Henley Centre's Time Use Survey of leisure (carried out by Public Attitude Surveys Ltd.) is based upon a regular quarterly sample (increased to 1,000 each quarter in 1994: therefore, an annual sample of 4,000 using "interlocking quotas for age, sex and class ... within each region"). The Henley Centre data for July 1993 to June 1994 identified 20% of the total sample as exercising at home at least once a week in Winter and Spring; and 10% participating in aerobics/Keep-fit/yoga away from home. Age differences were very noticeable for away-from-home fitness activity, so that the 10% of the total sample was seen as a misleading average, comprising only 2% of 60+s, 6% of those aged 45–59, and 7% of those aged 35–44, but 19% of 25–34 year-olds and 18% of those aged 16–24. Of those participating in aerobics, yoga and Keep-fit, men's average frequency of participation was close to a third higher than women's — 28.6 times, as opposed to 21.7 times per quarter; almost five times a fortnight for men as opposed to three and a half times per fortnight for women (Henley Centre, 1994: Tables 2.3, 2.5 and 2.8).

In the United States, similar patterns were evident. "Exercising with Equipment" peaked at the end of the early 1990s for men and for women, but fell off more strikingly for men:

"In millions of participants, participating more than once. Exercising with Equipment":

	Males	Females
1989	16.5	15.0
1990	18.6	16.7
1991	19.2	20.0
1992	19.1	20.3
1993	16.9	18.0

Source: Sports Market Place 1994 Update, July 1994: p. 29, reporting National Sporting Goods Association data published by Sportsguide Inc.

Of those 34.9 million USA citizens staying with the activity after the peak, most were from the adult age groups: 1.2% were 7–11; 8.7% 12–17; 45% 18–34; 32.4% 35–54; and 12.7% 55+ (*ibid.*, p. 30).

Patterns of participation in 'Aerobic Exercising' showed dramatic differences between men and women:

"In millions of participants, participating more than once. Aerobic Exercising":

	Males	Females
1989	4.2	20.9
1990	3.7	19.6
1991	4.4	21.5
1992	5.1	22.8
1993	3.5	21.4

Source: Sports Market Place 1994 Update, July 1994: p. 29, reporting National Sporting Goods Association data published by Sportsguide Inc.

For aerobic exercising, as with exercising with equipment, the early adult years were dominant, with almost half of the participants being aged 18–34 and close to a third being in the age group 35–54 (*ibid.*, p. 30). But despite some tail-off in total participation numbers, in 1993 6 times as many USA women as men continued to be active in aerobics. It is the quintessential growth activity for women — led by the combined motivations of health and fashion; 'do-able' in established slots of time and in places of convenience, including the home; unthreatening to male schedules, family-rearing demands and the traditional obligations of the wife and mother. Whatever its welcome progressive impact, the body boom as manifest in the rise and slight fall of aerobics must also be understood in terms of its inherent conservatism vis-à-vis established patterns of leisure participation, and traditional values of leisure cultures.

Local studies of particular activities, facilities and sites have demonstrated the persistence of patterns of women's participation, rooted in constraints rather than unbounded opportunity. In a study of pool use in East Hampshire, an area of the South of England (Lawrence, Magness and Standeven, 1992), 59% of users were also women. Users of two leisure centres in the South of England (Angel and Larkfield) were predominantly female (59.3%) (Lawrence and Standeven, 1991).

However, only 33.3% of these users stated that their main reason for coming to the centres was to take part in a sports activity themselves. The proportion bringing *children* to the centres or to train stood at 28.7% of the attendance figures. When comparing these findings with those of earlier studies, it appears therefore that overall attendance of sports and leisure centres has certainly increased for women and often outstrips men's. However, a big question mark remains over whether actual participation levels for women in physical activities have correspondingly increased. Factors impinging on this continue to be women's roles in servicing the needs of others, in particular by accompanying their children to participate rather than to participate themselves. The social dimension of attendance, too, is a major reason behind women's attendance at these centres, but the specific attraction of participation is less well-established.

The reasons and motives behind people's attendance and participation in sports and leisure activities vary according to gender. Examining data in East Hampshire on why respondents attend swimming centres, the great majority of women (94.7%) stated that they did so to escape home or family pressures or to take the children (74.4%). This contrasts with the majority of men (64.3%), although fewer in number, who stated that they attend to escape work pressures. Nevertheless, an almost equal proportion of women and men overall (52.6% and 47.4%) stated they attend because of the enjoyment factor. [Respondents were asked to specify a main reason and a 'second reason'. The data reported here are percentages derived from both choices of the respondents.]

Reflecting on more qualitative data gathered from group interviews in relation to the use of a 'Leisure Card' in the Brighton area, it was widely recognised by everyone in the group, irrespective of their circumstances, that leisure was both essential and therapeutic (Magness, 1990: p. 11), but particularly so for women:

> ... the importance of leisure seemed to be especially appreciated by women with young children, particularly those who were categorised as disadvantaged in some way. It gave them an opportunity to escape from the worries and concerns of everyday life.

Unlike the women, disadvantaged men, particularly those unemployed, did not share these sentiments. These men had a more blurred distinction between leisure and duty and, as a result, this left them less motivated to become more active in leisure (Magness, 1990).

A major barrier hindering women, particularly elderly women, from participating in activities outside the home, as a survey on Brighton's leisure facilities highlighted, is 'fear of the dark'. As Lawrence and Tomlinson noted, many people do not take advantage of Brighton's leisure facilities due to "fear of being in Brighton after dark" (Lawrence and Tomlinson, 1992: p. 29). Fear of the dark was regarded as a hindrance by 55% of respondents (major hindrance, 36%; minor hindrance, 19%). The survey found that the two particular sub-groups within the sample where 'fear of the dark' was a major hindrance were women and those people aged 65 and over.

Other local studies have identified this as a problem. Young females in the Stoke area commented, in the late 1980s, that hanging around town with boys "could be wrongly construed by men who imagined them to be prostitutes. The dangers for young women of hanging-around in public spaces was very apparent to female students and trainees" (Henson, 1994).

Walking was by far the most popular 'sport and exercise' activity participated in weekly (61% of all respondents), followed by visiting a sports centre, exercise or health facility, swimming indoors and dancing (Tomlinson and Parker, 1992: p. 30). However, this order of popularity was different if based on those who *never* did the activity: exercise or health facilities had the largest proportion (68%) of non-attenders. "People exercise/work out either regularly (addictively perhaps) or not at all" (Tomlinson and Parker, 1992). This obviously favours potential participants with the most control over time schedules and other commitments. Such patterns must be of concern to policy makers and providers, both from the point of exercise having an addictive effect, and in terms of the large proportion of the population which continues *not* to exercise regularly or at all, for many of the reasons already discussed in this section.

The number of respondents *not* engaging in any active sporting or leisure participation (Tomlinson and Parker, 1992), therefore, strikingly contrasts with the number that *did* participate. Although 41% of 18–34 year olds participated in active sports or leisure activities, 38% *never* attended leisure centres. Of the 35–54 age group 54% *never* attended, and 79% of the 55–69 age group *never* attended. These figures appear to reflect the increasingly sedentary life-style characteristic of modern society — i.e. home-based techno-logically-centred leisure activities such as television, video games/movies etc., as well as gardening. The major activities outside the home i.e. walking and visiting the pub are often carried out within the vicinity of the home. These influences are not conducive to great changes in the out-of-house participation patterns of women.

Nearly 12% of women surveyed in the East Hampshire study responded that 'lack of time' was a major reason for not attending and participating at swimming centres. And one in four women responded that transport was a problem. Clearly, all the promotion of health and exercise in the world, and enhanced facility provision, are of little use unless a transport infrastructure guarantees access.

The gender breakdown for transport use in East Hampshire is revealing, with 75.3% of all male respondents stating they had their own car, or one available for use, compared to 65% of all female respondents. Furthermore, 35% of all females stated they had no access to a car or to the availability of a car compared to only 24.7% of males. More women (73.7% of the sample) attended facilities as car passengers than men (26.3% of the sample). More women also travelled to the centres by foot or by bus than men.

It can be said — with some caution — that, for women, the accessibility of private car transport has increased since the early 1980s with in all likelihood a greater percentage driving themselves to centres. Nonetheless, private cars still remain less available for women in comparison to men. In addition, many women seek out friends to travel with and participate alongside at these centres. The social aspect thus reflects women's need for social networks both for their personal safety in alleviating fears as well as for purely social reasons, as found in the earlier studies.

In the East Hampshire survey, pool facilities such as adult and child learning, life-saving and survival swimming, family changing facilities, mother-toddler swim sessions and crèche facilities were recognised as important and essential by both sexes, but women saw these as more important in terms of community provision generally.

In drawing conclusions from the above review, there is evidence of sports and leisure facilities having generally improved over the past decade, with a corresponding increase in overall attendance/participation levels. However, it would be deemed dubious at best to equate this with increased levels of women's leisure participation, for the increased level of *attendance* by women at these venues seems to reflect more attenders *per se* as opposed to actual participants in active physical activities.

Attendance, especially for women still bound by a servicing and caring role in the family, is still far from synonymous with participation.

The major constraining influences upon women's participation were found to reflect those of earlier studies — marital status, employment, age, and class continue to influence participation. Domestic responsibilities, and difficulties with transport in conjunction with fears relating to being alone and out after dark, remain the most restrictive influences on women's participation in sports and leisure activities.

Single women in employment are not so constrained, and participated on a more regular basis. Being single, they not only have fewer domestic responsibilities, but in addition they have the confidence to assert their right to leisure. In doing so, single women have developed skills in negotiating for their own space, time and locale for leisure, have gained a sense of freedom from restrictive traditional mores, and are thus participating more in active sports and leisure activities. Education and employment have consolidated this sense of autonomy for these women, enhancing their social and economic advantages. But although there is evidence of an increase in the number of women attending centres — and for some this is clearly a positive and self-enhancing opportunity — it would be fallacious to conclude that, overall, women in the 1990s have more play and less work than their counterparts in earlier years.

Perceptions of the benefits of recreation are interesting to consider in terms of gender differences. An interview survey in the summer of 1993 with 250 respondents at four locations on the East Sussex Heritage Coast revealed marked differences between men's and women's responses. The outstanding feature which was 'liked best' was the Heritage Coast's 'scenery/ views/beauty', but 'peace and quiet' was particularly valued by women, half as many again women noting this in comparison with men. Proportionately more women also liked the 'unspoilt character' of the area (Clarke, Lawrence, Parker and Tomlinson, 1993/ 94). When asked to make general comments about the Heritage Coast area, 50% of the women respondents (as opposed to 29% of the men) reiterated a liking for the beauty of the area. Despite such appreciation of the area, though, women were more likely than men to say that they had no regular pattern of usage, and men were more likely than women to be visitors once a week.

Outdoor recreation might seem a long way from swimming in local facilities, but the dynamics and the meaning of participation are comparable: for women, regular out-of-home recreation cannot be so readily and frequently assumed, and the particular focus and value of the activity for women might be something that is not at first sight apparent. In the Heritage Coast survey it is the contemplative, aesthetic mode of involvement that is of more appeal for many women than for the males using the region. Men listed 'openness' and 'natural character' and 'opportunity for walks' more than did women, but did not prioritise the contemplative nearly so much.

Theorising gendered sports and leisure practices

Valuable as trend data and particular case-studies are, they need to be contextualised and theorised. Challenges to gender domination and women's oppression can be assured of no easy success, for the rootedness of male domination continues to be strong. Delegates were reminded of this at an event at the Warwick Centre for the Study of Sport and Society in September 1994, when four renowned researchers made presentations on the theme of 'Women in Sport'.

Jennifer Hargreaves argued that any claims to historical truth carry with them a large degree of uncertainty. This premise was linked to the charge that sports history discourse has been dominated by males, and that male authors continue to be in the majority, all too often working on sources which in themselves contain male biases and male emphases. Concentrating on women's sports between the First and the Second World War, Hargreaves portrayed a more widespread women's sports culture than many histories acknowledge; and, "before the advent of television and the rupturing of community culture", women were public performers in activities like galas and water cabarets. It seemed too that men and women mixed together in some sporting spheres, and women stars of sports shows could become well-known local celebrities. But old prejudices persisted and there were vociferous opponents of women's involvement in athletics and sports. The theory of constitutional overstrain still held sway in influential circles, with women being barred from the 800 metres event after the 1928 Olympics, on the basis of pseudo-scientific biological explanations. Whilst such prejudices persisted, initiatives such as the Women's League of Health and Beauty provided positive images of female physicality, and, Hargreaves added, helped place women on the sports policy agenda. Two particularly resonant examples, understood together, indicated the way in which cultural initiatives with a challenging potential can be constrained and inflected in ideological directions. The persistence of the ideology of constitutional overstrain confined challenging initiatives, such as the Women's League of Health and Beauty, to a culture of restraint rooted in the health rationale.

Eric Dunning employed the Eliasian figurational or process-sociological framework in raising questions about masculinity in sport and the consequences of the entry of women into sport. Dunning argued that figurational sociology, with its central emphasis on understanding the nature of the unwinding of the civilising process, provides a reality-oriented anti-ideological emphasis in sociological analysis. Responding to critics of the figurational approach — some of whom were described as "acolytes of Raymond Williams and Gramsci" — he called for theory-guided empirical (and as appropriate, comparative) research into issues. In exploring the connections between the civilising process and aspects of patriarchy, Dunning argued, some important aspects of the sport/gender relationship could be illuminated. These included the nature of male identities; the entry of women into the sporting sphere; and the development of socially acceptable forms of behaviour in sport. An idea of Elias' on how the "internalization of the group charisma of males" might affect relationships between men and women was provocatively outlined.

Sheila Scraton reported on a comparative research project focusing upon the experiences of sport in the life of women in four European countries — the UK, Germany, Norway and Spain. Reminding us that a lot is now known about the barriers to female participation, Scraton explained that the four-country project is exploring the ways in which some women integrate sport into their lives, through body image, concepts of the self and social relationships. What, the project was framed to ask, are the positive things about sport for those women who have overcome the barriers? The research was also planned to be qualitative, feminist, comparative and collective. Sixty open-ended in-depth (up to two-hour long) interviews have been conducted in each of the four countries.

Anne Flintoff rounded off the Warwick day with a version of her contribution to this volume.

In the final plenary session Celia Brackenridge picked up on Eric Dunning's reference to "the internalization of the group charisma of males", an idea developed in Elias' work on established and outsiders, and lively discussion ensued on how group values are generated, expressed and legitimated. Large numbers of females accept, Eric Dunning noted, the "superiority of males" in sport. Understanding the intricacies and subtleties of this social process calls for more than a model of crude power and accompanying oppression, he implied. Much of the discussion in this final session revolved around the issue of feminist epistemology. For Lincoln Allison (Director of the Centre and editor of *The*

Changing Politics of Sport, London: Manchester University Press, 1993) the idea of an epistemological basis to feminist study was worrying, carrying with it what he called a "tinge of ideology" and an element of "looking for sin". He argued the need for the development of a feminist case for liberal institutions. What would, he asked, constitute a fairer, freer and less oppressive structure of sport in forms conducive to feminist goals? Feminists were also challenged to provide or be alert to counter-evidence to their assumptions about the patriarchal basis of social institutions. Celia Brackenridge responded to such a challenge by asking why male researchers are not more involved in attempts to change things for the better, rather than urging feminists to seek out evidence of their own incorrectness.

The presentations at this event, and the full discussion and response to the presentations, were reminders of how much work remains to be done on both the analysis of the male-dominated institutions of sport from the perspective of women's experience, and the more projective task of shaping a less patriarchal sports culture for the future.

Although the presenters at the Warwick event recognised the pioneering thinking of Paul Willis (Willis, 1974 and 1982), his framework for the analysis of ideological processes at work in cultural forms or social institutions such as sport could have been more fully applied. For Willis, ideology (conceived as sets of values with distorting effects) can be countered, can be "seen through" in a process of cultural penetration, so that alternatives can be constructed. But ideology does not simply disappear in the wake of a challenge — the forces of the ideological/dominant can adapt or regroup (in the interests of, say, capitalism or patriarchy or, in terms of, say, a female-targeted fitness industry, both). The reassertion of the ideological can, in Willis' terms, be understood as the "situated rebirth of ideology". Applied to Jennifer Hargreaves' historical account of women's experience of sport in the 1920s and the 1930s, Willis' framework has a powerful explanatory dimension. Women achieved progressive strides in stating the case for their involvement in sport and physical activity, but a significant ideological continuity (pseudo-science confining them to a restrictive range of allegedly health-inducing physical activity) tempered the impact of the culturally challenging "seeing-through" .

The Willis framework is employed in comparable ways in this collection by Tomlinson, and by McFee and Smith. Many of the contributions in this volume could be theorised in similar ways. That this can be claimed in the middle of the 1990s is testimony to both the theoretical acumen and sophistication of Willis' pioneering framework, and to the need for continued empirically-grounded work on the gender dynamics affecting sports and leisure institutions and cultures. Seminal integrating works such as that of Jennifer Hargreaves (Hargreaves, 1994) or adventurous syntheses and applications [see pieces on gender in Henry (ed) 1994] are as much a guide to further work as final statements on women's experience of work and leisure, or the masculine context in which that experience is situated. It could still be concluded, on the basis of an ethnographic study in a multi-ethnic inner-city secondary school in the summer of 1992, that sport and physical activity remained unchallenged as a focus for the expression of an assertive traditional masculinity (Parker, 1992). In this study physical education was located as "a strategic site within the development of masculinity, speci-fically in relation to the violent, homophobic and patriarchal tendencies of those involved" (Parker, 1992: abstract). Interviewing 'hard boys', 'conformists' and 'victims' from two physical education class groupings in year three, it became clear that physical education and sport offered 'hard boys' an ideal setting for ridiculing 'victims' and 'conformists', sometimes in terms of sexual identity. 'Queer', 'fag' or 'faggot' labels would be stuck by boys on boys who made a mistake in sports/physical education lessons. Yet for both a 'victim' and a 'hard boy' the physical education lesson offered the opportunity to "have a good laugh" (Parker, 1992: pp. 122 and 141). A persisting theme in understanding women's experience of sport must be sport's continuing contribution to the formation of masculine identity.

Sport, leisure and gender: continuities and challenges

This volume brings together studies of sport, gender and leisure from a variety of contexts. The event from which the bulk of this volume is derived was a University of Brighton/PCFC-sponsored day seminar in June 1993. The papers by Carolyn Carr (and co-authors Anita White and Alan Tomlinson), Jim Clough, Anne Flintoff, Ilke Hartmann-Tews and Karen Petry, and Anita White were presented at that event. The papers by David Rowe and Anne Hall were presented at CSRC seminars in December 1993 and June 1994 respectively. Work by CSRC personnel — Graham McFee and Fiona Smith, Lesley Lawrence and Alan Tomlinson — informed the seminars and has been integrated into the current volume, as is the case with the paper by Mike Cole, Paddy Maguire and John Bosowski.

The volume is organised into four sections. In section one general issues of participation are raised, in the light of the influences upon change and the processes which act as constraints upon change. Clough, McCormack and Traill report encouraging increases in young girls' involvement in sports in Australia, and make the point that still more girls would become involved in sports if coaches were more available and encouraging. Hartmann-Tews and Petry, reporting on their studies in Germany, note large increases in women's involvement in sport, in the context of changing social trends which prioritise consumer-led and individualised modes of involvement. They point to new forms of freedom to become involved in sports, though remind us too that such freedoms are also affected by social class differences.

In the second section the three pieces deal with aspects of institutional and professional education. Anne Flintoff's piece draws upon her work on the values and ideologies at work in physical education teacher-training institutions. Based upon in-depth qualitative interviews with students and staff — and the observational insights so necessary in the production of informed case-studies — her analysis confirmed the deep-rooted gender stereotypes at work in the professional world of physical education ITT (Initial Teacher Training). These included forms of sexism among male students.

McFee and Smith, responding to Hanna's work on dance, sex and gender, apply such a critical approach to selected aspects of the professional training of physical education teachers. They explore the theme of dance as 'gender identity work', the need for appropriate 'theorised investigation of dance and gender', and the need for male students to be given time 'to understand dance at all'. Lesley Lawrence, drawing upon her study of the leisure aims of physical education teachers, shows how the personal and the professional can be linked; however, when a teacher makes assumptions about the benefits of leisure for others, this might cloud an understanding of the constraints affecting the leisure possibilities for those others.

The third part of the volume includes three pieces exploring the masculinist nature of selected forms of popular culture. Cole, Maguire and Bosowski apply selected aspects of Marxist and gender-aware theory to a single popular cultural form in the mid-1980s—BBC Radio 1. They demonstrate the masculinist and patriarchal nature of its discourses, and show the deep-rootedness of the politics of culture in the mid-Thatcher years. Rowe, commenting upon the expansion of image markets in a post-modern context, demonstrates the enduring nature of the connection between sport and hegemonic masculinity. He also considers the impact of challenges to hegemonic masculinity — in the shape of interventions by feminists and by gay men — and recognises that at levels of sport below the elite level "sport is now a rather less reliable ally of hegemonic masculinity'. Tomlinson's chapter examines the world of the soccer comic *Roy of the Rovers*, in the early/mid-1980s, and contextualises the meanings produced in that comic by also examining aspects of the fitness boom. In this contribution both these case-studies are theorised in terms of the culture-ideology dynamic.

The final section of the volume comprises three chapters. Carr, Tomlinson and White take three case-studies of the introduction of artificial playing surfaces in the South-East of England and examine the thinking and claims behind the policy process; the management practices involved in implementing the policy; and related aspects of women's participation. They illustrate how policy initiatives, particularly when not monitored in any systematic way, can be seen to fall short of their basic goals, and perpetrate the patriarchal basis of provision. White reviews some of the main developments in policy in the Sports Council (London). She looks at the move from 'targeting' ('Sport for All') to a concern with 'Sports Equity', and argues that the move towards equity "implies the redistribution of resources (including power) so that inequities are redressed". In the final article in the volume, Hall provides a comparative case-study of women's sports organisations. Case-studies are drawn from Australia, Canada, the United Kingdom and the United States. Hall shows how compromise and survivalism can be disruptive of initial campaigning goals, so that a "radical cultural politics" might give way to a "liberal gender equity framework for change" once funding becomes dependent upon "the state or the private sector".

Reporting data and case-studies, not just from Britain but also from Australia, Canada, the United States and Germany, this volume is offered as a modest contribution to a continuing debate on the continuities apparent in gendered sport and leisure cultures, and the impact of some of the most notable challenges to those continuities.

* I would like to thank Sue Mason-Cox for working on CSRC data-bases and important 1980s sources in providing the initial draft of the second section of this chapter.

References

Clarke, R., Lawrence, L., Parker, S. R. and Tomlinson, A. (1993/94) *Full report on recreational usage (Summer 1993) of the Heritage Coast (East Sussex)* (prepared for East Sussex County Council and the South-East Sports Council) Eastbourne: Leisure Research Unit, University of Brighton, Winter 1993–94.

Deem, R. (1986) *All work and no play: A study of women and leisure.* Milton Keynes: Open University Press.

Green, E., Hebron, S. and Woodward, D. (1990) *Women's leisure, what leisure?*, London: Macmillan.

Hargreaves, J. (1994) *Sporting females: Critical issues in the history and sociology of women's sport.* London: Routledge.

Henderson, K. A., Bialeschki, M. O., Shaw, S. M., and Freysinger, V. J. (1989) *A leisure of one's own: A feminist perspective on women's leisure.* Pennsylvania: Venture Publishing Inc.

Henley Centre for Forecasting (1993) *Leisure futures.* London: Henley Centre for Forecasting.

——(1994) *Leisure futures.* London: Henley Centre for Forecasting.

Henry, I. (ed) (1994) *Leisure: Modernity, post-modernity and lifestyles* (Leisure in Different Worlds Vol. 1), LSA Publication No. 48. Eastbourne: Leisure Studies Association.

Henson, M. (1994) *The leisure lifestyles of 16–19 year olds in Further Education.* M. Phil. Thesis, Department of Sociology, University of Staffordshire.

HMSO (1986) *General Household Survey 1983 — An inter-departmental survey sponsored by the Cultural Statistical Office of Population Censuses and Surveys Social Survey Division*, London: Her Majesty's Stationery Office.

——(1991) *Participation in sport* (by Jill Matheson), Office of Population Censuses and Surveys, London: Her Majesty's Stationery Office.

——(1993) *Social trends*, 23, Central Statistical Office, London: Her Majesty's Stationery Office.

Lawrence, L., Magness, A., and Standeven, J. (1992) *Market research report to identify swimming requirements in the Bordon/Whitehill area* (prepared for East Hampshire District Council). Eastbourne: Leisure Research Unit, Brighton Polytechnic.

Lawrence, L. and Standeven, J. (1991) *Angel Centre and Larkfield Leisure Centre: Report on users* (prepared for Tonbridge and Malling Borough Council). Eastbourne: Leisure Research Unit, Brighton Polytechnic, October.

Lawrence, L. and Tomlinson, A. (1992) *Brighton Leisure Card survey report (Phase three)* (prepared for Brighton Borough Council). Leisure Research Unit, Brighton Polytechnic, February.

Magness, A. (1990) *Report on research into the concept of a leisure card* (Phase 1: Group discussion). Leisure Research Unit, Brighton Polytechnic, December.

Mason-Cox, S. (1992) *A fair go: A critical look at gender equality in an Outward Bound Standard Programme*. Bachelor's Dissertation, School of Leisure and Tourism Studies, University of Technology, Sydney.

Mason-Cox, S. and Fullager, S. (ud) 'The feminine in sport', *Refractory Girl*, Vol. 1: pp. 21–24.

Parker, A. (1992) *One of the boys? Images of masculinity within boys' physical education*. MA Dissertation, Department of Physical Education, University of Warwick, September.

Philips, D. and Tomlinson, A. (1992) 'Homeward bound: Leisure, popular culture and consumer capitalism', in D. Strinati and S. Wagg (eds) *Come on down? — Popular media culture in post-war Britain*. London: Routledge, pp. 9–45.

Sports Council and Women's Sports Foundation (1992) *Women and sport — the information pack*. London: Sports Council and Women's Sports Foundation.

Sports Market Place (1994) *Update, July 1994*, Sports Market Place, P. O. Box 1417, Princeton, N. J. 08542 (Publisher/Editor Richard A. Lipsey).

Talbot, M. (1988) '"Their own worst enemy": Women and leisure provision', in E. Wimbush and M. Talbot (eds) *Relative freedoms: Women and leisure*. Milton Keynes: Open University Press.

Tomlinson, A. and Parker, S. (1992) *Life in the South: The paradox of prosperity*, Chelsea School Research Centre Topic Report 1. Eastbourne: Leisure Research Unit/Chelsea School Research Centre, University of Brighton, September.

Willis, P. (1974) 'Women in sport' (2) *Working papers in cultural studies 5*. Centre for Contemporary Cultural Studies, University of Birmingham, Spring, pp. 21–36.

Willis, P. (1982) 'Women in sport in ideology', in J. Hargreaves (ed) *Sport, culture and ideology*, London: Routledge and Kegan Paul, pp. 117–135.

Wimbush, E. and Talbot, M. (eds) (1988) *Relative freedoms: Women and leisure*. Milton Keynes: Open University Press.

I.

PARTICIPATION

A MAPPING OF GIRLS' PARTICIPATION IN SPORT IN THE AUSTRALIAN CAPITAL TERRITORY

Jim Clough, Coralie McCormack and Ron Traill Faculty of Education, University of Canberra Australian Capital Territory

Introduction

This paper discusses the participation of girls in sport in the Australian Capital Territory (ACT). This information was gathered as part of a research project conducted in 1992 which investigated the ways in which young people in the ACT are involved in sport. This research was jointly sponsored by the ACT Government's Office of Sport and Recreation, the ACT Junior Sport Council, the ACT Department of Education and Training, and the Australian Sports Commission.

The Research Study

The research involved surveying a stratified random sample of 1048 young people; approximately 80 were sampled from each of the thirteen year levels (Kindergarten to 12) of the government and non-government school systems in the ACT with equal numbers of male and female participants. A total of 17 schools was involved – nine schools for K-6 students, 4 schools for Years 7-10 students and 4 schools for Years 11-12 students.

Information on this sample was obtained through the administration of an eighteen-item questionnaire with many of these items having sub-items. Major variables included in the questionnaire related to: gender, age, year group and school; country of birth of subject and of parents; sports played in class time with family and friends, for a school, and for a community club; reasons for playing sport; use of leisure time; attendance at sporting events; attitudes about sporting facilities; attitudes about sports participation; sporting persons most admired; and involvement in competitive sport within the school and within the community.

This instrument was developed over a period of several weeks and involved close collaboration with a research project steering committee which was composed of representatives of the project's funding sponsors. The instrument was trialed with various age groups in a primary school (K-6), a high school (7-10), and in a secondary college (11-12). The administration of the questionnaire to the sample was tailored to the age and ability of the students. In the Years 7-12 groups, a researcher introduced the project, responded to any queries, and then asked the students to complete the questionnaire. In the case of Years 3-6 students, two researchers met with each group of students. After a brief introduction the researchers and students worked through the questionnaire together, question by question. For Years K-2 pupils a "buddy" system was employed. Year 6 students who had previously completed the questionnaire received additional guidance from the researchers; these students then administered the questionnaire to the younger children under the supervision of the researchers. This approach with the K-2 students worked extremely well and the researchers felt confident that they were able to report accurately the responses of these very young students to the issues raised in the survey instrument.

The questionnaire was administered during May and June 1992 and resulted in a considerable amount of information being available to the researchers on the involvement of these students in sport, and their attitudes to sport. The relational database management program Paradox 3.5 was chosen as the means of processing and analysing the data.

Information was therefore made available on 523 girls, with approximately 40 from each age group from Kindergarten to Year Twelve. Full details of the study are available in the research report on the project (Clough and Traill, 1992).

Results of the Mapping Exercise

Sports Played

The participation rates of the 523 girls in twenty-five different sports, most of which had one or more modified versions, was assessed. These data were collected to take into account sport which the girls might have played in four different contexts – in class time at school, with family or friends, for the school as in representative sport, or for a sporting club. As shown in **Table 1**, the most played sports in class time were Aerobics/Gymnastics (53%), Cricket/Kanga Cricket (48%), Volleyball (47%), Softball (46%), Netball (44%), Volleyball (47%), and Swimming (40%). With family and friends the sports most played

Table 1   **Sports Played by Females by Context - Percent (N=523)**

Sport:	In Class time at School (%)	With Family /Friends (%)	For the School (%)	For a Sporting Club (%)
Aerobics/Gymnastics	53	26	8	26
Athletics, Little Athletics	35	16	16	19
Australian Football	22	13	2	2
Baseball	27	12	5	2
Basketball	35	22	9	9
Bicycle Riding	10	80	1	2
Cricket, Kanga Cricket	48	27	7	2
Golf	5	26	0	1
Hockey, Minkey	36	10	11	7
Horse Riding	7	51	2	9
Lacrosse, Sofcrosse	15	2	1	0
Netball	44	28	32	24
Orienteering	19	9	3	3
Rugby League	12	16	1	1
Rugby Union	14	8	2	1
Skating	15	67	1	5
Skiing	7	32	2	2
Soccer	37	22	12	4
Softball	46	19	16	7
Squash	15	18	1	2
Swimming	40	77	21	20
Tee-ball	43	14	11	7
Tennis	29	45	4	14
Touch Football	28	20	3	1
Volleyball	47	24	10	3

were Bicycle Riding (80%), Swimming (77%), Skating (67%) and Horse Riding (51%). Participation rates dropped off quite dramatically in school representative and sporting club contexts. In school representative sport the highest participation rates were for Netball (32%), Swimming (21%) and Softball (16%). In the context of playing sport with community clubs the highest rates were recorded for Aerobics/Gymnastics (26%), Netball (24%), Swimming (20%) and Athletics/Little Athletics (19%). This sample of girls played most of their sports, therefore, either in class time sessions at school or with family and friends.

Data were also available on the average number of sports played by girls at different year levels. This information provided in **Table 2** shows that a wider variety of sports were played at the Year 10 level than at other levels. This is of interest to note when compared to research which suggests that females in the mid-teenage years tend to be less involved in sport. Perhaps these data suggests that in this particular sample an interest prevailed, but that it manifested itself through girls trying out several sports rather than concentrating on one or two sports.

Preferred Leisure Activities

In terms of a preferred leisure activity, sport ranked with "being with friends" from a list of seven activities (**Table 3**).

Table 2   **Average Number of Sports Played by Females by Context and Year Group**

Year Group	In Class time at School	With Family / Friends	For the School	For a Sporting Club
Year 3	2.6	4.8	0.8	1.7
Year 6	7.7	6.7	2.5	1.9
Year 10	11.0	8.2	3.0	2.3
Year 12	9.2	5.5	2.6	1.8

Table 3   **Average Rank for each Leisure Activity for Females**

Activity	Females
Playing or Listening to Music	4
Hobbies	4
Reading or Writing	5
Playing sport	3
Going to scouts, guides, a church or social group	6
Being with your friends	3
Watching television	4

Reasons For Playing Favourite Sport

The major reasons these girls gave for playing sport, shown in **Table 4**, were "It's fun" (98%), "It makes you feel good" (91%), "You make new friends that way" (82%), "It's something to do" (82%) and "People in this sport are really friendly" (79%).

Table 4 **Reasons Female Students Play their Favourite Sport (N=523)**

Reason	Yes	%	No	%	Other	%
My friends play it too	252	48	262	50	9	2
My parents encourage me to play	225	43	287	55	11	2
I do not have to travel far to play	191	37	325	62	7	1
Girls and boys can play it together	322	62	195	37	6	1
My mum plays/used to play it	129	25	384	73	10	2
It does not cost a lot to play	207	40	305	58	11	2
I am really good at this sport	368	70	133	25	22	4
No need for training sessions	147	28	368	70	8	2
It makes me feel good	477	91	43	8	3	1
The Coach is good	344	66	162	31	17	3
I am not likely to be injured	189	36	321	61	13	2
My dad plays, or used to play	104	20	403	77	16	3
It makes you look good	201	38	316	60	6	1
People are really friendly	414	79	100	19	9	2
Teachers encouraged me to play	137	26	379	72	7	1
I want to represent the A.C.T.	256	49	257	49	10	2
You can make a good living from playing this sport	240	46	266	51	17	3
It's fun	513	98	10	2	0	0
It could help me overcome a disability	176	34	332	63	15	3
I saw it played on television	228	44	288	55	7	1
Its helps you do well at schoolwork	177	34	337	64	9	2
I play this sport with my parents	140	27	367	70	16	3
You make new friends that way	431	82	85	16	7	1
I knew the coach	166	32	347	66	10	2
It's something to do	428	82	92	18	3	1

These reasons clearly relate to social considerations and suggest that for these girls this factor played a major part in their decisions to play a sport. While the boys in the study also rated the enjoyment factor as high, they tended to rate more highly than the girls reasons for playing which related to sporting ability and futures in the sport. Among other items of interest from this evidence, as shown in **Table 4**, are views of the coach: "the Coach is good" was an important factor (66%).

School Representative Sport

Forty-four percent (44%) of this sample of girls had represented their school in a competition against another school – as contrasted to 53.3.% of the boys in the study. The girls played in both girls only teams (55%) and mixed gender teams (43%). The teams were mostly coached by teachers (56.7%) or parents (13.4%).

Community Sports Teams

Gender differentiation in sporting participation for the children in this study was quite evident at the community club level. From the total numbers in this sample, 54% of the boys had played for a community club; however, only 37.7% of the girls had done so. As with school representative teams, most boys played on boys only teams (65.2%) as contrasted to girls who played in either girls only teams (50.7%) or mixed gender teams (45.1%).

Feelings When Playing Sport

The girls were asked to rate their feelings about playing sport in different contexts. This data are provided in **Table 5**. In class time at school "fun" (61%), "develops skills" (57%), "others take it too seriously" (44%) and "excited" (43%), rated highest. With family and friends, the girls rated their feelings "fun" (83%), "excited" (65%), "satisfying" (50%) and "develops skills" (47%), as highest. In school representative sport the higher ratings went to "excited" (56%), "fun" (56%), "develops skills" (49%), and "challenging" (47%). In sporting club contexts the higher ratings were for "excitement" (61%), "fun" (59%), "develops skills" (56%), and "challenging" (54%). In this data, in all contexts, these girls therefore commonly described their feelings when playing sport in terms of sport being "fun", "exciting" and "challenging".

Why Play Sport?

The children were given a number of reasons why they might play sport and asked to rank these reasons (see **Table 6**). The girls gave their higher rankings

Table 5   Female Students' Feelings about Playing Sport in Different Contexts — Percent (N=523)

How children felt about playing sport	In Class time at School (%)	With Family or Friends (%)	For the School (%)	For a Sporting Club (%)
Excited	43	65	56	61
Too organised	27	10	19	23
Boring	32	8	12	11
Fun	61	83	56	59
Satisfying	38	50	43	45
Too many rules	30	11	24	22
Dangerous	18	14	14	16
Others take it too seriously	44	18	35	33
Too competitive	23	11	29	30
Challenging	37	38	47	54
Develops Skills	57	47	49	56

to "improve my sporting skills" (88%), "be physically active" (86%), "make new friends" (84%), and "play close and exciting games" (77%). By contrast a higher proportion of boys than girls played sport to "compete against others" (83% boys, 66% girls), to "beat others in sport" (61% boys, 36% girls) and to "be like my sporting heroes/heroines" (boys 57%, girls 31%). In Year 7 a noticeably higher proportion of girls than boys played sport to make new friends – this was also true for the Year 10 and Year 12 levels.

Meeting members of the opposite sex was not of concern to younger students, boys and girls being similarly unconcerned with meeting members of the opposite sex when playing sport. In Year 9 a change occurred in that half the girls played sport to meet members of the opposite sex while this reason was given by only 37% of boys in this year group. While meeting members of the opposite sex remained at a similar level of overall importance for the oldest students (Years 10, 11 and 12) it was noticeable that the trend that emerged in Year 9 did not continue and that a higher proportion of boys than girls played sport to meet members of the opposite sex. This difference was at its greatest for Year 12 students; just over half of the boys played sport to meet members of the opposite sex while only one quarter of the Year 12 girls played sport for this reason.

Table 6   Females' Reasons for Playing Sport (N=523)

Reason	Yes	%	No	%	Other	%
Get medals and trophies	200	38	313	60	10	2
Beat others in sport	190	36	325	62	8	2
Make new friends	439	84	80	15	4	1
Compete against others	346	66	169	32	8	2
Play close and exciting games	405	77	109	21	9	2
Please the coach	222	42	289	55	12	2
Improve my sporting skills	459	88	59	11	5	1
Be physically active	450	86	68	13	5	1
Please my parents	241	46	272	52	10	2
Meet members of opposite sex	179	34	338	65	6	1
Be like my sporting heroes/heroines	165	32	351	67	7	1

Table 7   Female Students' Reasons for Playing More Sport (N=523)

Reason	Yes	%	No	%	Other	%
An indoor area was available	271	52	242	46	10	2
I had transport available	285	54	230	44	8	2
Sport did not cost me anything to play	325	62	188	36	10	2
I could play when I want to and not at a set time	332	63	186	36	5	1
My parents allowed me to play	290	55	228	44	5	1
If there was a competition available in one of my favourite sports that I do well in	371	71	146	28	6	1

What Would Prompt Girls to Play More Sport?

Of the reasons provided (**Table 7**) the girls rated more highly the factors of "if there was a competition available in one of my favourite sports that I could do well in" (71%), "I could play when I want to and not at a set time" (63%), and "Sport did not cost me anything to play" (62%), as the reasons for playing more sport.

Table 8   **Reasons Female Students would be Discouraged from Playing Sport (N=523)**

Reason	Yes	%	No	%	Other	%
Having a part-time job	200	38	311	59	12	2
My studies (lots of homework)	263	50	247	47	13	2
Having a poor coach	269	51	245	47	9	2
It costs too much money	253	48	258	49	12	2
Having to practise too much	132	25	384	73	7	1
The risk of being injured	150	29	365	70	8	2
More interesting things to do	189	36	320	61	14	3
My team losing all the time	122	23	392	75	9	2
Poor umpiring	244	47	266	51	13	2
Having barrackers and coaches yelling at me all the time	252	48	257	49	14	3
The season being too long	102	20	416	80	5	1
Having to travel all over the place to play matches	186	36	331	63	6	1
Coaches not really interested in the players, but just in winning	330	63	188	36	5	1
Coach only putting good players into the game, so that I miss out	342	65	172	33	9	2
My friends not interested in sport	115	22	403	77	5	1
My parents thinking I should not play so much sport	118	23	399	76	6	1
Having a disability and cannot play sport	209	40	304	58	10	2
Nowhere near where I live to play the sport I would like to play	237	45	277	53	9	2
Our school being more interested in academic subjects than sport	166	32	345	66	12	2
Having to do other things than play, e.g., umpiring, scoring	161	31	353	67	9	2

Reasons Which Discourage Girls From Playing Sport

Girls rated the major discouragements from playing sport (see **Table 8**) as: "The coach only putting the good players into the game, so that I miss out" (65%), "The coaches not really being interested in the players, but just interested in winning" (63%), "Having a poor coach" (51%) and "My studies (lots of homework)" (50%). It is interesting to note how highly adverse comments about coaches have been rated on this list. This became particularly noticeable in data collected from Years 10, 11 and 12 girls.

Sporting Heroes/Heroines

Both boys and girls in the sample were asked to identify their sporting heroes and/or heroines. Over 700 names were given. Three female "sporting heroines" were in the ten most given responses, Hayley Lewis, Lisa Curry-Kenny and Jane Flemming. However, when the girls in the sample were then asked if their heroes/heroines had influenced their sporting choices a majority of the girls (54.4%) felt that this had not been the case. By contrast, 54% of the boys felt that sporting heroes/heroines had in fact influenced their sporting choices.

Attendance at Sports Events

The majority of these girls rarely attended live sports events (see **Table 9**). However, when asked if they would rather attend a live sports event rather than watching it on television, most girls preferred to attend a live sports event, especially in the Years 2, 5, 7, 8 and 10 groups. Only the kindergarten girls preferred the "watch on television" option (see **Table 10**). The girls expressed a high level of satisfaction with the existing sporting facilities in their area – 78.4% of the girls believing this to be so.

Table 9   Females' Frequency of Attendance at Live Sporting Events as Spectators

Frequency	Number of Females	(Percent)
Never	142	(27.2)
Once or Twice a Year	179	(34.2)
Once per month	95	(18.1)
Once per week	92	(17.6)
Other*	2	(0.4)
Don't Know	4	(0.8)
No Response	9	(1.7)
Total	523	(100)

Table 10   Female Students' Venue Preference (prefer to attend a live sports event rather than watch it on TV) by Year Group : Percent*

Year Group	Percent of Females		
	Yes	No	Sometimes
Kindergarten	33.3	55.6	11.1
Year 1	50.0	47.5	2.5
Year 2	62.5	25.0	12.5
Year 3	40.0	22.5	37.5
Year 4	53.7	14.6	31.7
Year 5	61.0	7.3	31.7
Year 6	48.7	12.8	38.5
Year 7	65.1	7.0	27.9
Year 8	53.6	9.8	36.6
Year 9	42.9	7.1	50.0
Year 10	63.9	8.3	27.8
Year 11	44.4	5.6	50.0
Year 12	47.4	7.9	44.7
Total	50.5	17.2	30.4

* *excludes those who did not answer the question and those who answered "Don't know"*

Conclusions

What kind of profile then emerges on the participation rates and attitudes to sport of this random sample of just over 500 ACT girls? This profile appears to be:

* The girls in this sample were involved in a wide variety of sports. This feature became particularly noticeable at upper year levels (and contrasts with boys in the study who, at upper year levels, tended to focus on one or two major sports).

* The type of sports the girls played changed very much according to the context – in class time at school sports such as aerobics/gymnastics, cricket/ kanga cricket, volleyball, softball and netball attracted the highest

participation rates; but when with family and friends out of school hours, sports such as bicycle riding, swimming and skating recorded the higher participation rates.

- Most of their sporting involvements occurred either in the context of class time sport sessions at school or in playing sport with family and friends; school representative sport and playing in a community sporting club involved much lower participation rates.

- The social dimensions of sport were most highly valued by these girls. Having "fun" and "making new friends" typified the reasons girls gave for either currently playing a sport or for why they believed they should play sport.

- Adverse comments about coaches provided the main reasons for why the girls became discouraged from playing sport. Whereas these girls wanted to play sport "... that I could do well in" they believed they were discouraged by coaches "only putting the good players into the game so that I miss out" and "... not really being interested in the players, but just interested in winning".

This sample of ACT girls, then, emerges as having high rates of participation in sport and viewing this involvement in sport as of greatest value for its social interactions.

References

Clough, J. R. and Traill, R. D. (1992) *A mapping of participation rates in junior sport in the Australian Capital Territory.* Canberra, ACT: ACT Junior Sport Council, October.

INDIVIDUALISATION AND CHANGING MODES OF CONSUMING IN SPORT — SOME GENDER ASPECTS

Ilse Hartmann-Tews Institute of Sport Sociology, German Sport University, Cologne

Karen Petry Institute for Leisure Science, German Sport University, Cologne

Introduction

Over the past two decades there has been an enormous growth in sport participation in most (West-) European countries. This steady rise, especially in recreational sports, goes together with a slight reduction in the significance of sex, age and social class as discriminating factors in being active or not active in sport. Central features of this dynamic can be described in terms of pluralisation and differentiation of the demand, supply and ideological underpinnings of sport (Hartmann-Tews, in press).

There are several theoretical frames of reference that help to illuminate crucial aspects of this development. One of them goes back to early sociologists of 19th century Germany, and has been revitalised by Ulrich Beck with his book on the Risk Society, first published in Germany in 1986 (Beck, 1992). His proposition of processes of individualisation can shed light on changing demands in sport, and especially on trends towards individualised modes of participation in sport. For this purpose first of all some general features of participation in sport in the voluntary and commercial sectors will be outlined, then the most central feature of the notion of individualisation and its structural and cultural set-up will be presented in order to explain the most recent developments of growing (female) interest in products of the fitness industry and the commercially run sector of sport.

1. Organized sport in Germany: the voluntary and commercial sectors

The voluntary sector of sport in Germany is well-organized and dominated by the German Sports Federation (Deutscher Sportbund — DSB) as the umbrella organization of German sports. Sixteen sports federations of the constituent states (Landessportbünde), 55 governing bodies for single sports (Spitzenverbände) and some other federations with particular tasks have joined the DSB. At the grass roots of organized sports there are now approximately 76,000 sports clubs with a total membership of 23 million people (Deutscher Sportbund, 1992: p. 64)[1].

There has been a steady growth in membership over the past 20 years but the total number of persons organized in clubs is likely to be less than the data published by the DSB suggest because the statistics include multiple memberships. However, the evidence from various surveys on sport and leisure behaviour shows that 20% of the population claim membership at one or more sports clubs — suggesting that a real 'net' total of 13 million people are organized in clubs (Opaschowsky, 1987: p. 24). As regards gender differences, various data confirm that generally men participate in sport more than women. However, over the last 20 years women's increase in sports participation and in club membership has been even more impressive than among men — the proportion of women has risen continuously up to 35.1% in 1989 (see **Table 1**).

The proportion of women in clubs is lowest in small clubs made up of less than 300 members predominantly offering only one single sport (e.g. football)

Table 1. Development of clubs, membership and proportion of women within the German Sports Federation (Deutscher Sportbund, DSB)

year	clubs	membership DSB	% female
1970	39,201	10,121,546	23.1
1975	44,373	13,449,905	28.0
1980	53,451	16,924,027	32.0
1985	61,514	19,258,583	34.1
1989	66,652	20,965,422	35.1

and is highest in big clubs with more than 1,000 members offering wide ranges of sporting activities (Deutscher Sportbund, 1988). During the 60s and 70s physical training and sporting activities were located almost exclusively in voluntary clubs. Being predominantly competitive oriented, sport in clubs attracted more men than women, and more young people than older people. One of the most characteristic features of sports clubs is that running them depends heavily on the voluntary work and social commitment of members, thus creating a sphere of solidarity and community.

Alongside the traditional sports clubs there has been a steady growth of the so called 'commercial sector' of sport. Fitness-studios, health clubs and leisure centres now offer recreational and sporting activities within a multitude of new structures and arrangements. Several research projects have been conducted on the profile of the commercial sector in (leisure and) sport (Dietrich *et al.*, 1990; Sack *et al.*, 1989; Mrazek and Rittner, 1989). Their conclusion is that the commercial sector of sport "is no more but an amorphous category of a sparkling range of various contents and forms of supply as well as of different types of organizations" (Elpel and Elpel, 1990: p. 140).

The commercial sector consists of a wide range of centres and locations at which people can play sports and participate in various forms of physical exercise. An outline of the types of supply based on a content analysis of about 6,000 adverts of private suppliers over a period of one year is shown in **Table 2** (following page).

There is a large number of mainly small firms, usually single-activity enterprises, as well as multi-purpose centres: 450 private suppliers were identified of which 325 were sport related. Regarding the sports activities which are offered, it is remarkable that fitness-related activities are dominant: approximately one third of the enterprises fall under the heading of "fitness-club", "fitness-studio" or "modern gymnasium". For our purpose they are defined as single-activity enterprises. Most are based in premises which are especially equipped to provide opportunities for exercise and keep-fit with or without machines. A research project conducted in 1989 indicates that approximately 2,000 regular fitness centres and health clubs existed with a total number of approximately 750,000 customers (Mrazek and Rittner, 1989: p. 75). The evidence that the commercial sector is still growing rapidly is supported by the most recent reports of the Central Federation of Fitness Centres, giving a record of 4,500 of such centres in the old (West German) states (*Süddeutsche Zeitung*, 4 May, 1993).

Table 2.   Variety of private suppliers enterprises in the commercial sector

	no.	%
Fitness-clubs, body-building clubs: focus on fitness and/or body-building, but also offer e.g. martial-arts	60	13.3
Modern dance and gymnast-studios: mainly new forms of dance and movement	60	13.3
Single-track sport schools: traditional sports, e.g. sailing, horse-riding, swimming, boxing	44	9.8
Other sports venues: with a range offers, e.g. bowling	40	8.9
Large sport and leisure-centres: centres with a variety of sports and leisure activities, especially tennis and squash centres	32	7.1
Dance-schools: Ballroom dance, standard dance	23	5.1
Ballet-schools: focus on classical ballet	21	4.7
Martial-arts: focus on Asian-sport, further offers especially fitness and body-building	21	4.7
Travel companies: package-holidays with integrated sports activities	22	4.9
Single-person enterprises	79	17.6
Sports-offers from unknown suppliers	45	10.0
	450	100.0

[Source: Schubert 1991]

Commercially run clubs and centres attract more females than the voluntary sector. The proportion of women users reported in these surveys varies from 42% to 71% depending on the size of the sample and the area covered (Sack *et al.*, 1989; Mrazek and Rittner 1989; Rittner and Mrazek 1990; Dietrich *et al.*, 1990).

As regards age structure it is obvious that fitness centres and other commercially run centres are especially attractive to 20–40 year olds, whereas clubs in the voluntary sector are more attractive to young people and the elderly. A distinctive feature of the commercial sector is the provider-consumer relationship and the combination of several body-related services, not exclusively oriented towards active physical exercise — much the same as in Great Britain (Roberts *et al.*, 1988; Hartmann-Tews, 1991).

With this brief outline of the central characteristics of the voluntary and commercial sectors in mind two questions arise. The first asks for reasons for the impressive development of the commercial sector in recreational sport. The second asks for reasons for the rising interest of women in sport and their special commitment to fitness activities in the commercial sector.

2.   Indications of social change and individualisation

The argument that is put forward here is that recreational sport and the pursuit of fitness are heavily promoted by individualisation. The individualisation thesis contends that as a consequence of fundamental socio-structural and socio-cultural changes over the past decades a process of 'diversification' of life styles has been set in motion. The notion of growing individualisation has been widely acknowledged for its power to describe psycho-socio-cultural changes but it has provoked some criticism as regards the analytical precision of its arguments. For our purpose it seems to be most appropriate to focus on some central indications of social change that have strong effects on the individual as far as biography and identity are concerned.

Growing welfare and standards of living

The last four decades have seen increasing incomes, expanding amounts amounts of leisure time, rising standards of living and — up to the mid 1980s — a strengthening of the welfare state in Germany. The social process set in motion with these economic developments can be described as a form of collective upward mobility while the gaps between different income groups have persisted. A more general effect has been a democratization of formerly exclusive types of consumption and styles of living, such as the ownership of cars, furnishings, household appliances and leisure equipment accompanied by widening effect options of consumption.

Growing demands of the labour market and mobility

Linked with these changes in standards of living are changes in the labour market that require greater mobility. This includes local mobility as regards places of residence or employment; flexibility as changing demands of jobs and innovations constantly demands further (vocational) training and social mobility as the latter in turn very often initiates changes in social location. The effects of growing mobility include the experience of loosening of traditional social patterns and living arrangements.

Changes in duration and levels of education

Equalisation of educational opportunities from the early 1970s onwards has led to an enormous growth in the number of well educated young people — and women have profited disproportionally from this trend. The percentage of young people in secondary education (age 15+) has risen dramatically from 26% in 1960 to 64% in 1985 (Statistisches Bundesamt, 1990: p. 54). The effects of these developments are predominantly cultural. As schooling increases in duration, traditional orientations and ways of thinking are more and more replaced by universalistic forms of knowledge. Formal education in schools and universities provides — or at least makes possible — a certain degree of self-discovery, reflection and opportunity for individual identity work.

Size of households and family ties

A very poignant feature of modern times seems to be the changes in how people live together. More and more people tend to live in one person households: the proportion has risen from 19.4% in 1950 to 34.6% in 1987 (Statistisches Bundesamt, 1990). The total number of marriages has been falling, and at the same time the number of divorces has been growing and it is most interesting that predominantly women file for divorce. This development can well be interpreted in terms of a growing relevance of a 'rational choice' model that comes into play when the phase of enthusiastic romance has diminished and benefits and costs are more carefully weighed. If costs and benefits do not seem to be in due balance, the decision to terminate marriage is more frequently taken.

Two effects of these central aspects of social change are relevant to explain the growing interest in individualised modes of participation in sport and fitness activities. One relates to the economic and structural consequences of rising standards of living and welfare that allow more and more people to take part in leisure activities and sport, and to choose from an ever growing variety of such activities and offers.

The other one relates to the socio-structural and socio-cultural effects of social change. The documented social trends express a dissolving of traditional ties and values, a loosening of traditional commitments and a tendency towards social disintegration. In this context individualisation means that each person's biography is decreasingly determined by ascription (by class, gender and age) and by tradition, but more and more open to achievements by each individual and decisions that the individual can and has to make on his or her own. As a result biographies become more and more self-reflexive and open to decisions that individuals can and have to make by themselves (Beck, 1992: p. 91). The central effect is that: "...construction kits of biographical combination possibilities come into being. In the transition from 'standard to elective biography'" (Ley, 1984); "the conflictual and historically unprecedented type of do-it-yourself biography separates out" (Beck, 1992: p. 135).

In modern, advanced societies the individual must therefore learn to conceive him or herself as the centre of action with respect to his or her biography, abilities and, last but not least, his or her identity. This process contains a lot of ambivalence as, on the one hand, it provides freedom and various opportunities for the individual to create his or her own biography whilst on the other hand it implies a necessity and compulsion to decide — bound up with all the risks and uncertainties. For women this process of individualisation via better education and social and cultural change seems to have been even more crucial than for men. For women it has led to an intermediate status between 'freedom from' traditional role commitments and 'freedom to do' what they are more and more prepared to do, but as yet ambiguously conceded by the society.

3.   Individualised modes of participating in sport

Body enhancement

The proposition put forward here is that the phenomenon of individualisation has led to an increasing awareness of the body. There are several indications that there is a growing concern with the body, not only with its outer shape but also with the 'inner body' as well. Sport has always been body-centred and it is important to notice that growing interest in sport is predominantly centred on fitness, body-styling and body-shaping. Moreover, the growth of body-oriented therapies focusing on 'body-experiences' as well as people's concern for healthy and natural foods indicate that the body and body-related activities attract more and more attention. Taking into account that major illnesses nowadays are chronic and degenerative rather than infectious, health implies more than the absence of illness; rather it is an asset to be actively built. People from the middle-classes, and especially women, pursue lifestyles that are oriented towards fitness, health and body-awareness. As far as gender differences are concerned, sociological evidence suggests that women's elaborated interest in health and fitness, the fact that they are much more aware of signs of disease and symptoms than men, that they take greater care of their own and their families' health etc. are very much due to processes of socialisation. Processes of individualisation are based on these gender specific structures of somatic cultures.

Additionally the semantics of fitness seem to be instructive for our argument about individualisation and the growing interest — especially among women — in fitness activities. 'Fitness' seems no longer to be confined to physical fitness but refers to the general state of a person's psycho-physical well-being — mind as well as body — and advertisements of the fitness industry refer more and more to experiences of new dimensions of health, vitality and confidence (Glaser, 1989). They hint strongly at the effects of individualisation. As the construction of one's own identity becomes less structured by traditions and given patterns of biography, new identity generating sources are needed and searched for. In this context the body becomes the most private and very ultimate resort of identity; the most legitimate authority to express one's uniqueness (Bette, 1993).

Fitness and the notion of an ideal body are important for men as well as for women. However, women's identity is far more linked to the outer shape of the body than is true for men and women's body-concept not only differs from that of men but has always been a far more decisive part of female self-concepts (Hartmann-Tews, 1990). There is empirical evidence that women predominantly go to a fitness-studio in order to shape their bodies. Working on specific parts of the body that are perceived to be deficient — especially thighs, bottoms, breasts and bellies — are typically the most crucial elements in fitness training regimes (Mrazek and Rittner, 1986; Petry, 1989). Individualisation and the fitness movement have resulted in a new ideal of the feminine physique which involves a pulling together of several cultural antitheses: strength with beauty, muscularity with thinness, and hardness with curvaceousness (Glaser, 1989: p. 186). The effects of fitness-training and body shaping are in the promise of a more intentional selfhood and thus are part of identity-work. Femininity is no longer proposed as nature, but is read as work, a styled body, produced by a woman's own consciousness.

Uncomplicated consumer-provider relationship

The widespread and growing interest in the pursuit of fitness has led to growing participation rates in recreational sport in general. The question that rises is, why has the commercially run sector profited so much more from this development than the voluntary sector consisting of such a huge network of sports clubs?

Survey data on perceptions of the profiles of traditional sports clubs in the voluntary sector, and fitness centres in the commercial sector, provide some evidence of what makes the latter so attractive (Rittner and Mrazek, 1986; Dietrich and Heinemann Schubert, 1990). The most attractive feature of commercially run fitness-studios and health-clubs as perceived by the customers points strongly to effects of individualisation. It is the possibility of using the facilities individually and carrying out individually structured exercise programmes at individually chosen times, not being dependent on anyone else, that makes the facilities attractive. Once people have paid up, they appreciate the freedom to use facilities whenever and as often as they like, fixing their own special mixtures on the spur of the moment. People are well aware that fitness training in commercially run studios is a "fashionable activity", that "membership fees are relatively high" but "don't oblige for any regular engagement" (Rittner and Mrazek, 1986). Thus the uncomplicated provider-consumer relationship contrasts with the traditional club culture where voluntary social engagement and commitment to the organisation and community have been major constituent elements.

In addition, commercially run clubs attract and hold members by their friendly and supportive climates as well as by the higher standard of their facilities, especially the changing rooms and showers. Realising that membership fees are relatively high, customers look for offers and services that they consider value for money. In this respect customers become more discriminating and develop a more sophisticated consumer demand. The degree of specialisation and diversification in commercial health and fitness services appears to correspond much better to a new profile of individualised consumer demand than does the traditional structure of sports clubs.

Note

[1] As the development of sport and society over the past decades has been very different in the western and eastern parts of Germany we will concentrate our analysis on what are called the "old states", consisting of the 11 states of former West Germany.

References

Beck, U. (1992) *Risk society*. London/New York: Sage.

Bette, K. (1993) 'Sport und Individualisierung', *Spectrum der Sportwissenschaften*, Vol. 5, No. 1, pp. 34-55.

Deutscher Sportbund (1988) *FISAS 1986*. Frankfurt a.M.: DSB.

Deutscher Sportbund (1992) *Sport in der Bundesrepublik Deutschland*. Frankfurt a.M.: DSB.

Dietrich, K., and Heinemann, K., and Schubert, M. (1990) *Kommerzielle Sportanbieter*. Hofmann: Schorndorf.

Elpel, B., and Elpel, K.-P. (1990) *Der Neue Sport*. Hamburg: Ed. Akademion.

Glaser, B. (1989) 'Fitness and the postmodern self', *Journal of Health and Social Behaviour*, Vol. 30 (June): pp. 180–191.

Hartmann-Tews, I. (1990) 'Weibliche Körper-Verhältnisse — Kontinuitäten und Wandel', in N. Schulz and I. Hartmann-Tews (Hrsg.) *Frauen und Sport*. (Brennpunkte der Sportwissenschaft 4/2). St. Augustin: Academia Verlag, pp. 232-242.

Hartmann-Tews, I. (1991) 'Fitness-studios and health clubs — old wine in new bottles?', in J. Standeven, K. Hardman and D. Fisher (eds) *Sport for All into the 90s*. Aachen: Meyer & Meyer, pp. 310–316.

Hartmann-Tews, I. (1992) 'European diversity — a case for comparative research', in R. C. Wilcox (ed) *Sport in the global village*. Morgantown, WV: Fitness Information Technology, pp. 243–249.

Ley, K. (1984) 'Von der Normal — zur Wahlbiographie', in M. Kohli and G. Robert (eds) *Biographie und soziale Wirklichkeit*. Stuttgart: Teubner.

Mrazek, J. and Rittner, V. (1989): *Dienstleistungen von Fitnesstudios*. Köln: DSHS, Institut für Sportsoziologie (hektographiert).

Petry, K. (1990) *Fitneßstudios in geschlechtsspezifischer Wahrneh-mung*. Köln: Diplomarbeit DSHS.

Rittner, V. and Mrazek, J. (1986): *Sport, Fitness und Aussehen*. Köln: DSHS, Institut für Sportsoziologie (hektographiert).

Roberts, K., York, C.S. and Brodie, D.A. (1988) 'Participant sport in the commercial sector', *Leisure Studies*, 7: pp. 145-157.

Sack, H.-G. and Hennrich, R. (1989): *Kommerzielle Sportentwicklungen in Berlin (West) — Angebote, Nutzung, Stellenwert*. Berlin: Institut für Sportwissenschaft (hektographiert).

Schubert, M. (1991) 'Gewerbliche Sportanbieter', in H. Wieland and A. Rütten (Hrsg.) *Kommunale Freizeitsportanlagen*. Stuttgart: Nagelschnid.

Statistisches Bundesamt (Hrsg.) (1990): *Datenreport 1989*. Stuttgart.

II.

EDUCATION

LEARNING AND TEACHING IN PE: A LESSON IN GENDER?

Anne Flintoff
Faculty of Cultural and Education Studies
Leeds Metropolitan University, UK

Introduction

This paper draws on some of the data gathered as part of a larger study of the initial teacher education (ITE) of intending secondary Physical Education (PE) teachers in Britain (Flintoff, 1993a). The aim of this study was to critically examine the relationship between PE ITE and the reproduction of dominant images of masculinity and femininity and gender-appropriate behaviour[1]. This paper explores two key aspects of this research: firstly, the extent to which student teachers in PE are helped to become aware of the reproduction of gender power relations through schooling and PE, and to develop strategies for challenging this process in their teaching; and secondly a consideration of the process of ITE itself; how did it reflect, reproduce or challenge gender inequalities through everyday practices and classroom interactions[2].

The research context

The main part of the research involved an ethnographic study of two institutions involved in PE ITE. Qualitative methods of data collection were used, specifically those of observation, semi-structured interviews and document analysis. These methods were chosen in order to facilitate a full exploration of the ways in which gender power relations are reproduced at the level of social practice (see Connell, 1987). The two case study institutions central in the research offered both one-year, Post Graduate Certificate in Education (PGCE), and four year undergraduate courses, in secondary PE ITE[3]. They were chosen to reflect the separate and distinct historical development of the subject and are typical of the institutions currently involved in the training of secondary PE teachers[4]. The institution I have called 'Heydonfield' had been a former men's college of PE and is now part of a university, whereas 'Brickhill' had been a former women's PE college, and is now part of an institute of higher education. Both institutions had been co-educational for some years, a change imposed by the introduction of the European Law of Equal Treatment of 1976 (see Talbot, 1990), although the student cohorts at Brickhill, the former women's PE college, still had twice as many women as men students. This perhaps reflects the differing valuing of women's and men's activities and institutions.

The visibility and legitimacy of gender issues in the curriculum

How were students sensitised to the ways in which gender influences teaching and learning in PE? What kinds of legitimacy and visibility did gender issues have within the formal ITE curriculum, and how and where were they raised? Two main strategies were used; firstly, the inclusion of core units of work within the curriculum where gender inequalities were explicitly addressed, and secondly, through the permeation of such issues throughout the curriculum as a whole. In the permeation method, gender issues were discussed if or when they emerged in sessions other than those core sessions specifically allocated to this task.[5]

Core units

Both undergraduate courses introduced students to 'equal opportunity' issues in short, compulsory modules, situated within the second year Professional Studies element.[6] The fact that these units were situated so early in the students' course meant they did not contribute to work which was assessed for their final degree classification. However, opportunities did exist for a further, more in-depth consideration of gender in the later years of the degree courses, but this was within optional rather than compulsory modules, for example, sociology of education. This, one tutor maintained, was an appropriate structure, for he suggested that it would be "tedious to push such issues down students' throats by making such work compulsory".

Both members of staff in charge of the second year equal opportunities modules expressed some doubts about their role in running these courses; at one point the tutor at Brickhill even asked me whether I would be interested in teaching the module! The tutor responsible for running the unit of work at Heydonfield suggested that he had been given this role chiefly because of his interest in multicultural, rather than gender issues. The fact that neither member of staff with responsibility for these short modules showed a particular sensitivity or commitment to gender equality suggests it would be highly unlikely that the work would be successful in raising students' sensitivity to gender issues. Similarly, the location of the compulsory modules within the Professional Studies element of the courses — the area of work which students view as least relevant (e.g. Denscombe, 1982) — together with their 'one-off' nature, and their early placement within the course, are other factors likely to contribute to their overall ineffectiveness (Jones and Street-Porter, 1989; Shah, 1989).

The PGCE courses paid less attention to gender than the under-graduate courses, perhaps not surprising given the pressure of time on a one year course. At Heydonfield, one of the lectures within the Professional Studies element of the course specifically addressed 'gender stereotyping' in schooling. At Brickhill, the former women's PE college, the PGCE course leader suggested that they did not address gender because they had "always had more women". The issue for them, she suggested, was one of having to have "equal opportunities for the men ... we haven't been very good at that, like it was only last year that we got men's changing rooms". The danger in viewing gender in liberal terms of access, means that, as for this member of staff, for institutions or courses which have always recruited large number of women students, gender isn't seen as an issue!

Permeation of gender as a cross curricular issue

Many teacher education courses, particularly one year PGCE courses, use permeation as a means of addressing cross curricular issues such as equality issues (EOC, 1989). Permeation can be a valuable method of addressing equality issues, if it is part of a well structured, planned and evaluated package, and used alongside specific 'core' modules addressing equality issues (Cauldron and Boulton, 1989; Shah, 1989). However, it requires knowledgeable, sensitive and committed staff, and careful planning of when and where issues will arise, rather than leaving it 'to chance'. How then, did Heydonfield and Brickhill use permeation as a method of raising equality issues within other elements of the courses?

There was little evidence to suggest permeation was being used as an effective strategy for addressing gender issues in either case study institution. At Heydonfield, the former men's PE college, the head of PE admitted indifferently, that although the management team had made them aware of the issues, it was "up to individuals whether or not anything actually happened in practice". In contrast, the BEd at Brickhill in particular, specifically identified permeation as a method by which 'cross curricular issues' would be raised in the PE Subject Studies element of the courses. The course syllabus identified where, at least in theory, the permeation of 'cross curricular concerns' including race, gender and special needs would occur.

However there is a big difference between identifying where gender issues will permeate courses on paper, and how this is put into practice. Course documentation, for example, does not account for the difference between staff in terms of attitudes and value positions. As Ian Menter (1989) has noted, one of the major barriers to the implementation of anti-sexist and anti-racist work within ITE is the attitudes and value positions, as well as the interest and expertise, of the lecturing staff themselves. There were few examples during the observation period at both institutions of staff raising gender (or race) issues in a sensitive or informed way with students. On the other hand, there were many examples where stereotypical views of girls' and boys' physical abilities and behaviours were actually confirmed rather than challenged, by both male and female lecturers. Similarly, some staff were quite openly hostile to suggestions that gender issues should permeate their PE modules. The head of PE at Heydonfield, for example, suggested that in his opinion 'equal opportunities' received far too much attention and that this view had been echoed by the external examiner for the course that year. External examiners have important and powerful roles in making recommendations regarding course content and assessment procedures, and can have an important role in reinforcing the development of critical work. However, the opposite may be true, as suggested here. It does raise interesting questions, beyond the scope of this paper, about who get chosen as external examiners, and how this is done, as well as their expertise to act in this role.

This necessarily brief account shows how relying on permeation as a method of addressing gender issues can be problematic. However, although the examples used here have demonstrated resistance or apathy by staff to gender issues, it would be wrong to suggest that this was characteristic of all staff.

Whilst the study of teaching and teacher education as structures was central to this analysis, the practices of individual actors were also a vital ingredient, and it was clear that there were a number of different perspectives held by staff which need to be recognised and acknowledged. As Carol Smart (1984) has stressed, it is the study of individual actors which reveals the complexities of their ideological positions and the diversity of their practices, as well as their homogeneity and "it is these fragmentations and discontinuities which can give space to feminist ... struggles" (p. 152). A few staff were working hard to raise issues of equality in their work with students, particularly those women staff involved in teaching the Sociology and Curriculum Issues courses.

PE Subject Study

Although gender was given little official status in terms of the formal curriculum, nevertheless, it played a crucial role in the underlying values and structures of the courses. I was particularly interested to discover what kinds of physical activities were included in the PE curriculum, since the kinds of practical activities and knowledge students are introduced to in their training will undoubtedly be reflected in the shape and direction of their teaching, and the kinds of educational experiences they are able to offer children once in school. Were the institutions, operating on co-educational lines for some years, offering a co-educational PE curriculum?

The balance and range of practical PE activities included in the undergraduate courses reflected the gendered history of the institutions. Brickhill, as a former women's PE college, had retained its broad-based child-centred curriculum, which included a large emphasis on dance, gymnastics, and games. In contrast, the curriculum at Heydonfield reflected the games-based, skills orientated curriculum of the former men's PE colleges, with games making up almost half of the total time allocated to practical activities (see Fletcher, 1984; Kirk, 1990).

However, perhaps more significant than these differences was the differentiation of some of the PE activities by sex, and the rationales presented by staff for this. Although most activities were taught in mixed groups, male and female students were timetabled differently for some of the major games, specifically those which related to a social construction of 'appropriate' masculinity and femininity. Whilst interviews with staff suggested that a key rationale for introducing men and women students to these different activities was the preparation for their teaching practice in schools, further questioning revealed more deep-seated rationales tied to gendered ideologies. Activities which included physical contact and aggression, such as rugby, were seen as appropriate for men students, but not women; aesthetic activities, such as dance, were seen as important for women, but inappropriate for men and so on (see Flintoff, 1993b). The sex differentiated curriculum sketchily described here, both reflects, and reproduces, strong gender ideologies of men's and women's physicality and sexuality (see Messner, 1990; Scraton, 1987). Significantly, few students would have had access to the theoretical knowledge within their PE Studies which would help them challenge these. Despite very different course structures, both undergraduate courses marginalised socio-cultural knowledge at the expense of bio-behavioural knowledge (see Dewar, 1987; Flintoff, 1993a).

Despite the existing differences in curriculum content between the institutions, there was evidence to suggest that the move to co-educational was resulting in a male defined PE becoming dominant, a trend which has been noted elsewhere (Evans, 1990; Scraton, 1985). For example, complaints by male students at Brickhill about the amount of dance in the course had led to discussions on its reduction, or replacement for the men by a form of martial arts.

This trend is even more clear on the PGCE courses. The preoccupation of undergraduate PE programs with sport (e.g. Whitson and Macintosh, 1990), at the expense of a broader range of physical activities, including dance and gymnastics, affects the kinds of activities which can be included in PGCE courses. For example, at Brickhill, staff had decided to exclude dance from the curriculum, since so few students had experienced any dance in their under-graduate courses. The movement towards the PGCE as the main route into ITE PE therefore has important implications, not only for the amount of time students have to develop an awareness of wider educational issues, but also for the types of activities which become defined as 'PE'. It was significant to note the changes made by the Secretary of State for Education to the proposals for the PE National Curriculum (Department of Education and Science, 1991). These have eroded the suggested broad, balanced programme of experiences for children at Key Stage 3, making only games compulsory for this age group. The effects of these changes, together with the recent government moves to make training more school-based, suggests that the broad based PE characteristic of the women's tradition, is likely to be further eroded in the future.

Gender identities in PE

As well as analysing the nature of the formal curriculum, I was also interested in the ways in which gender influenced the everyday interactions and classroom practices. How did male and female students negotiate an identity within PE ITE and what effect did gender have on these experiences?

I have drawn here on Arthur Brittan's (1989) work on gender identity, who suggests that rather than seeing gender as a set of role behaviours unproblematically acquired (see Connell, 1987 for a critique of such 'sex role' theory), it is better seen as an accomplishment, something which is never static, and which is always subject to renegotiation and redefinition. A gender identity has to be worked at in every social situation and is always tentative. His work stresses the politics of gender identities, and the differentiation of behaviours and characteristics within gender groupings, as well as between them.

I should note here the difficulty of conveying through writing the ways in which gender power relations structure situations without reducing men to one cultural grouping and women to another (see Woods, 1984). Talking about men's or women's behaviour without care and detail can lead to the reinforcement of simple gender stereotypes (Askew and Ross, 1988). Here I have space only to note that institutions are involved in producing a range of masculinities and femininities, but that they are also involved in the processes by which particular ones become hegemonic (see Kessler, *et al.*, 1987).

Masculine identity work

A term's observation in each of the two institutions showed that a great deal of male students' behaviour revolved around 'doing' masculine identity work. This affected the ways in which they related to different curriculum activities, as well as to each other, lecturers, and women students. There were three key elements to this.

Firstly, male students' everyday behaviour involved actively competing with one another. There was a constant 'power play' underlying the interactions between one another — an ongoing process of positioning and a continual seeking of status and prestige. Competition seemed to be their primary source of motivation. Practical PE sessions were clearly useful and important vehicles for the demonstration of physical competition and the display of physical prowess — particularly those which demanded displays of appropriately 'masculine' physicality, such as in contact games, for example. However, even in non-competitive activity sessions, such as gymnastics, some of the male students would set up direct competitive challenges for one another, for example, daring one another to climb to the very top of a rope, or perform higher and higher dive forward rolls over a beam.

The effects of this kind of masculine identity work was a general reluctance on the part of some to involve themselves in pedagogical discussions, or in helping other students. I should add here that not all of the male students worked in this way during all of the practical sessions, nor was it the case that no female students displayed at least some aspects of this competitive behaviour. Since students' practical performance was formally assessed and contributed to their final degree classification at both institutions (and particularly at Heydonfield) it was in the students' best interests to practise and refine physical skills in this way. Interestingly, at both institutions, a student's performance in teaching could not help them improve their degree classification!

An alternative identity building strategy was the use of verbal put-downs, based on what Michelle Stanworth (1983) has called 'negative reference groups'. Women and homosexuals were used as negative reference groups, since as Michael Messner (1987) suggests, masculinity is defined in terms of what it is not — that is, not feminine and not homosexual. For example, one of the most common insults used to put-down or trivialise other men's perform-ances was to suggest they were performing like a 'right nancy' or like a 'girlie' (a derogatory term used by male students to describe women PE students). The effect of this second kind of masculine identity work was that male students distanced themselves from any behaviour or activity associated with femininity. For example, many male students went out of their way to demonstrate their lack of commitment to 'feminine' activities like dance by fooling around, and being generally disruptive. Homophobic comments were also common, acting to reinforce the display of appropriately 'gendered' behaviour by male and female students, but also to make virtually untenable the position of any student (or lecturer) whose sexual orientation was not heterosexual.

A third strategy of masculine identity work was to use the women students as a negative reference group. Throughout the fieldwork, I was struck by the lots of very subtle ways in which male students boosted their own confidence and status within the group by diminishing that of the women. As well as putting down their performances, with comments like 'just like a woman' etc., another important way in which women were controlled was through the explicit 'sexualising' of situations at their expense. Male students deliberately introduced jokes and sexual innuendoes into everyday classroom interactions, and the centrality of the body in PE meant that there were numerous opportunities for this to happen. For example, a partner stretch in gymnastics was suggested as a new sexual position, a progression for a flik flak involving thrusting the hips forward was a 'good exercise for later, lads', and a video of a young girl rolling in the gym provided an opportunity for female objectification by male students. Sexually appraising looks or gestures, often fleeting and very subtle, were also used. Whilst these incidents might be dismissed as trivial, and may be less extreme than some described by others within school environments (e.g. Mahony, 1985; 1989; Halson, 1989), nevertheless, they serve to reinforce the 'naturalness' of heterosexuality, and a construction of male sexuality based on objectification and conquest. These situations left women with little option but to 'go along' with the 'jokes', or risk being labelled as 'a spoil sport' — a situation commonly experienced by women in other settings (e.g. Burgess, 1989; Cunnison, 1989).

Given the little attention gender issues received in the formal curriculum, it is perhaps not surprising to note that these interactions were rarely commented on, or challenged by lecturers; indeed, although there is no space here to comment further, it is important to note that many male lecturers themselves were responsible for instigating a sexualised ethos within their sessions (see Flintoff, 1993a).

Being female in PE ITE

Negotiating an identity for the female students in PE meant ensuring, first and foremost, that they were recognised as heterosexual, feminine and attractive. Many of the women students, particularly in the early years of the undergraduate degree, took great care to emphasise their femininity and heterosexuality, for example through their dress and appearance, and through the way in which they avoided particular 'masculine' activities.

There were times when some of the women were clearly uncomfortable with being female in mixed settings in PE. I have already noted how some of the PE contexts were sexualised by male students and staff at women's expense. The potential for this was increased in some sessions where women's bodies were most clearly on display, such as swimming or gymnastics. Informal conversations with the students confirmed that their choice of wearing long tee-shirts over their swimming costumes until the last possible moment was an attempt to control the extent their bodies were 'on display'. Given the general lack of explicit recognition of sexuality within educational institutions generally (e.g. Holly, 1989; Kelly, 1992), it is perhaps not surprising that issues of sexuality have been similarly ignored within the PE profession. Scraton (1987) has suggested that PE needs to question whether, or indeed how, it contributes towards the image of 'woman-as-object'. This must include a consideration of current practice and policies within ITE. However, it is also important to note here that the reproduction of 'emphasised femininity' (to use Connell's 1987, terms) was not a simplistic, straightforward process, and there was evidence of women challenging, resisting and extending their gendered identities within PE. At one level, women's simple presence in PE represents an important challenge to ideas about their supposed fragility and passivity.

Overall, there was little evidence in my research to suggest that co-educational PE ITE has been a positive step forward for women, or that this form of organisation is contributing to a diminishing of gender differentiation and inequality within the profession. Rather, PE classes seemed to provide a context for the exhibition of strongly gendered interactions between students, with 'feminine' activities and contributions from women students being devalued and undermined.

Concluding comment

The development of the PE profession is, at least in part, influenced by the expertise of its newly trained members. Making PE an enjoyable, accessible and valuable experience for today's school children represents a difficult challenge for the profession. Teacher educators have a vital role in that process. My research suggests that gender equality is an important area within ITE where we need to improve our practice.

Notes

[1]   It is recognised that although the focus of this research was gender relations, these will be cut across and compounded by relations of class and 'race'. However as others (e.g. Dewar, 1990) have noted, it is often in terms of gender that an otherwise homogeneous group of PE students might be differently positioned. Certainly, since there were only very few black

students (or staff) at either of the two case study institutions, this research can only offer insights into white students' experiences of PE ITE. (See Siraj-Blatchford, 1991 for an account of how racism structures black students' experiences of teacher education).

2   I am using the term classroom broadly to include classes in formal lecture and seminar situations as well as practical sessions on the field, in the swimming pool or in the gymnasium.

3   The research focused on the training of intending secondary school PE teachers, not because primary school PE is less important, but because most of my experience had been with this age group.

4   There are now only approximately twelve institutions which offer initial teacher education courses for intending secondary, specialist PE teachers. Although the material presented in this paper derived specifically from fieldwork in the two case study institutions (and therefore it would be wrong to generalise about the findings) interviews with lecturers in other institutions revealed not dissimilar attitudes and value positions towards gender issues and curricular practices.

5   The term permeation is commonly accepted as a strategy for addressing equality issues by ITE institutions (EOC, 1989), despite, as Shah (1989) notes, a lack of clarity about what it is or what the method entails in practice for lecturers. John Coldron and Pam Boulton (1990) for example, suggest that the effectiveness of permeation can be assessed in terms of how far the professional legitimacy of a concern with gender is conveyed through all elements of the course.

6   ITE courses are currently made up of three key sections: PE Subject Study which includes both the practical and theoretical study of the subject, Teaching Practice, where students are practising their teaching in a school setting, and Professional or Educational Studies, which considers the broader context of education and schooling. It is significant, but not surprising, that the units of equality work were couched in terminology central to liberal feminist critiques of education. The limitations of such an approach, based on access and on changing stereotypical attitudes, are now well recognized (e.g. Arnot, 1981).

References

Arnot, M. (1981) 'Cultural and political economy: Dual perspectives in the sociology of women's education', *Educational Analysis*, Vol. 3, No. 1: pp. 7–116.

Askew, S. and Ross, C. (eds) (1988) *Boys don't cry: Boys and sexism in education.* Milton Keynes: Open University Press.

Brittan, A. (1989) *Masculinity and power.* Oxford: Basil Blackwell.

Burgess, R. (1989) 'Something you learn to live with? Gender and inequality in a comprehensive school', *Gender and Education*, Vol. 1, No. 2: pp. 155–164.

Cauldron, J. and Boulton, P. (1988) *The implementation and evaluation of an Action Plan to develop the PGCE curriculum so that the professional issues of Equal Opportunities are effectively addressed using a Focused Permeation Model.* Sheffield: Department of Education, Sheffield City Polytechnic.

Connell, R. W. (1987) *Gender and power.* Cambridge: Polity Press.

Cunnison, S. (1989) 'Gender joking in the staffroom', in S. Acker (ed) *Teachers, gender and careers.* London: Falmer, pp. 151–167.

Denscombe, M. (1982) 'The hidden pedagogy and its implications for teacher training', *British Journal of Sociology of Education*, Vol. 3, No. 3: pp. 249–269.

Department of Education and Science (1991) *Physical Education for ages five to sixteen, Proposals of the Secretary of State for Education and Science.* London: HMSO.

Dewar, A. (1987) 'The social construction of gender in physical education', *Women Studies International Forum*, Vol. 10, No. 4: pp. 453–465.

———(1990) 'Oppression and privilege in physical education: struggles in the negotiation of gender in a university programme', in D. Kirk and R. Tinning (eds) *Physical education, curriculum and culture: Critical issues in the contemporary crisis.* Basingstoke: Falmer, pp. 57–99.

Equal Opportunities Commission (1989) *Formal investigation report: Initial Teacher Education in England and Wales.* Manchester: EOC (June).

Evans, J. (1990) 'Ability, position and privilege in school physical education', in D. Kirk and R. Tinning (eds) *Physical Education, curriculum and culture: Critical issues in the contemporary crisis.* Basingstoke: Falmer, pp. 139–167.

Fletcher, S. (1984) *Women first: The female tradition in English physical education 1880–1980.* London: Athlone.

Flintoff, A. (1991) 'Dance, masculinity and teacher education', *British Journal of Physical Education*, Vol. 22, No. 4: pp. 31–35.

———(1993a) One of the Boys? An Ethnographic Study of Gender Relations, Co-Education and Initial Teacher Education in Physical Education. Unpublished PhD thesis, School of Education, Open University.

————(1993b) 'Gender, physical education and initial teacher education', in J. Evans (ed) *Equality, education and physical education*. London: Falmer, pp. 184–204.

————(1993c) 'One of the boys? Gender identities in physical education initial teacher education', in I. Siraj-Blatchford (ed) *'Race', gender and the education of teachers*. Milton Keynes: Open University Press, pp. 74–93.

Holly, L. (ed) (1989) *Girls and sexuality: Learning and teaching*. Milton Keynes: Open University.

Jones, C. and Street-Porter, R. (1989) 'The special role of teacher education', in M. Cole (ed) *Education for equality: Some guidelines for good practice*. London: Routledge, pp. 211–229.

Kelly, L. (1992) 'Not in front of the children: Responding to the right wing agenda on sexuality and education', in M. Arnot and L. Barton (eds) *Voicing concerns: Sociological perspectives on contemporary education reforms*. Wallingford: Triangle Books, pp. 20–40.

Halson, J. (1989) 'The sexual harassment of young women', in L. Holly (ed) *Girls and sexuality: Learning and teaching*. Milton Keynes: Open University, pp. 130–142.

Kessler, S., Ashenden, D., Connell, R. and Dowsett, G. (1987) 'Gender relations in secondary schooling', in M. Arnot and G. Weiner (eds) *Gender and the politics of schooling*. London: Hutchison/OU Press, pp. 223–236.

Kirk, D. (1990) 'Defining the subject: Gymnastics and gender in British physical education', in R. Tinning and D. Kirk (eds) *Physical education, curriculum and culture: Critical issues in the contemporary crisis*. Lewes, Falmer: pp. 43–66.

Mahony, P. (1985) *School for boys? Co-education reassessed*. London: Hutchison.

McKay, J., Gore, J. and Kirk, D. (1990) 'Beyond the limits of technocratic physical education', *Quest*, Vol.42, No. 1: pp. 40–51.

Menter, I. (1989) 'Teaching practice stasis: Racism, sexism and school experiences in initial teacher education', *British Jnl. of Sociology of Education*, Vol. 10, No. 4: pp. 459–473.

Messner, M. A. (1987) 'The life of a man's seasons: Male identity in the life course of the jock', in M. S. Kimmel (ed) *Changing men: New directions in research on men and masculinity*. London: Sage, pp. 53–67.

Scraton, S. (1985) 'Losing ground: The implications for girls of mixed physical education', paper presented at the British Education Research Association, Sheffield.

————(1987) 'Gender and physical education: Ideologies of the physical and the politics of sexuality', in S. Walker and L. Barton (eds) *Changing policies, changing teachers: New directions for schooling?*. Milton Keynes: Open University Press, pp. 169–189.

————(1992) *Shaping up to womanhood: Gender and physical education*. Milton Keynes: Open University Press.

Shah, S. (1989) 'Effective permeation of race and gender issues in teacher education', *Gender and Education*, Vol. 1, No. 3: pp. 221–245.

Siraj-Blatchford, I. (1990) 'A study of black students' perceptions of racism in initial teacher education', *British Educational Research Journal*, Vol. 17, No. 1: pp. 35–50.

Smart, C. (1984) *The ties that bind: Law, marriage and the reproduction of patriarchal relations*. London: RKP.

Stanworth, M. (1983) *Gender and schooling, A study of sexual divisions in the classroom*. London: Hutchison.

Talbot, M. (1990) 'Sex discrimination in Britain: Implications for the delivery of physical education, recreation and sport', in S. Scraton (ed) *Gender and physical education*. Victoria: Deakin University Press, pp. 99–117.

Whitson, D. (1990) 'Sport in the social construction of masculinity', in M. A. Messner and D. F. Sabo (eds) *Sport, men and the gender order: Critical feminist perspectives*. Illinois: Human Kinetics, pp. 19–29.

Whitson, D. and Macintosh, D. (1990) 'The scientization of physical education: Discourses of performance', *Quest*, Vol. 42, No. 19: pp. 40–51.

Wood, J. (1984) 'Groping towards boys' sex talk', in A. McRobbie and M. Nava (eds) *Gender and generation*. London: Macmillan.

LET'S HEAR IT FOR THE BOYS: DANCE, GENDER AND EDUCATION

Graham McFee and Fiona Smith
The Chelsea School, University of Brighton

Introduction

Two anecdotes will remind readers of the (widely familiar) central concerns of this paper. In writing a book on dance, one of the authors faced the standard problem of the apparently gendered character of singular pronouns in English: but, more importantly, it became obvious that one common solution (that of using "she" in one chapter, "he" in the next) was inappropriate. For such a procedure would support the (mistaken) view of dance as 'for girls': every other chapter would be explicitly for "she" and "her". Second, when the cover of the book was under discussion, the publishers offered an abstracted image of a dancer, obviously female (and obviously balletic). Perhaps they envisaged this as a suitable marketing strategy: certainly it gave the wrong 'messages' both about the book and about dance more generally.

If dance is, in this way, centrally seen as a 'feminine' activity (and valued accordingly?), that is a fact of central importance when the place of dance in education is under discussion; and, since the formulation of the National Curriculum for England and Wales, such discussion in the UK will focus on the place of dance within physical education. As Anne Flintoff rightly records:

> ...the majority of feminist research on the role of schooling in the reproduction of gender relations has concentrated on making girls' and women's experiences central and visible. (Flintoff, 1991: p. 31)

As such, these researches have naturally supported a (necessary) push for the kinds of reverse discrimination that might be hoped to begin improving the situation. No doubt far more than this is required, but this is at least a starting point — a first practical step, at least if handled properly (Scraton, 1993). Yet that is not precisely the situation in respect of dance: for dance, the production of a non-gendered physical education does not in the same way require the reinstatement of women's experience. Indeed this fact is implicitly conceded by Sheila Scraton when, in an excellent book about gender and girls' physical education (Scraton, 1992), she pays little attention to dance — even referring to it as "a traditional female activity" (p. 48).

Nor can it be realistically doubted that the 'stereotype' of dance as feminine is pervasive: for example, in a 'contribution' to the debate about the place of dance in the curriculum in the UK, the (then) Minister for Sport Robert Atkins[1] said: "I think there is a possibility of dance as a cop-out — a sixth-form disco as a substitute for physical activity. I don't think I agree with that." There is, of course, a difference between a genuine class and the kind of recreational activity the Minister may have had in mind, but two further assumptions on his part show here: first, that only this form of dance (disco) could possibly have a place for boys and, second, that it would not constitute genuine physical activity — a clear sign of his regular attendance at dance class! So one important thread here will connect discussion of the educational role (and significance) of dance in the context of schooling with the (emergent) research literature on dance as such.

In what follows we will consider the nature of dance in its relation to gender by discussing some ideas from Judith Lynne Hanna's *Dance, Sex and Gender* (1988) before turning to the application of these ideas to education — in particular, to the training of physical education teachers. Throughout, we will be concerned to insist on the need to theorise these matters: that the alternative would be to slip into repeating old platitudes. So we will comment briefly on some theoretical frameworks of possible application here. And our commitment to dance as a valuable, human, value-laden activity should also be clear throughout.

As will be obvious, our thinking on this topic is still at a preliminary stage: we are here assembling reminders as to points that should not be forgotten, and theoretical notions (often already in use in related areas) which might have application here too. We offer these ideas in this spirit.

Gender-identity as a Topic in Dance

The usual starting place for discussions of dance and gender is one Judith Hanna records as a central theme of her book[2]:

> ...to enrich the discourse on male/female body images and social change by spotlighting and clarifying how gender is socially and culturally constructed and transformed in a critical medium of human communication — the dance. (Hanna, 1988: p. 241)

Moreover, she wishes to do this as part of a focus on:

> ...the continuing reconstitution of gender roles and meanings that bear on the perpetual human struggle with questions of self-identity and interpersonal relationships. (Hanna, 1988: p. 241)

And we will turn to some of her comments on such issues in the next section. Here, though, we consider another matter Hanna raises: the place of gender-identity as a topic within dance. What must be seen is how a suitable dance form — a kind of 'Right-on' dance — might be thought to offer a non-gendered dance opportunity. For there is a curious isomorphism between this issue and the other. The famous Romantic ballets, such as *Swan Lake*, may be seen as presenting just the stylisation of gender roles under consideration: men as princes (and enchanters), women as idols (and victims), etc. It would not be far-fetched to see the Petipa/Ivanov *Swan Lake* as simply reinforcing these roles, and the relations of dominance/subservience they contain. Indeed, as Hanna notes, such ballets were seen in just that way. Recognising that, as Marcia Siegel (1977: p. 104) puts it, the male dancer's "main job is to lift the ballerina and look noble", Erik Bruhn choreographed "a 'corrective' version" (Hanna, 1988: p. 220) of the ballet for the National Ballet of Canada in which the hero is presented with a clear choice between spiritual and sexual love, and "meets his downfall by choosing spiritual over sexual love" (Hanna, 1988: p. 220; Siegel, 1977: p. 106). Here we see a rebellion against (or at least a contestation of) traditional images of masculinity and femininity. In this way, dance recognises its own position in the construction of images of gender-roles as well as in the articulation of those roles in dance[3].

More recently, Mats Ek has produced a version of *Swan Lake* (1987) which more directly confronts gender-construction, by taking it as a central theme of the ballet. Here, the Prince — offered a fiancé who is a pale image of his mother/stepmother — goes in search of the rich complexities offered by another *person*, as opposed to a mere cipher. Of course, the 'girl of his dreams' is initially conceptualised uni-dimensionally. But he learns (some of) the errors in this way of relating to others, for this is a world more like our own, "where, even with swans, everything is not black or white" (McFee, 1994: p. 80). So that the enchanter who holds the swans in thrall turns out not merely to be a woman, and not only to be the mother/stepmother, but also to be nude. Moreover, the 'happy ending' provided, with the Prince marrying the White Swan-Princess, is suitably equivocal: following the end of the White Swan's train comes the Black Swan-Princess (danced here, as traditionally, by the same dancer). The Prince has clearly married them both! It is clear that they will not 'live happily every after' in any straightforward fashion. Rather, they will need to negotiate the relationship in just the same ways as other people. All-in-all, this work might fit an account Hanna gives of a possible future, where danced-images of women "…combine the virgin and the bacchante: indeed, one finds complex women expressing many different facets." (Hanna, 1988: p. 216).

A fuller discussion of this case would talk about *how* it is achieved in the dance itself: both in its playful use of the traditions of the form and of the production-values standardly in place in this dance, and in its range and character of movement. (For are the 'dumpy' swans, some of who are male and all of who are ungainly, working against our expectations of balletic movement, or of *Swan Lake*? Of course, the answer is, "both"!)

Gender and Expectation

We turn now to explore some central ideas on the nature of dance drawn from the discussion in Hanna's book. Among her conclusions is that:

> More attention should be given to how images of dance and its production affirm and challenge basic social arrangements and doctrines about them. (Hanna, 1988: p. 250)

And notice here that this conclusion permits both affirmation and challenge. (We will come later to how this might be explained.) The first step in Hanna's argument is to emphasise both the importance of dance and what, precisely, makes it challenging (in her view). She tells us that "dancing motion attracts attention": and does so because "…the instrument of dance and of sexuality is one — the human body" (Hanna, 1988: p. 13). We are to infer that it is *because* of this connection between its instrument and sexuality's that dance is challenging: that there is some connection here between sexuality and challenge. (Notice that this is no argument: the same body is used for walking etc.) But, if this kind of emphasis is granted, we still need to locate more clearly the impact of dance here.

Hanna offers a "theory of vicarious learning" (Hanna, 1988: p. 11) at this point. Following Bandura (and earlier Kohlberg), she urges that:

> ... an individual tends to reproduce attitudes, acts, and emotions exhibited by an observed model ... A model may be cognitively registered and used or remain in subconscious memory until a relevant situation activates it. (Hanna, 1988: pp. 10-11)

Notice that this theory does not confine itself to what is explicitly learned, but also emphasises what is 'picked-up' — and may therefore remain part of one's consciousness. We might, with a proviso noted earlier [4], see this as a kind of 'role-model' analysis.

Our first major point grows from here. For a central question posed by such a conceptualisation of dance concerns the degree to which one can conceive dance movements as imbued with gendered characteristics. Hanna takes this for granted, though its extent and detail she sees as requiring further research, following-on from some of the work recorded in her book. She has begun to articulate a set of characteristics which might (arguably) provide a way of classifying what is (typically) to be vicariously learned. Such 'descriptors' would, if well-validated, give us a clear and thorough method for analysis of dances. Hanna is especially concerned about the large-scale (potential) impact of television, so her plan for future research identifies a need:

> ... to systematically describe the images of televised dances that have the potential to reach the entire nation. Illustrative descriptors could include gender identification for who is passive and assertive; who uses relatively larger or smaller movements in space; who is the subject and object of pushing, propelling, lifting, dipping, grasping another's body parts; who throws the body, clings, or leans, or supports; who cries or frowns; who moves a limb as a unit or in parts, takes a wide or narrow postural stance, and uses strong or weak effort. (Hanna, 1988: p. 250)

(And that is just the beginning of her list!) We might well question the methodological integrity of this approach: for instance, could any useful cross-cultural descriptors be conclusively identified? But here we are just noticing the ways this conception of dance permits the construction of 'role-model' movements.

Our second point brings in the relation between the sexuality of those in the dance world, whether as dancers or choreographers. For Hanna, an issue at one time concerned why — given that "... many of the greatest male dancers and choreographers, especially in the twentieth century, have been homosexual or bisexual" (Hanna, 1988: p. 226) — dance had typically not explicitly addressed, as a *topic* of dance, the nature of such sexuality. Now, the situation has perhaps changed since the time of the views Hanna quotes (they are from the seventies): indeed, she gives examples to suggest this. But this is not our point. For, if *our* concerns are with involving males in dance (both as performers/choreographers and as teachers), one might think it unlikely that the appeal of such themes will be strong. Indeed, one might suspect that this perception of dance (at least at the highest level) as a province of the gay and bisexual is one reason for its failure to attract a larger number of male participants. Certainly, it would not be the only such factor — opportunity for suitable experience, for instance, would clearly be another. But it might be taken as indicative.

So we have identified here two considerations: first, certain movements or movement patterns (roughly, those considered on Hanna's list of 'descriptors'?) are taken as feminine; second, the sexuality of (established) dancers is identified as gay or bisexual. And these two mutually reinforce. So that, as Hanna records, a movement pattern expressing "...male powerlessness or refusal to compete becomes imbued with the imagery of homosexuality" (Hanna, 1988: p. 136). Revealing this is not just an issue for dance. In a similar vein, Brittan (1989: p. 75) notes:

> A successful sportsman cannot afford to be 'soft' or 'passive'. Both in his muscular presentation and his behaviour he will embody an explicit aggressiveness. (also quoted Flintoff, 1991: p. 33)

Here Hanna cites, from Graham Jackson, the view "... that gay men can be macho dancers as well as dainty ones" (Hanna, 1988: p. 227). And, of course, one can agree. But that is not quite the issue, for it only addresses the sexuality of the dancers, not the 'qualities' of the movement.

In the same spirit, Hanna asks (also drawing on Jackson) "...why a woman can make herself glamorous and appealing as possible, but a man flaunting his sexuality is considered improper." At this point, we should remind ourselves (as noted above) that Hanna's argument drawing the connection between sexuality and dance is misconceived: that this connection is not well-established. And this seems the beginning of insight: perhaps what is at issue is not so much the flaunting of sexuality as something else. If this is accepted, it may create room for a role for a (more traditional) denial of feeling or emotion — that is, of the 'expressive' role of dance. Yet this is arguably central to the nature of dance[5], at least as it can (justifiably) appear in education.

Some Useful Theory

At this point, it must be acknowledged that our reflections are insufficiently theorised. And this consideration will be important since there are many issues and unclarities that our remarks thus far bring to the fore. However, we can now expand our discussion thus far by reminding ourselves of some of the disparate (if familiar) threads that a complete analysis might bring together, and some theoretical or analytical tools that might have a part to play. (And some of those tools will, of course, have already been utilised in respect of physical education though not — or not extensively[6] — for dance.)

Situated Rebirth of Ideology

One aspect which we have already noted is the way in which dance's apparent challenges to gendered orthodoxy are absorbed or accommodated by traditional positions. But how is this to be understood? One possible way forward would draw on an analysis of ideology (by Paul Willis [1982]) that is both generally revealing and could have special relevance in respect of dance. It comprises three elements. First, we recognise the ideological force of definition, "a general account of what the ideology 'says', as if indeed it were a manifesto" (Willis, 1982: p. 124). So 'we' think of ourselves in terms of, for example:

> ...the justice of meritocratic advancement as well as, of course, the natural superiority and aggressiveness of men coupled with the weakness and caring/emotional nature of women. (Willis, 1982: p. 124)

Moreover, conceptions of femininity in physical activity run along with such views. Such conceptions might be lampooned as 'women don't sweat'!

Second, Willis invites us to recognise contestations in selected (social) situations: "felt discrepancies which the actors involved are puzzled by and cannot adequately account for" (Willis, 1982: p. 125). In terms of our lampoon, 'we' must confront sweaty women in sport and, crucially, in dance.

What is the ideological response to such cases? Clearly, the outcome is not typically one of wholesale ideological revision[7]. In response, Willis introduces the third aspect: *the situated rebirth of ideology*. Consider one of Willis' examples (Willis, 1982: p. 130), the place of women as sportspersons in tennis. Here the situated rebirth of ideology might operate in one of two main ways: the women might be seen as reinforcing the gendered image (say, through media presentation which emphasised their prettiness, the design of their knickers, their roles as mothers or some such). In this way, the activity in tennis reinforces the central images of femininity for the women tennis players — so the 'definition' is not thereby contested. Equally, some tennis players are simply accommodated within these central images through their assimilation into the masculine images: their virtues — say, of speed and strength — as incorporated as 'mimicking' those masculine characteristics, and thereby failing to challenge the ideological definition.

Whatever one makes of this analysis for sport more generally, it provides useful categories for understanding dance. For it highlights at least one way in which increased involvement by males in dance would not really constitute a major[8] way forward. One might introduce the point by noting that a 'dance-artist-in-education' programme had, as an aim, the "... intention that boys be involved as fully as possible" (Briginshaw *et al.*, 1980: p. 19). As a result, one element of the project consciously used Robert North's dance *Troy Game* (1974) as a topic of study *because* it was an "... exciting and athletic dance for men" (Briginshaw *et al.*, 1980: p. 5). The degree to which such a strategy might be successful is, of course, to be sorted-out case-by-case. But it is clear that there is no *automatic* route to success here. For if we seek to make dance more accessible to males by ensuring "... masculinity through athletics in dance" (Hanna, 1988: p. 217) we are in danger of simply reinforcing traditional images of masculinity: thereby bringing about no more than the situated rebirth of ideology. And this danger is an especially live one for teachers. As one respondent in Sheila Scraton's research remarked:

> Dance is fine for boys as long as you use appropriate themes. They would need to do stronger, more assertive movements probably with a more dramatic element. (Scraton, 1992: p. 46)

Our point here is to use Willis' theoretical notion as a way of 'flagging-up' the dangers in this way of proceeding. If you make large numbers of such changes, you make dance 'for the boys' at the cost of destroying what made you want to teach it in the first place (the ideology is reborn).

Hegemony

Further, we have seen how it is inappropriate to conceptualise in purely adversarial terms the power relations that are reproduced (and explored) through dance. For the potentiality for revision or contestation is — as we have noticed — inherent in (at least) the artistic possibilities of dance. But what theoretical tools are required to handle this fact? One candidate here — Gramsci's account of power and domination, which introduces the concept of hegemony — seems to have much to offer (Willis' work might also be seen as growing from here). By the term "hegemony" is meant (roughly[9]) the capacity of the dominant group in a society to win the active consent of other groups in their own domination[10]. The details are complex and need not detain us. But two features of this notion give it promise in analysing gender relations and dance. First, it recognises that "… power relations … are a matter of negotiation" (Hargreaves, 1992: p. 270). In particular, applying this concept will preclude any simplistic analysis on which females are entirely powerless: "parties to negotiations cannot participate meaningfully without possessing some significant degree of power" (Hargreaves, 1992: p. 270). Such ideas have promise in the analysis of the development of dance in the twentieth century (chiefly in the USA) which, as Hanna notes, can usefully be understood in terms of three notions: *indict, dismantle, create* (see Hanna, 1988: p. 131). And all of these imply a negotiation around power relations.

Even more central to Hanna's account is dance as a (possible) site of female power/influence. As might be expected of any area to be analysed in terms of hegemony, contrary images abound here. For example, "… the toe shoe raised women above the herd and out of the house" (Hanna, 1988: p. 125), despite the fact that the very same toe shoe "… restricts natural movement and perpetuates the ethos of female frailty" (Hanna, 1988: p. 125).

The point to be drawn from this discussion is a rejection of any simplistic account of the relationship between dance and gender: no doubt there are power relations at work here. But that story will need a very careful telling — certainly more subtle than it has typically received.

The second crucial idea is that hegemony should be thought of as a continuous process of negotiation, rather than something attained: or, at most, as attained only for a time. As such, it also has direct application for our understanding of masculinity as well as femininity. It is in this spirit that we should, for example, read Anne Flintoff's remarks[11] on the ways in which male students may be engaged in "...an almost continuous process of confirmation and construction of their masculinity" (Flintoff, 1993: p. 195).

A Social Super-Ego

One might feel that both the theoretical notions suggested thus far cannot explain what we have noted — that they focus too exclusively on social-structural considerations, or concentrate too exclusively on the "structure" side of Giddens' 'structure and agency' dynamic (Giddens, 1984: pp. 281-284). For what can seem more *individual* than one's response to an art-form such as dance? So should we not therefore be recognising the place of the individual *psyche*?

Much here will turn, of course, on how the *psyche* is understood. Thus a theoretical notion which might usefully be invoked here is the Freudian idea of a *super-ego*, at least on some ways of understanding that notion[12]. For Freud, the super-ego developed in a way that was heavily social — as a kind of embodiment of (learned) social values. It is for this reason that it is only slightly misleading to see the super-ego as one's conscience: one learns moral values (and similar) in acquiring a super-ego: as Freud (1973a: p. 92) puts it, "...in general it represents the claims of morality". But, as Freud (1973b) recognised, the development of moral sensibility (in particular, the content of morality) would necessarily be heavily dependent on the time, place and circumstances of one's growing up:

> The super-ego ...represents more than anything the cultural past ...[p. 443]. It represents the influence of a person's childhood, of the care and education given to him by his parents and of his dependence on them ... And ... it is not only the personal qualities of these parents that is making itself felt, but everything that has a determining effect on them themselves, the tastes and standards of the social class in which they lived ... [p. 442]

By stressing the *social* reading of these (and similar) remarks, we have a way of explaining both the personal importance of dance — seeing what Hanna called "vicarious learning" in terms of the development of the super-ego — and its inherent capacity for evolution: just as hegemony is not (typically) permanently achieved, so one's super-ego development need not be finally rounded-off.

In this section, we have sought to remind readers of notions which, in a fuller discussion, might play a central role. But an element of their interest here is that their precise contribution remains unclear — partly, no doubt, because most have not been concretely applied to dance: indeed, even the possibility of using these notions in combination requires argument not provided here.

Dance and the Physical Education Student

Given, then, that the discussion in the previous sections sheds some light on issues from dance more generally, what morals might be drawn for the training of physical education teachers — who, under the provisions of the National Curriculum in England and Wales, will have responsibility for dance teaching in schools? Flintoff (1991) begins with some comments on dance by male students engaged in Initial Teacher Education (ITE); these are the predictable responses:

> ...dance is not an important priority for us men as you might have gathered! ...a man doing dance is a threat to his masculinity whereas a woman doing football is not a threat to her femininity. (Flintoff, 1991: p. 31)

Much that we have said about dance here might be taken to support the kinds of explanation Flintoff offers of such attitudes — in terms of "... the role of PE in the reinforcement and reproduction of hegemonic masculinity ..." (Flintoff, 1991: p. 34). [Her analysis of PE as such could usefully be supplemented from the work of John Hargreaves and David Kirk[13], who have urged, respectively, the centrality (for contemporary PE practice in the UK) of idealised versions of the body with their attendant conceptions of the masculine and feminine, and the roots of such practice in a "Scientific Functionalist" conception of PE which had dominated male-only physical education institutions.] But if this is broadly accurate, what is to be done?

Flintoff accurately charts two major worries here: the potential disappearance of dance "...in the coeducational PE ITE context" (Flintoff, 1991: p. 34), and the possible contribution of the PE teacher to this disappearance. Both are worries we share — indeed, the first motivates our concerns in this paper! On the second issue, Flintoff writes:

> Not many PE teachers, particularly male teachers, are prepared to offload their prejudices enough to make dance teaching attractive and relevant. (Flintoff, 1991: p. 33)

This is correct. But it is important to recognise — as we have already seen — that "attractive and relevant" here must not *simply* mean that one reproduces standard masculine characteristics through the dance (Brittan's "masculine identity work"). For to do so is likely to amount to a "situated rebirth of ideology": dance is included, but shorn of some key characteristics. As Flintoff records (see also Scraton, 1992 p. 48), a standard reaction to mixed-sex teaching has been "… to change everything: the music, the choice of material, the praise and feedback …" (Flintoff, 1991: p. 34). But this precisely does *not* address the issue. If the previous music, material etc. was educationally suitable for a single-sex group, it might be expected to continue to be relevant for the mixed-sex group. So we begin to identify one *inappropriate* strategy here.

One unsatisfactory aspect of this account is the way it leaves the ITE institutions as passively responding to what goes on in schools. (And this is, of course, in line with the present Government's policy whereby teachers-in-training will spend very large parts of that training in schools.) Now, it is certainly not true that all ITE institutions have insight and all schools lack it. (Neither part of that is true!) So that some schools are clearly well advanced in terms of, say, equal opportunities compared to some ITE institutions. But one role for ITE institutions is to use students as 'agents of change' as a way of updating PE (and other) curricula; as shapers of school practice, by arguing for and exemplifying good practice.

Perhaps it helps to be clearer on some of the gendered aspects of dance: as Flintoff remarks, dance has a "…potential for providing non-traditional images of girls as active and independent, rather than passively feminine" (Flintoff, 1991: p. 34)[14]. And we have drawn on Hanna's discussions (and Mats Ek's dance) to point out that dance's role may be even more challenging to traditional images. Also, it is important to see that the 'stereotype' response of the male teacher-in-training (which Flintoff records above) is not the only one encountered. So there are at least some signs of (actual or possible) contestation. For example, here are comments by male students on ITE courses in physical education in our institution:

> Once you get over the initial embarrassment dance is really good — it's not what I thought it would be at all.   I thought it would be boring and tedious, that I'd look silly and have to be a tree ... I was very pleasantly surprised .... I'm not embarrassed at all now: I want to be involved and to teach it.

Of course, it would be foolish to conclude from such comments that the problem has 'gone away': there is nothing representative about this sample of comments, and — even if there were — they represent at most a contestation of the stereotypical view, not its overthrow.

Our position, after teaching dance to numerous male students and listening to their comments as they progress through their training, and working in collaboration with male teachers trying to introduce and promote dance in their schools, is therefore broadly this: that there is another side to the story — or, rather, that the full story has not yet been told, or listened to. In particular, we are considering two main questions:

The *first* asks what (we might speculate) explains the differences between the responses from students that we have reported and those Flintoff quoted. One answer must relate directly to the exposure to dance of these different groups of students. For we have recognised constraints here: the presentation of dance must not simply reproduce dominant gender images, but it must still reflect traditional virtues of dance. From experience, it is possible to teach dance to males in a way that does *not* compromise artistic integrity (crucial if an 'artistic account' of the educational justification of dance is to be sustained [see McFee, 1994: pp. 156-158]) but *does* acknowledge what those males will bring to the subject in terms of years of social exposure, and preconceptions about the nature of the activity.

At its heart (and unsurprisingly) the issue here has much to do with knowledge and experience. For example, a recent evaluation by two first-year groups on the completion of a 30-hour dance module[15] showed a drastic shift in positive attitude towards dance. On analysing this very sizeable shift, it became clear that the majority of students who had never participated in dance prior to the course began that course with a very unrealistic opinion of what was to be expected, an opinion (as far as we could tell) based wholly on preconceptions about the activity — since they had never experienced it! This being the case, opinions soon shifted once students appreciated the true nature of the activity they were being offered. But, of course, this is merely indicative of the nature of the problem, without offering any concrete solution.

Moreover, it would be inappropriate to *assume* that these students had escaped once-and-for-all from the misconceptions they brought to the activity — as our analytical tools remind us! For the (potentially gendered) nature of dance represents an area of contestation: one where the negotiation around power characteristic of *hegemonic* relations is operative. And we must be alive to the possibility that this is just the *situated rebirth* of the dominant ideological 'stereotype'. In addition, such broadly structural considerations might be understood as integral to the development of the students' *super-egos*: and hence as centrally personal. Indeed, this degree of alteration at the individual level — which might be expected to inflect *understanding* — seems crucial to any hope that the students' classroom (that is, studio) activities prove genuinely educational. In summary, then, we must recognise that the possibilities for student satisfaction (on the part of male students) depends on their coming to see the activity as *other than* reproducing dominant gender images: and we would emphasise this possibility, without being blind to the difficulties that beset those who attempt it.

The *second* of the questions that (as noted above) arises from reflection on our practice has theoretical and practical dimensions: what considerations are important for the training of the ITE students in physical education? As well as looking for explanations (in terms of attitudes based on dominant images of masculinity and the 'gender-identity-work' of male pupils) for the failure to recruit large numbers of males to dance, or to an unwillingness to become teachers of the subject, teachers in ITE need to review their own practice — especially, perhaps, where females are teaching male students, for it is clearly crucial precisely how dance is introduced, presented, and so on. (In part, therefore, this issue connects with that identified above.)

The results here, while unsurprising, are worth recording. Asked what they had expected of their dance module, replies by male students included:

"I expected it to be really girlie — like ballet."

"I thought it would be all slow and boring."

"I imagined it would be a nightmare, lots of tutus and lycra tights."

Overcoming the preconceptions these views represent will clearly be a complex matter: how might it best be done?

It was clear that those who favour an 'in at the deep end' approach certainly run the risk of developing negative attitudes — and attendant confrontation or absenteeism — that may be difficult to reverse. The students interviewed felt very strongly that initial experiences were essential in setting positive attitudes to the subject for the future — like the child learning to swim, they needed to feel safe and comfortable in the 'new environment'; and that required the possibility of success and enjoyment in ways that were not threatening. In this sense, the initial dance experiences should not be offering a direct challenge to their 'masculinity'. For this reason, the majority of students favoured the 'gentle wade in' approach, predominantly teacher-led, with readily accessible themes and with physical challenge of paramount importance. These students identified a danger here: if an emphasis on the creative possibilities were interpreted so that students were left to their own devices — for example, to select dance ideas and/or music, or to decide on progressive tasks — they would have been overwhelmed, and never have gained any mastery. Of course, this general point might apply quite widely to beginners. But our reflections have highlighted one special problem: namely, that the recognition of considerations of gender intensifies the need for the tutor to be making key decisions concerning the presentation of material — that to leave these decisions in the hands of beginner students is to invite stereotypical reactions.

Conclusion

This paper began from differences between dance and (the rest of) physical education (as it is seen in the UK): that the issue for dance was not centrally that concerning the installation of a women's perspective — if anything, such a perspective was arguably already in place in much dance study. In its tentative fashion, the paper has offered three lines of conclusion:

- Substantively, the 'dance world' constitutes a social arena for gender-identity work both through the practice of dance and through the themes of dances. We have noted some difficulties (for a gender-neutral account of dance) flowing from each of these ideas. Attention to dances as exploring the nature of human sexuality can readily be transformed into attention on the sexualities of dancers: and these may reinforce misconceptions as to the 'feminine' nature of dance.

- Methodologically, we have shown the need for a fully theorised investigation of dance and gender, and suggested some analytic tools (familiar elsewhere, but not extensively employed in dance study) that might well have a place.

- We have presented a practical warning (if an obvious one): modes of delivery of dance courses in higher education (ITE) will be crucial for the eliciting of appropriate responses from male students — since (we have suggested), if those students are to understand dance at all, they must be given time to do so before being subject to dance ideas and dance practices potentially confrontational in respect of gender identity.

One might take further the speculations from which this paper began: is dance still seen as a female 'domain', as a site for feminine 'identity work'? If it were, as the male students' preconceptions suggest, that might begin to explain the relative paucity of analysis of dance in relation to gender-issues. For it might be thought that there is no *question* here at all: that what will be at issue for dance studies will concern the construction of masculinity, a comparatively neglected topic.

Finally, to return to our starting point, consider the outcome for the cover of the dance book (mentioned originally). Recall, the original suggestion from the publishers was for an image both obviously female and balletic. Yet what occurred? In the end, there was a revealing lack of a complete resolution: the final image was arguably not female, and obviously not balletic. So that final image might be taken to apply to humankind, and to avoid the most misleading of the unwanted inferences — for this was not a book on ballet! But that outcome just illustrates how key gender questions can be taken (mistaken?) as less central for dance studies than other issues.

Notes

1 Reported in *The Times Educational Supplement* 7 February (1992) p. 1.
2 N.B. This is not one of her more extreme works (such as Hanna, 1978) and is chosen as representing a plausible set of views.
3 In this way of putting the matter, the term "roles" is not intended in any precise sense: in particular, there is no commitment to a solely role-based account of gender.
4 The point here, as above, is to accommodate other analyses: for example, that of Arthur Brittan, 1989.
5 See the 'artistic account' of the nature of dance and of its educational role in McFee (1994).

6   Consider, for example, Adair (1992).

7   As Willis recognises, we should not pessimistically conclude "...that located actors are doomed carriers of ideology. A sufficiently strong repossession of the definition of the situation can reverse the process" (Willis, 1982: p. 129). But such an occurrence should be seen as the exception, rather than the rule.

8   There might be other virtues here, not discussed in the text; for instance, increased participation by males might have a long-term effect. But that is not the topic in this passage.

9   It can only be rough because the precise articulation of the concept is a matter for prolonged scholarly debate. For an account of some of this, see Hargreaves, 1992, esp. the references.

10 Compare Bocock (1986): esp. pp. 32-37.

11 Flintoff (1993) is here giving exposition of Brittan (1989).

12 The account offered here is substantially that of Wollheim, 1984: pp. 200-221.

13 Hargreaves (1986): esp. Ch 8; Kirk (1992): esp. Ch 4, Ch 6.

14 Here Flintoff also cites with approval Angela McRobbie (1984) writing on *Flashdance*.

15 These were students on a full-time ITE degree course: Flintoff's data are from ITE students on a PGCE course.

Bibliography

Adair, C. (1992) *Women and dance: Sylphs and sirens*. London: Macmillan.

Bocock, R. (1986) *Hegemony*. London: Ellis Horwood/Tavistock.

Briginshaw, V., Brook, J. and Sanderson, P. (1980) *Dance artists in education: Pilot projects 1980*. London: Arts Council of Great Britain.

Brittan, A. (1989) *Masculinity and power*. Oxford: Blackwell.

Flintoff, A. (1991) 'Dance, masculinity and teacher education', *British Journal of Physical Education* (Winter): pp. 31–5.

Flintoff, A. (1993) 'Gender, physical education and Initial Teacher Education', in J. Evans (ed) *Equality, education and physical education*. London: Falmer Press, pp. 184–204.

Freud, S. (1973a) *New introductory lecture on psychoanalysis (Penguin Freud Library Vol 2)*. Harmondsworth: Penguin.

Freud, S. (1973b) *An outline of psychoanalysis (Penguin Freud Library Vol. 15)*. Harmondsworth: Penguin.

Giddens, A. (1984) *The constitution of society*. Cambridge: Polity Press.

Hanna, J L. (1978) *To dance is human*. Austin: University of Texas Press.

Hanna, J L. (1988) *Dance, sex and gender*. Chicago: University of Chicago Press.

Hargreaves, J, (1986) *Sport, power and culture*. Cambridge: Polity Press.

Hargreaves, J. (1992) 'Revisiting the hegemony thesis', in J. Sugden and C. Knox (eds) *Leisure in the 1990s: Rolling back the welfare state* (LSA Publication No. 46). Eastbourne: Leisure Studies Association.

Kirk, D. (1992) *Defining physical education*. London: Falmer Press.

McFee, G. (1994) *The concept of dance education*. London: Routledge.

McRobbie, A. (1984) 'Dance and social fantasy', in A. McRobbie and M. Nava (eds) *Gender and generation*. London: Macmillan, pp. 130–161.

Scraton, S. (1992) *Shaping up to womanhood*. Milton Keynes: Open University Press.

Scraton, S. (1993) 'Equality, coeducation and physical education in secondary schooling', in J. Evans (ed) *Equality, education and physical education*. London: Falmer Press, pp. 139-153.

Siegel, M. (1977) *Watching the dance go by*. Boston, Mass.: Houghton Mifflin.

Willis, P. (1982) 'Women in sport in ideology', in J. Hargreaves (ed) *Sport, culture and ideology*. London: Routledge and Kegan Paul, pp. 117-135.

Wollheim, R. (1984) *The thread of life*. Cambridge: Cambridge University Press.

ADDRESSING THE ISSUE OF GENDER INEQUALITIES IN LEISURE: ILLUSTRATIONS FROM A CASE STUDY OF A PHYSICAL EDUCATION TEACHER

Lesley Lawrence
School of Tourism, Travel and Leisure
University of Luton, UK

[Physical education] teachers need to look more critically at both structural constraints and the realities of everyday experiences for women in physical leisure activities. (Scraton, 1992: p. 110)

Introduction

There has been a growing volume of literature citing evidence of constraints on women's personal leisure (e.g. see Shaw, 1985; Deem, 1986; Wearing and Wearing, 1988; Wimbush and Talbot, 1988; Woodward *et al.*, 1989; Green *et al.*, 1990). For example, in their revealingly entitled book — *Women's leisure, what leisure?*, Eileen Green and her colleagues examine in detail the structural constraints, that "operate to limit both the form and frequency of women's leisure opportunities" (Green *et al.*, 1990: p. x). It is not the intention here to examine at any great depth the constraints on women's leisure and more generally, gender inequalities in leisure. Rather, this paper will examine Sheila Scraton's contention that physical education teachers' leisure aims fail to address adequately such inequalities. She argues that, "the failure [of PE teachers] to assess realistically the problems of using leisure as a relevant and useful concept for women produces a contradictory and, in many ways, an unachievable aim for physical education" (Scraton, 1992: p. 110). Though not disputing the importance of the aim, Scraton questions the appropriateness of 'preparation for leisure' for adolescent young women. Whilst the women PE teachers she interviewed saw the aim as important, she considers it a "dubious objective for young women's PE" (Scraton, 1987: p. 177), particularly in the light of constraints on women's leisure, the structural limitations and the reality of everyday experiences for women in physical leisure activities.

Evidence from my own research findings[1] on teachers' professional leisure aims and practices (Lawrence, 1991) would, on the whole, support Scraton's concerns over the lack of attention given to gender inequalities in leisure by the so called 'leisure educators' in schools — from only a minority of teachers questioned did such concerns emerge. In the second half of the paper, one such case —that of Louise, a teacher in the case-study phase of the study — will be used to illustrate how one teacher's awareness of constraints on women's leisure from her own life experiences in conjunction with her perceptions of constraints on her South Asian girl pupils' opportunity to take part in sport now and in the future, permeated through and affected her professional leisure practice. First though, the research findings from my study of teachers' leisure aims will be used to set the scene, giving a general overview of teachers' leisure aims and practices. This will be followed by a brief account of some of the major criticism levelled at leisure delivery in secondary school PE, and then some discussion of possible reasons for the apparent lack of attention paid to gender inequalities in leisure by the PE teacher.

General overview of leisure aims and practice

Some of the basic findings from my study (Lawrence, 1991) will provide the context for the discussion to follow on PE teachers' approaches to the issue of gender inequalities in leisure. These can be summarised as follows:

1. Some form of leisure aim existed in the teaching of PE.
2. The leisure aim was fairly narrowly construed: *teachers hoped pupils would participate or continue to participate in sport/physical activity on leaving compulsory education.*
3. *The leisure aim was regarded as a very important aim by the vast majority of the teachers.* Such evidence though, conflicts with those observers (e.g. Whitehead and Fox, 1983; and Tozer, 1986) who would argue that fundamentally the leisure aim is non-essential, or a mere by-product of other more important aims which are unique to 'Physical' Education.
4. Significantly for many teachers, *the leisure aim had increased in importance since they had started to teach.* Two key inter-related reasons for this

emerged: first, the consequences of the high profile of leisure in society as one teacher explained — "growing trends in life towards increased leisure time has meant a greater need for "leisure" preparation through schools"; second, the concerns expressed over inactivity, health and use of time.

5. *The level of importance of the aim was found to be a function of pupil age*, namely, that the leisure aim became more important in the final years of schooling.

6. Contrary to the general views expressed in the literature, *there was notable variance in the way that an apparently commonly held leisure aim was being translated into practice* by the teachers. Yet there were common elements and the findings supported the literature which points to three such areas of practice:

a. *the structure of the PE programme itself*: for example, with as wide a range of sports and physical activities as possible. This is particularly expressed in the form of some options scheme in the senior years with the choice element playing a prominent role;

b. *the facilities and opportunities to participate*: for example, community links with clubs and facilities, a school's extra-curricular clubs. The most popular type of practice was teachers facilitating and encouraging pupils to join clubs outside of school where they could participate in their chosen sports;

c. *the nature of the PE experience itself*: for example, as being enjoyable, and satisfying. This last area of practice might either be aimed at making the experience enjoyable, satisfying and motivating as a strategy to promote future activity — as a means to an end; or merely aimed at encompassing the notion of 'PE as leisure' — enjoyable and allowing a degree of freedom possibly acting as a break from the more academic subjects in the curriculum.

7. An additional area of leisure practice was identified — one case-study teacher referred to this as 'progressive leisure practice' — namely, the area of health-based PE and thus, *the health benefits of participation*. The assumption here is that participation will continue if pupils understand the value of health, of exercise in life. This reflects the growing influence of the health-related fitness movement in PE (see, for example, contributions in a text on 'Issues in Physical Education', Armstrong and Sparkes, 1991).

8. *Differences in leisure practice priorities and emphases were discovered.* Three inter-related elements were offered as reasons for this — the teachers' working situation; teachers' career; and teachers' own meaning of leisure; this last personal factor from the teachers' own life emerged as central to understanding both teachers' leisure aims and their practice emphases in their teaching.

9. Differences between female and male teachers, in for example, Kane's (1974) 'ranking of PE objectives' question, and the historic and traditional distinction between men's and women's PE, led to expectations in the early stages of the research that there might be gender differences in teachers' leisure aims and practices. In the event, very few statistically significant differences were found concerning the leisure aim and these tended to be related to status in the department — e.g. male heads of department gave a higher importance rating to their leisure aim than did female assistant teachers. *No gender differentiation was found in terms of teachers' leisure practice.*

Criticism of leisure practice

The failure of PE teachers on the whole to address the issue of gender inequalities in leisure opportunities and the problems their pupils might face in taking part in sport should they wish to, is just one of a number of criticisms made of traditional leisure practice in the PE literature over the last 15 years. Not surprisingly given the growing climate of accountability in schools and concerns with the status of PE, the main criticism directed at school leisure programmes in general and senior programmes in PE, has been their recreational rather than educative nature (e.g. Borrett, 1982; Hendry, 1986; and Robinson, 1990). It has also been argued that the teacher is as much an administrator as a teacher (Williams and Jenkins, 1988). Additionally, the traditional menu of activities within the PE curriculum and in option schemes may be contrary to pupils' own favoured activities; choice is based on value judgements being made on the types of activities which are good for the pupils. The Physical Education Association considers, for example, that PE contributes to "the purposeful use of leisure time" (PEA, 1987: p. 242) and this is just one example of a reforming zeal underlying much debate on the worthwhile-ness of leisure; yet we know that much of one's leisure time could be and often is spent in non-constructive, informal, non-purposeful activity. Faced by evidence of misuse of leisure time and non-acceptable forms of leisure activities, leisure education in secondary schooling is regarded as responding to such problems in society.

Why are constraints on women's' leisure/gender inequalities in leisure not addressed?

This paper began with Sheila Scraton's recommendation that teachers "need to look more critically at both structural constraints and the realities of everyday experiences for women in physical leisure activities" (Scraton, 1992: p. 110). Whilst research examining the reasons for the general failure to address gender inequalities and constraints on women's' leisure would be welcome, in the meantime, it is worth speculating on some possible contributory factors.

One such factor relates to the teachers' reality in a turbulent educational climate with changing and often increasing demands, and "the teacher's increasingly diffuse role and a fragmented occupational culture" (Hargreaves, 1980). Significantly, even before the advent of the National Curriculum in PE, commentators such as Evans and Davies (1988: p. 4) were remarking that, "never before" have teachers had to "deal with so many pressures for change from different sources". The findings from my own study suggested that the leisure aim may be regarded by many teachers — both female and male — as highly important, yet, in practice it is often overtaken by other more pressing matters and priorities. As one teacher commented: "I feel I would like to make it more important, but longer term considerations are overtaken by 'day to day' routines and tasks. Also, so little time is given to exercise by youngsters that I feel all available time be given to its practice in lessons" [*m, oh, 35*][2]. Is it realistic to expect teachers to spend much time on addressing gender inequalities and constraints on women's' leisure, given today's pressures and demands?

Teachers also lack guidance from sources within the PE profession on 'good practice' or issues to consider where leisure aims and practices are concerned. In my study, only 8% of teachers had received any guidance, for example, from their Local Education Authority, on 'leisure aims in PE'. Just over one half (51%) of the teachers would have welcomed some guidance, yet even with the advent of the National Curriculum, discussion or guidance on the leisure role in PE by policy makers is not prioritised (Lawrence, 1993). It is therefore not surprising to find that individuality of leisure practice is promoted, as noted earlier.

Another contributory factor relates to the lack of evaluation where the leisure aim is concerned. Were ex-pupils, for example, participating or continuing to take part in sport/physical activity? Were they having problems in doing so? From his work on physical education curriculum planning, Underwood (1983: p. 132) contended that "most heads of department do not regularly and systematically evaluate their original aims". In my own study, just under a quarter of the teachers responding to the questionnaire survey (23%), admitted they made no attempt to judge the success of their leisure aim. One of the case-study teachers tried to find out on a casual basis from the community school recreation staff, "how many come in at weekends to do extra things"; she admitted that there was "no real follow-up once pupils had left school". Of those making an attempt, 84% professed to having difficulty in judging the success of their leisure aim. This suggests teachers are not obtaining feedback, and are therefore not aware of possible problems.

Perhaps the most plausible explanation lies in the type of people PE teachers themselves are as a group, and in the interplay between teachers' professional and personal lives. Woods (1984: p. 239) for example, believes that "a teacher's self, in part at least, both finds expression in and gives expression to a curriculum area". I would contend that the majority of PE teachers lack real awareness of the problems many women experience in taking part in sport and physical activity, due to their own background and positive experience of sport. From my personal experience in sport throughout schooling and adult life, and from the years spent training to be a PE teacher and teaching the subject, I would suggest that: PE teachers on the whole have a deep-rooted love for sport; they have or have had strong motivation to take part; many will have benefited from parental and monetary support; and they themselves might not have experienced any great problems in terms of opportunities to take part. Indeed, when the teachers in the study were asked what had influenced their views on their leisure aims and how important they were in their teaching, a number — both female and male teachers — referred to their own positive experience. For example, one teacher had been influenced by her own "personal participation in sport associated with opportunities presented for socialising, travel, self-confidence" [*f, oh, 40*]. Another considered that, "since I have a very active and full life and gain a lot of enjoyment from my leisure time activities, this has influenced me in my methods of teaching and overall aims [*m, a, 25*]. Ninety five percent of the teachers questioned in the study (n=158) were currently involved in some form of active participation. As one teacher commented, "to me leisure means doing something active and practical and enjoyable whenever possible" [*f, a, 31*]. Even the older teachers, many of whom perceived themselves as less active, were still highly active.

Related to this, and also a contributory factor are the women PE teachers' personal meanings of leisure. In the study, no discernible differences were detected in leisure meanings when the teachers' responses were differentiated by gender. Some difference might have been expected given criticisms levelled in the Leisure Studies literature, of a failure to differentiate as regards gender (e.g. by McIntosh, 1981; and Deem, 1986). Such commentators consider traditional, objective conceptualisations of leisure as inappropriate for women; McIntosh (1981), for example, argued that Parker's (1971) dimensions of time and activity did not apply to women. Yet, such an argument clearly did not hold true for the group of women PE teachers in the study; time and activity dimensions to leisure were prominent in female and male teachers' meanings of leisure. To the majority, leisure itself was viewed objectively as 'doing things', as 'use of time'. In the case-study phase when the whole question of meaning of leisure was examined in depth, leisure for the teachers was primarily seen as use of time other than that of paid employment with perceptions of work playing a key role. The evidence suggested that being employed in the work force as 'physical education teachers' overrides any gender factor influence in teachers' personal meanings of leisure.

Yet the argument that positive personal experience is influential and has some bearing on teachers' failure to address gender inequalities in sports participation in leisure, can be seen to be somewhat flawed with the realisation that a number of PE teachers in the study *did* speak of the lack of time to take part in sport and to do as much as they wanted. Likewise, the female teachers in Scraton's study (Scraton, 1992) had also described the problems they faced concerning family and domestic responsibilities which restricted their opportunities to spend more time on extra-curricular activities or personal leisure pursuits. Importantly, such problems did not just apply to the female teachers in my own study. One of the male case-study teachers — John[3], for example, bemoaned the lack of time for leisure over the last two years, related largely to time and financial constraints. In his early thirties, married with two young children, he had to teach adult evening classes to help make ends meet and the rest of his time he wants to spend with his family rather than pursuing his own sporting pursuits. His was a clear example of what Roberts (1981) calls, 'dramatic changes' in leisure habits, heralded by marriage and parenthood: "Family responsibilities mean that the amounts of free time and money available to maintain outside interests diminish. Establishing a home becomes a central preoccupation" (Roberts, 1981: p. 77). Yet John, at the same time, did not appear to appreciate that this might be a problem for his pupils when they left school, or consider other constraints which would curtail sporting participation. His leisure aim was that pupils choose to follow on with participation in sports. The concern was with improving skill levels, and knowledge in order that the pupils knew what they were choosing from and would continue taking part in their chosen sport. Along similar lines, Scraton comments upon the certain irony of women PE teachers from her study who, whilst recognising problems and limits on their own leisure time and opportunities on the one hand, at the same time, consider leisure as a realistic objective for young women (Scraton, 1992).

Let's move now to Louise, the case-study teacher in the study who did address gender inequalities in leisure and whose leisure practice, clearly, was affected by this awareness. The interplay between her professional and personal lives was certainly visible. In telling this teacher's story, it must be stressed that the intention is not to be overly critical of the accuracy of her perceptions and reasoning behind many of her beliefs and actions against evidence from the literature. There is certainly a tendency for Louise to fall into the various traps of ethnocentrism, racist stereotyping and false universalism (for such discussion in the sport and leisure context, see for example, Lovell, 1991; Carroll and Hollinshead, 1993; and Fleming, 1993). Importantly, the following passage reveals what *Louise* believes in, how *she* defines the situation and how *her* practice is affected by these beliefs. Whether 'occasionally mis-informed awareness' is better than 'no awareness' remains a contentious issue to be argued elsewhere.

The case of Louise

Louise has been head of the girls' PE department in a large urban community comprehensive in the midlands of England (11-18) for twelve years. Although the school is mixed sex, she teaches only girls' lessons. When she had first come to the school, it could be described "as a multi-racial school"; within the last few years it has increased to 80% South Asian and in 1st year as high as 90%. She believed that the Head teacher's strategy of introducing the language punjabi to all pupils two years previously — a failed venture — had accelerated the change and had contributed to a falling role with non-Asian pupils being removed by parents. This changed population had a number of consequences for the girls' physical education department. For example, "the fitness, co-ordination of the Asian girls is far less, so we really have had to put more emphasis on HRF [health-related fitness] than we've done in the past. And I think we've had to go back to basics very much more".

As for Louise's own personal life and leisure, she was 39, divorced, recently re-married with no children. Her first reaction, when asked what leisure meant, gives an immediate pointer as to the significance of leisure in her life: leisure was precious and scarce. Leisure was:

> ...time which is *my* time: time which I can devote to *my* interests, time which I can use for *myself.*

She divided this time up predominantly for sporting interests, but also liked to read, to garden, and knit; her idea of leisure was when she wasn't working, "when I've got my own free time, time that I can devote to the interests that I've got".

To Louise, 'devoting time to herself' seemed critical when she spent the majority of her time teaching, travelling to work, and running the house. Louise found her weekends full of what she called 'work' — decorating at the moment, washing and ironing, preparing meals, and "school stuff". The highlights of the week where leisure was concerned therefore were what she called 'my nights': two nights when she went to a recreational fitness club and a badminton club respectively. More important than the activities themselves and all the benefits, was the feeling that "they're *my* nights ... and nobody's going to take them off me". Partly responsible for this attitude had been seeing the experiences of many of her women friends whose lives revolved round the 'man in their life', with severe consequences when the marriage breaks down:

> He goes off ... he's got his golf club, football team and she folds up. She's lost her friends, she's never developed herself as a person, she has no interests, or she's tied down with kids and can't get out.

Louise was very much aware of the woman's right to work and to have leisure. Having your 'own' life is important in helping you to "have identity, [it] helps you know who you are, to take a pride in yourself". She felt strongly that married women must think of themselves.

I'm a person, I *should* have interests, I *should* have hobbies, I *should* have things around me other than close family.

Her husband had his own interests and a number of sports, going out to the Rugby Club and Round Table two nights a week; while he was going out to these, Louise had no intention of giving up her nights or her extra-curricular clubs at school (the latter she saw as leisure — chosen to do in her own time). In addition to the satisfaction of 'doing her own thing', Louise's two club nights lacked compulsion, they were enjoyable, she was able to relax, and the social element was important meeting up with fellow club members and friends other than husband; she was "able to get something out of it". She also ate out so had no cooking to do. For Louise, this was what leisure was all about. "The only real leisure I get is on these two nights". As well as an opportunity to assert her own identity as a woman, her two nights were seen as both precious and necessary, an important function being restorative:

I think without them I probably wouldn't cope ... I wouldn't be as well adjusted if you like, or as fit to cope with the pressures of what I do.

Time permitting, she would like to ski at a local dry ski slope, play golf (develop this with her husband as they have separate sporting interests), learn a language, go to upholstery evening classes, but "you don't have the time. That's why I've made those two nights my nights and I would not go without them".

Thus, given the importance of having her 'own life' and this conviction of the need to assert herself and the need for other women to do so, it is not surprising that this strongly shows up when she talks about her aims for the girls in a predominantly South Asian school population and the importance she places on a leisure aim for her pupils. She considered the curriculum to be geared to the leisure aim of developing sporting interests that could be continued throughout adult life, participation in sport being one means by which she is herself able to have time of her own and assert herself as a woman.

Believing South Asian women to be particularly disadvantaged and "not expected to have any interests outside" — it was important to her that the girls should have some time of their own to follow some leisure activity. She saw her role as trying to establish extra-curricular habits at school so that in adulthood, "my life involves going somewhere else and taking part outside of my work time" (employment or housework):

> If you don't get that when they're children, they're not going to do it as
> adults. Not girls ... men might I think ... you've got to really begin as
> you mean to carry on. If you can get them doing things in their leisure
> time right from the start, then I think it's going to rub off later on in life.

Preferably this would entail some form of sports participation, but she also showed
interest in pupils' passive leisure interests out of the home environment and
encouraged these. Central to Louise's leisure practice was attempting to establish
favourable attitudes towards physical exercise and sport 'now in school', in the
belief that if this fails, "then it's not going to happen". With the South Asian pupils,
"you were setting off at a disadvantage" because their families give little priority
"towards girls' health and fitness ... and getting girls interested in sport". She
feared parents' attitudes being reflected. Consequently she perceived her role as
changing attitudes—"they're not going to be there established for us". It was due
to such beliefs that she thought it important that "we do attempt to instil positive
pupil attitudes; that we get the parents in, we get them interested and get the girls
going from as early an age as possible". She also considered that instilling positive
attitudes towards sport and educating future parents (South Asian girls *and* boys)
could help. Hence her pushing for mixed PE from 1st year onwards despite the
potential cultural resistance from some parents.

Louise is very concerned that the numbers of pupils participating in the clubs
she runs is dropping, seen as corresponding with the higher percentage of South
Asian pupils in the school. "You're fighting a lot harder. You're having to push
and push and encourage as much as possible". She is largely pessimistic in
terms of how her aim to establish favourable attitudes to sport and exercise and
extra-curricular habits is likely to progress, in particularly pointing the finger at
cultural barriers faced.

Should she ever succeed in instilling positive attitudes and interest in sport,
Louise foresees enormous problems for her South Asian girls in actually
pursuing an interest in sport in 'their society'. Revealing a blatantly Eurocentric
perspective, she sees South Asian women:

> "... as subservient to men terrifically within their society, they're tied to
> the home, they're not expected to have any interests outside. Their
> opportunity to do something for themselves is, — really there is none
> you know, it's totally deficient in their lifestyle. It's bad enough for
> *women* to pursue sport."

Concluding comments

Louise's case has been used to illustrate how one teacher's perceptions of gender inequalities in leisure and awareness of constraints on women's leisure from her own life experiences, in conjunction with her perceptions of constraints on her South Asian pupils' opportunity to take part in sport now and in the future, has affected her professional leisure practice. As we've just seen however, Louise has expressed doubts over whether she will be successful; she feels she is fighting a losing battle to instil favourable attitudes and extra-curricular habits. The important point to make however, is that this particular teacher exhibited awareness — whether 'academically' informed or otherwise — of the problems many women, and in particular South Asian women face in taking part in sport, and was attempting to do something about it in a positive manner. Evidence suggests that such an outlook is rare amongst PE teachers. It could be argued that it was the combination of a number of factors in Louise's personal and professional life, the strength of her convictions over the right for women to have their own leisure time, that has accentuated for her the problems of participation in sport by women and her pupils, and caused her to prioritise her leisure aim.

Scraton suggests that "teachers need to look more critically at both structural constraints and the realities of everyday experiences for women in physical leisure activities" (Scraton, 1992: p. 110). Whilst concurring with this, but also being mindful of the demands and pressures on teachers, should this apply just to the teachers? From my own examination of teachers' leisure practice, the notion of '*education*-awareness of leisure' was suggested as an additional form of leisure practice — one which would incorporate a critical awareness factor *about* leisure whereby the individual and their values, attitudes and what enhances or constrains the leisure experience would be prioritised; pupils would leave school with more informed attitudes about the structure and operation of leisure in society (Lawrence, 1991). A rare example of thinking along these lines in the study was provided by one of the female teachers who ran a Leisure Advice Course (the course had received a Schools Curriculum Award). The teacher felt that "I do, at last, feel that we are getting to grips with preparing our 5th year girls for coping with their free time both now, and once they have left school" [*f, gh, 33*]. The six week course for 5th year girls contained a wide range of practical exercises associated with the 'hows' and means of taking advantage of leisure provision; importantly, it also dealt with constraints — one of the course objectives being to encourage pupils to challenge the reasons for the low status of sporting leisure pursuits for women. Whilst creating awareness amongst pupils, this type of practice also begins to approach Kirk's (1989: p. 143) call for teachers to help pupils develop:

> ... a critical awareness of the pre-packaged, commodified forms of leisure activities currently in vogue in the "health, fitness and leisure industries" and so supplying them with the critical capacities to create their own leisure-time pursuits and also to create their own industry.

If teachers themselves lack awareness of the issues of gender inequalities and constraints on women's leisure, or perceive them as irrelevant or unimportant, then there is a problem with this educ-awareness proposal. Yet, as Scraton points out, "preparation for leisure is a dubious objective for young women's physical education unless it is approached through a critical analysis" (Scraton, 1992: p. 110).

In bringing this paper to a close, the evidence does suggest that PE teachers, on the whole, lack critical analysis and fail to address the real problems that many girls and women face in taking part in sport/physical activity, should they wish to do so. The example of Louise, can be regarded as an exception rather than the rule. Why there is this failure, given the importance that so many teachers give to a leisure aim — one which clearly indicates that teachers hope that pupils participate or continue to participate in sport/physical activity on leaving compulsory education — is a matter for concern and debate within the PE profession. Several possible contributory factors have been proposed in this paper, including: the lack of teacher guidance from the PE profession on leisure aims and practices; teachers having other priorities in teaching; lack of evaluation of the leisure aim by teachers; and PE teachers' positive leisure experiences in their own lives. It could be argued that the influence, throughout life of positive experiences in their own leisure, overrides any current constraints on teachers' own personal leisure, and results in leisure practice which fails on the whole to address problems in taking part in sport and physical activity. Research undertaken on this would certainly provide useful insights.

Acknowledgement

Thanks are due to Dr Scott Fleming, University of Brighton, for his comments on an earlier draft of this paper.

Notes

[1] In a two phase study, an extensive questionnaire on aspects of teachers' leisure aims and practices was mailed to teachers (both female and male teachers) in secondary schools in 6 local authorities in England in May 1988 — responses from 165 teachers in 61 schools were analysed. In the subsequent case-study phase in late 1989, there followed greater in-depth investigation of six individual teachers' leisure aims and practices, and influences on practice. The teachers were shadowed and observed, interviewed over a period of 2-3 days.

[2] To give some indication, albeit brief, of the experience and gender of the teachers making direct comments, quotes are followed (in brackets) by an *indication of gender* (m/f); *status in the department* (oh = overall head of department; gh = girls head of department, and a = assistant teacher); and *age in years*.

[3] All interviewee names used here are 'fictional' substitutes for the respondents' real names.

References

Armstrong, N. and Sparkes, A. (1993) (eds) *Issues in physical education*, Cassell, London.

Borrett, N. W. G. (1982) Leisure and Education — Towards a Leisure Education Programme in Schools with special reference to Sport and Physical Education. Unpublished MSc dissertation, South Bank Polytechnic, London.

Carrington, B. and Williams, T. (1988) 'Patriarchy and ethnicity: The link between school Physical Education and community leisure activities', in J. Evans (ed) *Teachers, teaching and control in physical education.* Lewes: The Falmer Press.

Carroll, B. and Hollinshead, G. (1993) 'Equal opportunities: race and gender in Physical Education: A case study', in J. Evans (ed) *Equality, education and physical education.* London: The Falmer Press.

Deem R. (1986) *All work and no play? — A study of women and leisure.* Milton Keynes: Open University Press.

Evans, J. and Davies, B. (1988) 'Introduction: teachers, teaching and control', in J. Evans (ed) *Teachers, teaching and control in physical education.* Lewes: The Falmer Press, pp. 1–19.

Fleming, S. (1993) 'Ethnicity and the physical education curriculum: Towards an anti-racist approach', in G. McFee and A. Tomlinson (eds) *Education, sport and leisure: Connections and controversies* . University of Brighton: CSRC, pp. 109–123.

Green, E., Hebron, S., and Woodward, D. (1989) *Women's leisure, What leisure?*. Basingstoke: Macmillan.

Hargreaves, D. H. (1980) 'The occupational culture of teachers', in P. Woods (ed) *Teacher strategies — explorations in the sociology of the school*. London: Croom Helm, pp. 125–148.

Hendry, L. B. (1986) 'Changing schools in a changing society: the role of Physical Education', in J. Evans (ed) *Physical education, sport and schooling: Studies in the sociology of physical education*. Lewes: The Falmer Press , pp. 41–69.

Kane, J. E. (1974) *Physical education in secondary schools*. London: Macmillan Education.

Kirk, D. (1989) *Physical education and curriculum study — A critical introduction*. London: Croom Helm.

Lawrence, L. (1991) Understanding Teachers' Leisure Aims and Practices in Secondary School Physical Education. Unpublished PhD thesis, Brighton Polytechnic.

Lawrence, L. (1993) 'Leisure in physical education', in G. McFee and A. Tomlinson (eds) *Education, sport and leisure: Connections and controversies*. University of Brighton: CSRC, pp. 134–148.

Lovell, T. (1991) 'Sport, racism and young women', in . G. Jarvie (ed) *Sport, racism and ethnicity*. London: Falmer Press, pp. 58–73.

McIntosh, S. (1981) 'Leisure studies and women', in A. Tomlinson (ed) *Leisure and social control*. LSA Publication No. 19. Eastbourne: Leisure Studies Association, pp. 93–112.

Parker, S. (1971) *The future of work and leisure*. London: MacGibbon & Kee.

PEA (1987) *Physical education in schools. Report of a Commission of Enquiry*, London: PEA.

Roberts, K. (1981) *Leisure, work and education* (prepared for the Course Team). Milton Keynes: The Open University Press.

Robinson, S. (1990) 'There has to be more to it than that!', *The Bulletin of Physical Education*, Vol. 26, No. 2: pp. 23–26.

Scraton, S. (1987) 'Boys muscle in where angels fear to tread — girls' sub-cultures and physical activities', in J. Horne, D. Jary, and A. Tomlinson (eds) *Sport, leisure and social relations*. London: Routledge and Kegan Paul, pp. 160–186.

Scraton, S. (1992) *Shaping up to womanhood — gender and girls' physical education*. Buckingham: Open University Press.

Shaw, S. (1985) 'Gender and leisure: inequality in the distribution of leisure time', *Journal of Leisure Research*, Vol. 17, No. 4: pp. 266–282.

Sherlock, J. I. (1979) 'The evaluation of leisure programmes in secondary schools', *Journal of Psycho-Social Aspects, Occasional Papers No 5*. Edinburgh: DCPE.

Tozer, M. (1986) 'To boldly go where no subject has gone before', in *Trends and developments in physical education*, Proceedings of the VIII Commonwealth Conference on Sport, Physical Education, Dance, Recreation and Health, Glasgow. London: E. &F. N. Spon, pp. 178–184.

Underwood, G. L. (1983) *The physical education curriculum in the secondary school: Planning and implementation*. Lewes: The Falmer Press.

Wearing, B. and Wearing, S. (1988) '"All in a day's leisure": Gender and the concept of leisure', *Leisure Studies*, Vol. 7, No. 2: pp. 111–123.

Whitehead, J. R. and Fox, K. R. (1983) 'Health related fitness in schools', *Bulletin of Physical Education*, Vol. 19, No. 2: pp. 21–30.

Williams, A. and Jenkins, C. (1988) 'A curriculum for a fit state? The National Curriculum proposals and physical education', *Physical Education Review*, Vol. 11, No. 2: pp. 123–132.

Wimbush, E. J. and Talbot M. (1988) (eds) *Relative freedoms — women and leisure*. Milton Keynes: Open University Press.

Woods, P. (1984) 'Teacher, self and curriculum', in I. Goodson and S. J. Ball (eds) *Defining the curriculum — histories and ethnographies*. London: The Falmer Press, pp. 239-261.

Woodward, D, Green, E. and Hebron, S. (1989) 'Bouncing the balls around ... or keeping them in the air? The sociology of women's leisure and physical recreation', in S. Parker (ed) *Work, leisure and lifestyles, Part 1*, LSA Publication No. 33. Eastbourne: Leisure Studies Association, pp. 36–51.

III.

POPULAR CULTURE

RADIO 1 IN THE 1980S: DAY-TIME DJs AND THE CULT OF MASCULINITY

Mike Cole
School of Education, University of Brighton, UK

Paddy Maguire and John Bosowski
School of Historical and Critical Studies, University of Brighton, UK

Introduction

The original paper, on which this chapter is based, was written in 1984 and entitled 'The Happy, Happy Sound? Day-Time Radio 1 DJs and the Cult of Masculinity'. It arose from our alarm at the contemporary — minatory — political climate and from our concern that, while a new and undesirable political order ('Thatcherism') was being constructed, many of the 'ordinary people' of Britain were being cynically manipulated, both by those organs directly under the control of the *political* and by the less *evidently* political, but still essentially establishmentarian, views of the management and other key workers of national organisations such as the BBC. This manipulation of the audience took a variety of forms. In a subtle way, day-time Radio 1 lulled its (passive) audience into complacency and cultural comfort with the 'happy, happy sound', as their jingle put it. More actively — but no less subtly — preconceptions about individual rôles in this developing society (particularly, though not exclusively, those determined by gender) were transmitted, reinforced and reproduced via the significant productive capacity possessed by any effective medium of mass communication. Thus, the audience was being simultaneously anaesthetised and acclimatised to the economic and political objectives of Thatcherism.

The paper was written as a contribution to the series 'Young People and the Crisis: Some Radical Analyses', held at what was then Brighton Polytechnic. The audience was a general and popular one, rather than specialist or 'academic', and no assumptions were made, therefore, about prior theoretical knowledge. The request to adapt the paper for inclusion in a ('scholarly') book to be published in the mid-1990s, therefore, presented us with a dilemma. Should we present it, untouched, as illustrative of an historical moment in Thatcher's mid term of office? Or should the paper be rewritten in order to reflect a decade's change in party politics or to consider developments in Radio 1 itself? Perhaps we should address changes in academic theorising since the mid 1980s? Given the import of Thatcher and Thatcherism we decided on a middle course. The chapter has been rewritten so as to be more readable in the 1990s, but we have not addressed the post-Thatcher era. This means that no post-1984 perspective on Radio 1 is provided (including possible changes in attitude of those DJs mentioned in the empirical analysis). It also means that in this paper we do not address the challenges to marxism from postmodernism and poststructuralist feminism (but see, for example, Cole and Hill, 1994; 1995a; 1995b; Hill and Cole, 1995).

Further, despite the fact that there is no systematic analysis of relevant developments since the paper was first prepared, we do believe that the cultural constructs — individual and structural— that we were concerned with (particularly gender stereotyping and the dominance of 'masculinity') are equally, if not more embedded in the language and attitudes of the media and popular cultural artefacts, now as then. However, it may well be the case that the programming and broadcasting attitudes of Radio 1 are no longer, primarily, or even particularly, the vehicles of such attitudes. Impressions derived from recent (non-systematic) listening suggest a far greater "political" rectitude than a decade ago. Nevertheless, the location and exploitation of such undesirable stereotypes and the reinforcement of male, patriarchal, power are more than ever visible in both 'tabloid' and 'broadsheet' journalism, and post-Thatcherite managerialism in relation to the public and private sectors (if such a distinction is any longer feasible![1]). Similarly, it is possible that these 'reasonable' standards in national broadcasting are not replicated in some local and regional stations. It may also be the case that in their efforts to increase 'market share' and boost sales and profit, many of the media, in reinforcing consumer self-image, providing security and avoiding criticism, are reinforcing the "anaesthetising effect" referred to earlier, by pandering to the buyer.

Finally, and on a less pessimistic note, the proselytic tone of the original article (evident with hindsight and in the light of subsequent positive development) should be seen as itself a reflection of the need we felt at the time to recognise some neglected concerns. These were to ensure that the ideological and specifically political debates which engaged us took proper account of the importance of gender construction and relationships. This endeavour, at least in these debates, has become more (if not necessarily *fully*) acknowledged.

Capitalism, patriarchy and popular culture

With the notable exception of some works, (particularly of the Centre for Contemporary Cultural Studies[2]), analyses of the media, be they conservative or radical, tended, in the main and until (approximately) the late 1970s, to concentrate on 'serious matters', such as the news, current affairs, programmes about science and 'the arts', or party politics. These topics seemed to deserve more attention and consequently were a greater focus of critical analysis than forms of 'popular' culture. Thus TV soap operas, sit-coms, popular music (either of the Radio 1 or Radio 2 sort) or the forms of cinema designed for mass audiences, were ignored or were simply categorised as entertainment, fantasy or escapism — "the illusory construction of pleasure — pleasure in a created complacency" (Barrett, 1982: p. 19). This possibly reflects on the part of conservative critics their judgement of only elite or more sophisticated forms of 'Culture' repay analysis. On the other hand some radical or 'leftist' critics might be accused of operating with a rather over generalised notion that because they are so easily categorised, popular forms are easily dealt with. (This reflects a sort of cultural discomfort with popular form that is admitted and agonised over by many radical critics). It is interesting too that the dismissal or general casting off of mass audiences even with the traditions of 'enlightened' cultural analysis is often tinged with moralism (Barrett, 1982: p. 55):

> Television and the popular cinema are seen as pandering to a reprehensible desire on the part of the audience for romance, violence, identification, a good yarn, an illusion of stability and closure.

Much work subsequently has (from the vantage point of 1994) redressed this and acknowledged the notion of 'mass' as a key cultural term, recognising sport, recreation and other forms of popular (and populist) entertainment as key determinants of social and cultural identity.

Quite apart from questions of 'moral purism' which are discussed for example in the article by Barrett, we would argue that popular forms are indicative of much more than a vague unspecified audience's 'reprehensible desires'. In particular, the content and *language* of Radio 1 in the mid-1980s were an important manifestation (of such popular forms) and offer a ground for the analysis of certain historical trends as well as for the understanding of attitudes and preconceptions which are prevalent in the society. Furthermore, such forms are a means of demonstrating how meaning and social attitude are related to underlying social structures. This relationship is complex and involves consideration also of the history and development of Radio 1.

At this stage a short theoretical excursus is necessary. Some marxists have argued for a simple correspondence between the economic base of society and other levels such as the ideological, the educational. A classic example of this line of arguing is Bowles and Gintis' *Schooling in Capitalist America*[3]. Here they argue that what happens in education in the United States *corresponds* with the requirements of the economy, for example, industry requires docile, rule-following workers used to a hierarchy, *therefore* schooling creates such workers.

An alternative (neo-marxist) interpretation is provided by Stuart Hall. As he puts it (Hall, 1977: p. 56):

>...the more Marx examined in depth the capitalist mode of production, the more he observed the internal complexities of its laws and relations: and the less he thought this complex whole could be expounded in terms of the immediate correspondence between one of its circuits and another, let alone one of its levels and all the others... He [became] concerned with the necessary complexity of the social formation of advancing capitalism and of the relations between its different levels... with the 'unevenness', the non-immediate correspondences, between these levels which remain, nevertheless, connected.

The economy (the thrust for the accumulation of capital) may be thought of (Hall, 1977: p. 60):

>...not as specifying in detail the content and forms of the ...[other] levels...and thereby 'determining', but as providing the governing move-ments (including the contradictions and crises in that self-expansion, and the 'solutions' which permit capital to continue to accumulate while reproducing its antagonisms at a more advanced level of composition), dictating the tempo and rhythms of development in the other parts of the social formation: setting limits, as it were, to what can or cannot be

a solution adaptable to capital's self-expanding needs, and thus as
determining through the repertoire of solution (political, social,
ideological) likely to be drawn on in any particular historical moment or
conjuncture.

Our position is that the problem is not necessarily polarised into the economy
'setting limits' on the one hand or 'simple correspondence' on the other; that
there are times when the correspondence is 'non-immediate'[4] and indeed times
when it is 'simple'.

Specifically, we want to argue that the relationship between capitalism
and the formation of BBC Radio 1 exemplifies the fact that there is a cor—
respondence, but that this correspondence is uneven and contradictory.
Capitalism, in this case consumer capitalism, although it did not 'determine'
Radio 1's development in any straightforward sense, did 'dictate the tempo and
rhythms of its development'.

Thus the creation of this set of uneven and contradictory circumstances, viz
Radio 1, has provided a dominant ideological force which sits easily with the
forces of capitalism. It also, and this is the central argument of this chapter, sits
easily with the forces of patriarchy.

Capitalism is, of course, very dependent on and interrelated with patriarchy.
The cheap labour of women in paid work, and the unpaid and essential labour
of women in the home have always been crucial features in the development of
capitalism and continue to be so. At the moment, for example, women are
increasingly being used as cheap, flexible, part-time labour in the metropolises
of the west and in appalling sweatshop conditions, particularly in 'the third
world' (Mitter, 1994a; 1994b).

However, patriarchy has also an autonomous dimension. As Zillah Eisenstein
(1978: p. 22) has argued:

> ...oppression and exploitation are not equivalent concepts, for women or
> for members of minority races, as they were for Marx and Engels.
> Exploitation speaks to the economic reality of capitalist class relations for
> men and women, whereas oppression refers to women and minorities
> defined within patriarchal, racist and capitalist relations. Exploitation is
> what happens to men and women workers in the labour force; woman's
> oppression occurs from her exploitation as wage-labour but also occurs
> from the relations that define her existence in the patriarchal sexual

hierarchy — a mother, domestic labourer, and consumer. Racial oppression locates her within the racist division of society alongside her exploitation and sexual oppression. Oppression is inclusive of exploitation but reflects a more complex reality. Power — or the converse, oppression — derives from sex, race, and class, and this is manifested through both the material and ideological dimensions of patriarchy, racism and capitalism. Oppression reflects the hierarchical relations of the sexual and racial division of labour in society.

We reject the notion that there is always a simple correspondence between the requirements of capitalism and those of patriarchy. To take a straightforward example, at certain historical periods, the forces of patriarchy may require women in homes and capitalism may need them in factories; at other times the forces of both patriarchy and capitalism may, albeit for different reasons, attempt to keep women off the labour market. However, we would argue that there are times when there is a simple correspondence between capitalism and patriarchy. In fact we would go as far as to say that there *was* a simple correspondence between Thatcherism (acting in the general interests of international capitalism), patriarchy and the rhetoric of Radio 1. Radio 1, moreover, in true Thatcher style, took this correspondence of interests directly to the people (even if they did not always listen).

This is the final dimension to our argument — the political. In the analysis which follows, we try to demonstrate the relationship between the Government which is but one arm of the state and Radio 1, a state institution or, more precisely, echoing Althusser (1971), a 'state apparatus'. We do not see the state as synonymous with government, but rather as comprising a number of institutions *in addition* to central and local government, such as the hierarchies of the Civil Service, the judiciary, the military and the police as well as the cultural and ideological apparatuses, such as the education system and the various branches of the state-owned media, such as Radio 1[5].

The Creation of Radio 1

In order to demonstrate its position as a 'state institution', we need to look both at the place of Radio 1 in the moral and ideological traditions of the BBC and at developments in British consumer capitalism. The right-wing version of the moral purism, which may be seen to represent an attempt to preserve cultural hierarchies, is well exemplified in the statement by Frank Gillard (*BBC*

Handbook, 1957: p. 20) who was, in 1957, Director of Sound Broadcasting at the BBC:

> The medium [radio] has been accorded a standing in Britain which has safeguarded against the erosion and decay so evident in some other countries where radio today is not much more than a mechanism for the wider dissemination of the jukebox record and the sensational news headline. It is against degradation of this kind that the BBC sound broadcasting has continually to be protected.

The quotation very much reflects the tradition, particularly moral, of the BBC which of course in itself was part of another tradition in British history. And this tradition had a lot to do with 'improvement', of disdain and distrust for the popular, or moral policing and licensing of some popular manifestations at the expense of others. It might also, from the institutional point of view, be worth reflecting here that it was hardly accidental that the economic foundation of the BBC was and is such a characteristic ruling class form, the licence, which is also a licensing of cultural monopoly and political power. Right from the start, first as the British Broadcasting Company and then as the British Broadcasting Corporation, the BBC has been strongly marked not just by its terms of reference (the Charter) but also by the reluctance of the state to permit that the diffusion of communications (as a form of production as opposed to one of consumption) could be beyond its control. This monopoly was to be consistently challenged by the growth of consumer capitalism, of the youth market, and the consequent need to advertise.

Before coming to the events of the 1960s, which eventually resulted in the formation of Radio 1, it is worth pointing out that this was not the first time that the BBC had faced competition from commercial radio. It had had the same experience in the 1930s for broadly similar reasons (that radio provided a major advertising potential) when, revealingly, it had attacked one of its major competitors, Radio Normandie, as acting in a "blatantly American manner" (Briggs, 1985: p. 353). Then it had responded by utilising the Post Office to attack commercial operators, seeking government assistance in outlawing them and, ultimately, by reordering its programming by introducing the Light Programme to compete directly with the appeal of such as Radio Luxembourg. The response in the 1960s would be similar, culminating in legislation as the BBC sought to reassert its monopoly.

In fact, by the 1960s the audience for radio broadcasting had both contracted and expanded — contracted under the onslaught of TV, which largely restricted 'mass' audiences to daytime, and expanded with the wider diffusion of radios, particularly the transistor radio and the burgeoning market for car radios. As early as 1960, the Committee on Broadcasting had pointed to the dangers and advantages of such developments, in particular to the tendency (which would soon be more than a tendency) to respond by programming along lines which assumed that "there are large numbers of people who like only one kind of programme" (HMSO, 1960: p. 25). At the same time the music industry particularly, but not exclusively, at the 'pop' end of the spectrum, had grown enormously, also aided by technical developments, portable record players, juke boxes etc.. A handful of 'labels' dominated existing outlets, particularly broadcasting outlets provided by Radio Luxembourg. Here, sponsored airtime was controlled by the four major record companies (EMI, DECCA, Pye and Phillips) who also accounted for 99% of all record sales in 1962. These developments need to be seen in the light of the post-war boom. In particular the long boom, from the end of the war to the 1970s, heavily based on the expansion of credit and the production of consumer goods and services, had particularly benefited young consumers, the fastest growing wage rates being for young females, the lowest for skilled adult males. 'Full employment' and the substantial narrowing of differentials between adult and 'juvenile/youth' labour had massively stimulated the young consumer market — i.e. the time of life before marriage and children (and the probable, if temporary, switch from two to one income base, mortgage, etc.) had eroded real purchasing power. Such a potential was of interest to more than record manufacturers, even if music of a particular type became its characteristic consumer identity.

It was into this highly complex and highly lucrative market that the commercial (i.e. pirate) radio stations moved[6]. Able to draw on a wide range of advertising sponsorship and to operate through an already highly commercialised medium ('pop' music) they proved enormously successful. In its first eighteen months, Radio Caroline grossed over £750,000 in advertising revenue; after just two months on the air, Radio London (the pirate radio station, that is) had grossed £200,000. Commercial radio was big business, and big business threatened to undercut the BBC's audience, the audience which was the justification for the licence and therefore for its existence. Not surprisingly, it was worried. In 1964 its own research department was asked to investigate the

'Caroline phenomenon' and found that one in five listeners were regular commercial radio listeners and that 70% of those were under 30 (Silvey, 1974: pp. 212–213). (Unfortunately the relative male/female figures are not available.)

Two years later, a Government White Paper indicated "a need for a new service devoted to the provision of a continuous popular music programme". At the same time, the Government was proceeding with legislation to outlaw the so-called 'pirate stations', like Radio Caroline, operating outside British territory but aiming at a British audience. The outcome of this was Radio 1, begun on 30th September 1967, and celebrated by the Director in the following year, as a "rather bouncy new radio network", one which it was apparently 'difficult' to name and which would, therefore, simply be referred to as Radio 1 (BBC, 1968: p. 21 and p. 48). The direction in which this was aimed was quite clear as "the image is designed to be youthful, friendly and fast-moving", with a stress on constant (daytime) pop, and on 'presentation'. The last was deemed to be particularly important because "the manner of delivery is all important. This must be both professional and personal" (*ibid.*, p. 22). That however presented particular problems to the BBC. A compromise between British values [sic] and popular demand seemed inevitable. It meant that to make their new network viable they were heavily reliant on personalities such as the Emperor Rosko and Kenny Everett and where could they obtain them but from the existing (but soon to go out of business) commercial sector? To that extent, Radio 1 not only inherited much of the format but also many of the actual personnel of the pirate stations. At its inception, no less than seventeen of its presenters were ex-pirates (*The Listener*, Oct. 5, 1967). A particular symbiosis between commercial and public radio was therefore created.

A crucial factor in the subsequent development of Radio 1 relates to the fact that, unlike the pirates, the BBC was constrained by agreement with the Musicians Union as to the amount of 'needle-time' (i.e. of commercial records broadcast) permitted in any one day. As the gap between records needed to be filled, and could not be filled by advertising messages, it was perhaps inevitable that it would be filled by presenters, particularly as this was a cultural form readily available through the United States experience. The presenter as (male) superstar was therefore in the process of formation from the very outset.

Before turning to our empirical data, it is probably worth making one further point regarding the language of Radio 1. Some ten years after its opening, Radio 1 introduced a new programme, 'Newsbeat'. Its ethos was spelt out as "specifically designed to appeal to younger listeners ... pioneering a new kind of radio journalism" (BBC, 1977). Gillard's 'sensational news headlines' had come home to roost. In a sense, the pressures, internal and external to the BBC, which had led to the founding of Radio 1, had dictated a kind of commercial radio without the commercials[7], with all that implied in terms of primacy of 'personality', the constant search for increased audiences, the servile relationship to the music industry and, above all, the constant avoidance of anything genuinely controversial or 'serious' — that no doubt come under the BBC's heading of 'minority interests', a heading which appears in every issue of its annual handbook.

If the values of the new station could not, like the Light Programme before it, reflect the BBC Establishment's conception of (high) culture, then it needed to ensure that the music for the masses was not accompanied by a politics of the masses. In a programme on Channel 4, in 1984, a member of the group UB40 was emphatic that popular musical success did not necessarily bring with it any opportunity to make political points and he quoted the fact that whatever the content of a particular song, it would probably be sandwiched between bland or politically irrelevant songs in its chart placing. To put the same point perhaps more clearly, the political connotations of the phrase 'Flying Pickets' were of obvious significance at the time of the 1984 Miners' strike, but the 'musical' product of the singing group of that name appeared to have no connection whatsoever with these connotations, whatever the personal points of view and political contributions of the members of the group themselves.

It is also questionable to what extent oppositional forms would be 'acceptable' to the Radio 1 daytime audience as constituted at the time (there *were* attempts to discuss serious issues in the evening). The French marxist Louis Althusser has coined the phrase "the interpellation of subjects" (Althusser, 1971: pp. 171–183) to describe the way in which we act and respond to ideology as if we were the originators of the ideas and values within it. When Radio 1 or the *Sun* or the *Daily Mail* speaks about 'what we all know', this strikes a chord with all the other organs of dominant ideology — the rest of the media, the various apparatuses of the state — referred to above. Because we are largely trapped with one view of the world — capitalism/patriarchy/racism — it all 'makes sense' to us. This is not to say that forms of resistance cannot be developed[8].

The Cult of Masculinity and Thatcherism

We can see then, how, from the history of its inception, from the way in which it was obliged to find its DJs, Radio 1 assisted in the development of a national form of the dominant ideologies — we will call this 'the cult of masculinity'[9]. This cult of masculinity, we will argue, is intimately connected to the Conservative approach to managing capitalism and particularly intimately connected to the approach of the Radical Right epitomised by Thatcher[10]. In fact, according to Raphael Samuel (1983: p. 12):

> One of the unifying strands in contemporary Conservatism is anti-feminism. It can be seen not only in the extraordinary outburst of venom which has been directed at the women of Greenham Common — 'social misfits', 'the Lesbian army' and, according to Mrs Thatcher, 'partly to blame' for the rising crime rate (*Mail on Sunday*, 13 March 1983) — but also, more subliminally, in the negative symbolism of female attributes, and the positive exaltation of the male.

Conservative rhetoric, he states, is by and large structured on the opposition between the hard (attributed to masculinity) and the soft (attributed to femininity). This is the case whether the sphere is the economic, the political, the cultural, the educational or the religious. In all situations the soft is identified with weakness and surrender. Tory rhetoric is 'tough minded' rather than tender-hearted (Samuel, 1983: p. 12):

> It uses military metaphors when speaking of the economy, and homo-erotic ones when extolling the virtues of nuclear weaponry. 'Feather-bedding' is said to have 'emasculated' private enterprise in industry; 'mollycoddling' to have stifled the competitive urge; privatisation will give 'vibrancy' to small businesses. The male notions of honour and glory are uninhibitedly championed.

The anti-feminist venom of the new Tories relates, Samuel goes on, to that "tremendous sense of fun", whether man-of-the-world or boyish, which the Tory male is always proud to exhibit. Putting women down is all part of the fun — all part of being one of the boys — being a man. Elsewhere he refers to the ways in which Conservatism has always fed on male companionships, on the hunting field, in the courts, in the gentleman's clubs and the other all-male clubs. He continues (Samuel, 1983: p. 14):

The atmosphere of masculine exclusiveness is nowhere more apparent than in that great seminary of Conservative politicians, the Victorian public school. It can be seen not only in the enormous amount of importance attached to organised games, 'a kind of legalised toughness', and the association of 'manly pastimes' with moral virtue — in school sermons, a favourite preacher's trick was to emphasise the close connection between 'virtus' (virtue) and 'vir' (man) — but also in the symbolic importance attached to Classics, an exclusively male form of learning. (Readers of *The Mill on the Floss* will recall Tom's sovereign contempt for Maggie Tulliver because girls were 'too silly' to learn Latin.)

It is somewhat ironic that the arrival of a woman to the leadership of the party strengthened the party's masculine bias. All her real enthusiasm went to men. She surrounded herself with men in her cabinet and she clearly delighted in posing for photographs with soldiers — in the Falklands, in Northern Ireland. Moreover, she showed real enthusiasm for paramilitary interventions in domestic affairs, sending the SAS into the Iranian embassy and recommending rubber bullets and water cannon for the youth of Toxteth. And the enormous popularity which she enjoyed with the Party 'bloods' (even those who found her economic policy too 'liberal') was because she had the 'guts' to wage war.

Mrs Thatcher presented herself from the start as a warrior rather than a healer. She came to the leadership pledged to shake Britain free of what she called "a prolonged course of sedation" (Samuel, 1983: p. 15). Mrs Thatcher was never happier, Samuel goes on, than when castigating opponents for being cissy. "She takes a robust, no-nonsense view of hanging". "Unarticulated notions of masculinity", he concludes, underpinned all aspects of government policy (p. 15).

In the mid 1980s, Radio 1, which was but one arm of the ideological apparatus upholding capitalist patriarchal Britain, fitted neatly into the Thatcherite scenario.

In reinforcing patriarchal notions of sexuality and gender, Radio 1 also worked to maintain capitalism and racism and specifically Thatcher's vision of British Society[11]. It did this primarily through the rhetoric of its DJs, through the cult of masculinity which is enabled by male access to power and oppression. Radio 1 DJs not only reflected, through the form and content of their language, dominant social assumptions and ideologies, they also assimilated (potentially) oppositional assumptions and ideologies.

In fact the station was, at the time, imbued with a chauvinist nationalism where 'British is best', all foreigners are funny and workers know their places (the patronising way in which DJs talk to those who phone in). Indeed, Radio 1, at the time, may be thought of as specifically aimed at the young (white) working-class (both in the work place and the home). There was moreover (and perhaps still is) on Radio 1 an overall macho ambience which is difficult to put into words, but easily recognisable by men (and we suspect by women); it resembles the atmosphere of a pub or of a factory. (Incidentally, DJs are always talking about pubs/drinking/getting drunk — this is part of the image.) There were a great number of 'in-jokes' which were difficult or even impossible for listeners to understand — this is part of male style. Certain adjectives recurred to describe men — 'macho', 'brawny', 'dark and hunky', 'big and bulky' while a different set of terms were used for women — 'beautiful', 'adoring young lovelies', 'cute people' 'singing cute little numbers'. Women were over-whelmingly 'little' and 'wonderful'. Men 'leapt in' to do things, women were 'shy and giggly'. These terms were often used in jest — but that does not matter.

Even more difficult to describe verbally are forms of verbal pornography — in 'soft' form like Steve Wright's 'heavy breathing' woman, or even more worrying, in 'hard' form, his 'screaming woman', which followed an impersonation of Clint Eastwood.

Two days in the life of Radio 1

The research is based on daytime Radio 1 over a period of 2 days — 29th February and 1st March 1984. Radio 1 is aimed primarily at young people. This is, of course, not to say that older people are not among its audience. But there are other stations catering for their needs. Radios 2 and 3 are also music stations. However, Radio 2 is less obsessed with the charts and tends to cater for an older age range; Radio 3 plays almost exclusively 'classical' music, which has no mass appeal among the young (or other age ranges for that matter). Radio 4 is not primarily a music station; it contains a *variety* of programmes, with music forming only a small part of the menu. Its mixture of serious (and not so serious) items are clearly not aimed at young people. Another thing to note is that, like Radio 2, Radio 1 is background music[12]. This means that people can go about their business without actually listening to it with concentration; 'housewives' can get on with their housework, the young unemployed can move about the house or chat wherever it is being played, without having to stop what they are doing. Workers in factories or workshops can listen and carry on working.

Since Radio 1 is primarily background music, the implications are that some of its messages are missed. However, we want to argue that since it works so consistently and constantly to present specific messages, it acts as a powerful ideological reinforcer. If you miss something, you get the same treatment relatively soon after.

A large part of the rhetoric of DJs is aimed primarily at young women, but also works to uphold male visions of self. In fact, we would argue that, in the period of the research, such messages worked at two levels:

(i)   DJs talking about women;

(ii) DJs talking to women (both through the radio and on the phone).

We will deal with each in turn.

DJs talking about women: reinforcing the stereotypes

Ninety-nine red balloons is, to our knowledge, the first feminist protest against nuclear warfare to get to No. 1 in the charts. We describe it as 'feminist' since it contains verses like:

> 'THIS IS WHAT WE'VE WAITED FOR, THIS IS IT BOYS THIS IS WAR.
> EVERYONE'S A SUPER HERO, EVERYONE'S A CAPTAIN KIRK WITH
> ORDERS TO IDENTIFY, TO CLARIFY AND CLASSIFY'

So what were DJ Adrian John's comments about the song after having played it? Typically, he said nothing about the words[13], but concentrated on the singer. On the breakfast show which used the jingle 'tune in and off to work you go' he described Nena as "a very tasty lady" and let his (male) listeners (just off to work?) know when to tune in to television if they "want[ed] to see her" (The Breakfast Show: 29th Feb. 1984). Later on (for 'the housewives') Simon Bates explained that "One of the interesting things about Nena is that she is actually a fully-trained jeweller who makes all her own jewellery". It is obviously so important that this is the message that we get from Nena and her song that he repeated this the following day (Simon Bates Show: 1 March, 1984)[14].

Thus, for Radio 1 DJs in the mid 1980s, women have a far more limited range of possibilities as human beings than men.

As a clue to his Celebrity Trivia Quiz, Steve Wright asked his 'listeners' to "name the movie which starred Ann Margaret *topless* and Art Garfunkel", while later in the same show we were informed that Dudley Moore was back with *leggy and tall* Susan Anton (Steve Wright in the Afternoon: 29th Feb. 1984).

Women were usually referred to as 'ladies' or 'girls' and were then described by male-defined stereotypical adjectives, like 'tasty' or ' shy and giggly'. Referring to a female recording artist, Simon Bates let us know that she was also working as a 'front lady' on an afternoon T.V. show and "looking good doing it as well" (Simon Bates Show, 29 Feb., 1984), while Gary Davis informed us that the reason Radio 1 was broadcasting proposals over the air on leap year day was for the benefit of "those girls too shy to pop the question themselves" (The Gary Davis Show: 29th Feb. 1984).

In a similar vein, Mike Smith (The Mike Smith Show, 29th February 1984) talked about a listener by the name of Little Sheena: "...who is probably blushing and giggling at this moment as she hears me say this"[15]. So, 'ladies' are tasty and 'girls' shy and giggly. We do not think that it is a question of age: 'ladies' and 'girls' are the same women but in their different (male-defined) roles.[16]

Women are overwhelmingly reduced to sex objects for men: "She had long black stockings on, that lady, and I'd never seen long black stockings and suddenly I knew what being a man was all about" (The Simon Bates Show: 1 March 1984)[17]. They are also helpless creatures in need of men's protection. Listen to Simon Bates (The Simon Bates Show: 29 February 1984), this time in a different vein: "Lizzy's in love — you can't get a sensible word out of the girl". Moreover, women in their role as sex objects are fair game for men's advances. Commenting on a woman who failed her driving test because she pretended she had wooden legs, Gary Davis (The Early Show: 1 March 1984] commented: "I could think of a way [to see if her legs were wooden or not]". In their role as helpless creatures, the male DJ was there to calm women down. Following a tape of 'a giggling woman', Steve Wright (Steve Wright in the Afternoon: 1 March 1984) urged: "Calm down love, calm down".

Daytime Radio 1 DJs, in the mid 1980s, were, if nothing else, 'masculine' and 'fun loving'. They tended to get involved in football matches, driving fast cars and motorbikes and parachute jumping; the idea of men exhibiting 'female' characteristics repulsed them. Just as women's identity is stereotypically determined by men (falling back on the resources of our language and culture), so too challenges to stereotypical images are ridiculed and assimilated by being reduced to one or two categories.

Take the case of Boy George and Marilyn. Steve Wright (Steve Wright in the Afternoon: 29 February 1984): "Joan Rivers is the funniest woman I've seen in my life apart from Boy George". Simon Bates (The Simon Bates Show: 1

March 1984): "Now either Boy George is gonna be the stewardess or he's gonna be the pilot".[18] Introducing a record by Marilyn, Adrian John (The Adrian John show, 29 February 1984) stated: "… and, up to 31, minus handbag, Marilyn"[19].

On Radio 1, 'macho' was a term of endearment. All the women 'fancied' the DJs because they were macho and male listeners were encouraged to emulate their behaviour in order to impress 'ladies' who were, of course, easily impressed, for example by sports cars. Simon Bates (Simon Bates Show: 29 February 1984) once again: "If you wanted to be really trendy and impress your lady you bought yourself a Spridget, a BLMC sports car" [a combination of Austin Healey 'Sprite' and MG 'Midget'].

Other stereotypes about women were abundant — for example, they lie about their age. Simon Bates (The Simon Bates Show: 29 March 1984), again: "Happy Birthday to Debbie, who is sixteen years old today, which means she must be four times older than that".

Women were also said to be 'after men' and this brings us on to the second level at which the messages work.

DJs talking to women: reinforcing the cult of masculinity

Unlike teenage magazines such as *Jackie* which are preparing girls for their 'destiny' — settling down with 'a nice boy'[20] — daytime Radio 1 addresses itself in the main to a slightly older audience. Many of its women listeners will already have 'settled down' and Radio 1 works to provide an outlet at the level of fantasy as to what things could have been like. Macho Radio 1 DJs are readily available. After playing a song which keeps repeating the words, 'What do I do if I wanna get through to you' Adrian John (The Adrian John Show: 29 February 1984) informed his female listeners: "What'll I do if I wanna get next to you? Well you just wander over here if you like. I'm not fussy. In fact, I like the idea".[21] In a more flippant, but just as suggestive way, Simon Bates (Simon Bates Show: 29 February 1984) urged Librans, said to be in an affectionate mood on the day in question, to: "…come and cuddle my diodes".

Radio 1 DJs were 'manly', men of the world, and had all the trappings (money and possessions) which 'ladies', who are by nature materialistic, were after. They were romantic, macho, rich, and fun to be with. They had no trouble 'getting girls'. They were, in the words of the Gary Davis Show, 'young, free and single'. However, they were also, as we have said, readily available to their listeners. Even Steve Wright, who often mentioned his girlfriend, was available to his listeners (Steve Wright in the Afternoon, 29 Feb., 1984): "Oh ya I'd like to make it with you. Come on darling — over here. Yes. Just let's have a rest for a minute and think naughty thoughts [pause]. Very nice eh!"

So Radio 1 DJs personified the unlikely combination of 'getting' any woman they wanted and being available to every woman listener (although the availability was, of course, at the level of fantasy)[22]. They were in fact 'available' to all women listeners except the much-hated feminists denigrated as 'women's libbers'[23] and, of course, the stereotyped 'spinster' who like all women (at heart) wants to get her man, but in her case is never able to.

According to Adrian John (on Leap Year day) women have the *privilege* (sic) of being able to propose marriage to their partner:

> ... however, if refused, they are, according to tradition, to be given a silk gown as a consolation prize [pause]. So what that means ladies is if you know you've got no chance you just go up to any guy in the street and say [silly 'female' voice] "Hi, my name's Sarah. I'd like to marry you". [Male voice[: "I don't wanna marry you". [Silly 'female' voice]: "Where's my gown, gimme my gown, I want it" (Adrian John Show: 29 February 1984).

The Serious Business

> TAKE YOUR BABY BY THE HAIR AND PULL HER CLOSE
> AND THERE THERE THERE. TAKE YOUR BABY BY THE EARS
> AND PLAY UPON HER DARKEST FEARS (Dance Hall Days by
> Wang Chung)

Although the flippant talk is based around sex, the real centre of importance, the fulcrum of women's lives, is considered to be 'romantic love'. Sex is primarily about fun and is for men (black stockings, wet T-shirts, 'tasty ladies', etc.) while romance is serious — the real thing — and for women (c.f. its centrality in *Jackie*). This came through in an 'ideal type' form in Simon Bates's 'Our Tune'; although there are other items on other shows. 'Our Tune' was introduced by very sentimental music and featured true life stories of heartbreak and romance. In many ways it complemented *Jackie* — but stressed how things could have been (for the older age range) as well as how they could be, with the DJ acting as surrogate lover. Simon Bates (Simon Bates Show: 1 March, 1984): "Every single [Our Tune] is for real. Every single one is a letter from you or a person like you" .

In many cases the stories are genuinely tragic, involving physical and emotional abuse, even the death of loved ones. However, what is the message which came across about love? After the Eagles' number 'After the love has gone', which was 'Our Tune' for a woman who had lost her loved one, Simon Bates (Simon Bates Show, 1 March 1984) informed his listeners (as the sentimental theme tune of 'Our Tune' returned) that:

> Her whole world was shattered. All she's got now is the ring that [he] bought her and a lot of great memories and a message maybe for you — it's her message as well — Please tell anyone that if they've got love make the most of it because when it's gone you realise [pause] that its the most important thing in the world and when its gone you've lost it [pause] forever....'

What we wish to point out is that romantic love is for (women) listeners to Radio 1 — like younger readers of *Jackie* — presented as *all there is*. The ultimate form of assimilation is reached when individual possibilities are stereotyped and thereby incorporated into the dominant and dominating cult of masculinity.

Conclusion

The above analysis is not a comprehensive analysis of Radio 1 in the mid 1980s. We have not touched upon women Radio 1 DJs, night-time Radio 1 DJs or the production of the programmes; we have only briefly mentioned the content of the music, and the composition of the audience. We have not considered what the DJs *thought* they were doing, what they were told to do and say or what they were told *not* to do or say. We hope, however, that we have centralised a neglected and crucial field for analysis.

We are also aware that we've presented a particular analysis of Radio 1 but, as regular listeners to Radio 1 at the time, we suggest that the discussion is illustrative of the nature of day time Radio 1 in the mid 1980s. Radio 1 may have changed since, but other areas of the media continue explicitly or implicitly to reinforce particular (often repressive) attitudes. This type of analysis, in terms of both the communications medium and the content of the medium's broadcasts, is essential to recognising the fact of the social and political significance of the mass media (their historically unprecedented complexity as well as their universal pervasiveness). Furthermore, what the media (as 'modes of production') produce is effective, at a number of levels, in reinforcing gender and other stereotypical preconceptions and attitudes.

Of course, just as the media may act as vehicles for maintaining the existing order, so too they have the potential to change it. Our 1984 paper concluded, perhaps naïvely, by suggesting that those who found cause for concern in the language and attitudes that certain Radio 1 DJs displayed and reinforced should write and complain to the BBC. That is, of course, still an option. But, ten years on, there are more avenues of access to the media than ever before. The platforms and products of such media are now more accessible, and accountability ('chartism', consumer protection and a range of 'control' and audit mechanisms — although often of dubious origin) is taken seriously. Technological advances and availability mean that the gap between 'home-made' or 'DIY' and professional programmes is narrowing. Therefore, with proper organisation, the power and the networks of the media could themselves be used for the promulgation of radical, alternative and challenging views.

Acknowledgement

We are grateful to Myrene McFee for her help with the reworking of this chapter.

Notes

1   The progressive undermining of the 'public' by denying any remotely *democratic* apparatus for the provision of health-care, welfare provision, transport and some forms of education (particularly further and higher) spring to mind.

2   For details, contact the Department of Cultural Studies, University of Birmingham, Edgbaston, Birmingham B15 2TT (UK); Tel. 0121-414 6060.

3   Samuel Bowles and Herbert Gintis, *Schooling in Capitalist America*, RKP, 1977. Following a number of neo-marxist critiques of this work (for example see Madan Sarup, *Marxism and Education*, RKP, 1978), Bowles and Gintis attempted to refine some of their earlier arguments. See Mike Cole (ed.) (1988) for their reply, for some critical appraisals of the work of Bowles and Gintis, and for a reply from Bowles and Gintis to their critics.

4   Unless Marx's analysis of capitalism is rejected *in toto*, there must always be some correspondence. As Hall explains, "When we leave the terrain of

[economic] 'determinations' we desert, not this or that stage in Marx's thought, but his whole problematic" (1977: p. 52).

5   Notwithstanding its contradictions, what we believe is particularly significant about the advent of Thatcherism is the way in which the aims of the state were brought closer together and the extent to which they were quite brutal and unambiguous in their intensified assault on the working-class as a whole, and on the black and Asian communities.

6   For a (rose-tinted) summary of the emergence and activities of the pirate stations see M. Baron, *Independent Radio*, Terence Dalton, 1975: pp. 35-55.

7   The possible logic of the situation, of commercial radio minus the commercials, did not long escape some opponents of the BBC. As early as 1968 it was being suggested that the BBC could usefully supplement its income by carrying advertisements on Radio 1 as, in the words of Lord Denham, "they would fit well into the patter of the so called disc jockeys...", (*New Statesman*, 19 August 1968). That kind of threat developed a more serious impetus with the Conservative victory in 1970 and the lobbying over commercial radio — which would result in the establishment of local commercial radio stations — even to the extent of considering the 'privatisation' of Radio 1, (*The Listener*, 7 January 1971). The possibility of advertisements on Radio 1 has been suggested a number of times.

8   The strengths of the structuralist marxism of Louis Althusser are that it allows us to identify the constraining structures of capitalist society and stresses the power of these structures. However, in order to break through these structures we need to centralise the power of the human will and the possibilities of counter-hegemony (humanist marxism). One should neither over-emphasise structuralist marxism as this can lead to defeatism, nor over-emphasise humanist marxism as this can lead to idealism.

9   This term recently came to light in a contemporary report by the independent Policy Studies Institute and referred to the racism and sexism of the Metropolitan Police.

10 For this reason, it would be particularly interesting to analyse to what extent Radio 1 has changed since the advent of Thatcherism.

11 We are aware, of course, that Radio 1 forms but one instance of the mass media. We do not underestimate the important effects of local radio stations and all the other forms of the media; TV programmes and advertisements, newspapers and magazines, and videos. Our concentration on radio relates

to its aforementioned relative neglect. The reasons for our concentration on Radio 1 are discussed below.

12 By its nature, Radio 4 allows people to choose to *listen to* certain programmes. Radio 3, however, caters for those who are likely to have a serious interest in music. Radios 1 and 2 also cater for those with a serious interest in popular music. However they also cater for those who do not have such a serious interest. They do not *demand* concentrated attention from their listeners. They can be just there — as a background.

13 Words of songs were usually only mentioned if they could be used by DJs to project their images.

14 It is worth pointing out that it seems that certain stereotyped assumptions are made about men going 'off to work' and women being 'housewives'.

15 Women and things associated with women are often described as 'little'. For example, referring to the imminence of 'Our Tune' (discussed below), Simon Bates (The Simon Bates Show: 29th February 1984) promised "a great little letter" — obviously from a woman.

16 Sometimes the term 'girl' is used to describe woman in her 'sex object' role, as the quotes from Tony Backburn exemplify (see Footnote 17).

17 There did seem to be a limit as to how far you could go on Radio 1. Talking to a 'phone-in listener' about 'centrefolds', Mike Smith suggested that they move away from a discussion of whether her husband thought of her as a centrefold "before we get censored" (The Mike Smith show: 1 March 1984). There did not seem to be the same restrictions on BBC Radio London. Complaining of being held back on Radio 1, DJ Tony Blackburn, who worked for both Radio 1 and BBC Radio London , felt that on the latter he could 'talk freely on serious subjects like sex'. What he meant by this was that he could 'go over the top' and 'get away with it': "It's wonderful being able to flirt when the girls ring up. I can say 'I'd like to come and grope you' and 'Are you wearing stockings and suspenders?'" (*News of the World*, 11 March 1984). On another occasion he said:

> Okay, Natalie from Kensington High Street is on the line. Hello? Natalie? What kind of shop do you work in my love? A *leather* shop. Ooooh! I bet that's a turn-on, eh Natalie? I thought so, but to be truthful leather isn't really my thing. Is it yours? It is. Why's that? Because when you wear it you can hear it creaking as you walk. What a *lovely* girl you must be Natalie... Now tell me, is there anyone in the shop who's actually wearing leather? Your

friend Michelle is? Okay, ask her to move a chair near the phone and when she sits down put the phone near her bum so we can all hear her skirt creak... She won't do it? Ah! that's a shame. Never mind. Thanks for calling Natalie and let's move on to Jane in Finsbury Park, and Jane, I'd love to move on to you..

Blackburn, moreover, had very definitive views about women's liberation (*New Musical Express:* 18 February 1984):

The trouble with the British people is that they are obsessed by not talking about sex. What's wrong with it? It's a natural function and I don't feel like I'm corrupting anybody. Also, I'm taking the micky out of the Women's Lib movement because to me the women libbers have become crushing bores. In fact, if we get any complaints we tend to get complaints from men, who I think are just jealous of what I'm doing.

[18] Note that he even changes the words of the song in order to make his remarks.

[19] Incidentally, Simon Bates was so eager to make this cheap joke that he hardly gave the woman he was talking to over the phone time to answer the question he had asked her.

[20] The banality of the remark does not detract from its underlying assumptions.

[21] For an interesting and informative analysis of Jackie see Angela McRobbie 'Jackie: an ideology of adolescent femininity', in Bernard Waites, Tony Bennett and Graham Martin, *Popular Culture: Past and Present*, Croom Helm, 1982.

[22] Marilyn was a male recording artist. After the record Adrian John commented, "and isn't it beautiful".

[23] Because of this availability, there were bound to be some heartbreaks! On the Simon Bates Show, a man, with an East Anglian accent, told us in rhyme that after Peter Powell and Mike Smith had visited East Anglia 'with pop music enough to make them teenagers rave', they would leave behind "some happy memories and maybe even one or two broken hearts". (The Simon Bates Show: 29 February 1984).

[24] See, for example, Tony Blackburn's comments (Note 17).

References

Althusser, L. (1971) *Lenin and philosophy and other essays*. London: New Left Books.

Baron, M. (1975) *Independent radio*. London: Terence Dalton.

Barrett, M. (1982) 'Feminism and the definition of cultural politics', in R. Brunt and C. Rowan (eds) *Feminism, culture and politics*. London: Lawrence and Wishart.

BBC (1967) *BBC Handbook*.

BBC (1977) *BBC Handbook*.

Bennett, T. and G. Martin (1982) *Popular culture: past and present*. London: Croom Helm.

Bowles, S. and Gintis, H. (1977) *Schooling in capitalist America*. London: RKP.

Briggs, A. (1985) *The golden age of wireless*. Oxford: Oxford University Press.

Cole, M. and Hill, D. (1994) 'Resistance modernism: emancipatory politics for a new era or academic chic for a defeatist intelligentsia?', paper to the conference 'New Visions of Post-Industrial Society', University of Brighton, July.

———— (1995a) 'Games of despair and rhetorics of resistance: postmodernism, education and reaction', *British Journal of Sociology of Education* (Spring).

———— (1995b) 'Postmodernism, education and contemporary capitalism: a materialist critique', in O. Valente, A. Barrios, V. Teodoro and A. Gaspas (eds) *Values and education*. Lisbon: Faculty of Science, Department of Education, University of Lisbon.

Eisenstein, Z. (1978) 'Developing a theory of capitalist patriarchy and socialist feminism', in Z. Eisenstein (ed) *Capitalist patriarchy and the case for socialist feminism*. New York: Monthly Review Press.

Hall, S. (1977) 'Rethinking the "base-and-superstructure" metaphor', in J. Bloomfield (ed) *Class, hegemony and party*. London: Lawrence and Wishart.

Hill, D. and Cole, M. (1995) 'Materialism and the postmodern fallacy: the case of education', in J. V. Fernandes (ed) *Proceedings of the Second International Conference of the Sociology of Education*. Lisbon: Fundaçaõ Calouste Gulbenkian.

Mitter, S. (1994a) 'Organizing women in casualised work: a global overview', in S. Rowbotham and S. Mitter (eds) *Dignity and daily bread: New forms of economic organising among poor women in the third world and the first*. London: Routledge.

———— (1994b) 'What women demand of technology', *New Left Review* Vol. 205 (May/June).

Report of the Committee on Broadcasting (1960) [Cmnd. 1753, para. 74, p. 25]. London: HMSO.

Samuel, R. (1983) 'Boys will be boys', *The New Statesman*, 18 (March).

Sarup, M. (1978) *Marxism and education*. London: RKP.

Silvey, R. (1974) *Who's listening?*. London: Allen and Unwin.

BIG DEFENCE: SPORT AND HEGEMONIC MASCULINITY

David Rowe
Department of Communication and Media Arts
University of Newcastle, New South Wales, Australia

Introduction

Critical sports theorists have long regarded masculinity and sport as the most willing of bedfellows. Sport has been shown to operate in diverse ways as a crucial institution in the making of men. From early boyhood socialisation, through teenage male bonding and identity formation to the often segregated leisure patterns of adult men, sport has been of enormous importance in helping to define and differentiate the meaning and practice of masculinity (Messner, 1992; Messner and Sabo, 1990). Sport has been of particular significance as a domain in which both legitimate and illegitimate violence is committed in the process of becoming 'manly' (Sabo and Runfola, 1980). It is by means of such a sport-centred rite-of-passage that Colin Ward (1989: p. 182), in his autobiographical account of British soccer hooliganism in the seventies and eighties, can claim that, "When I was a young man, getting punched in the mouth at football seemed just a part of growing up". Nick Hornby (1992), in a more warmly nostalgic personal history of football fandom, has provided an equally detailed and probably more representative account of how an intense relationship to sport substantially shaped the gender identity of young men of his generation (those born in the fifties and early sixties).

This intimate linkage between sport and maleness has never produced absolute exclusivity or completely clear lines of difference. As a number of 'herstories' reveal (Blue, 1987; Fletcher, 1984; Hargreaves, 1994; Howell, 1982; Stell, 1991), women's continued (and much underestimated) involvement and interest in sport has long entailed a keen contestation of its gender boundaries, while the accelerated de-stabilisation of social categories, relationships and identities under what we might characterise as late or postmodernity (Crook, Pakulski and Waters, 1992; Lash and Urry, 1994; Miller, 1993) has made it more difficult for traditionally hegemonic groupings to 'seal off' cultural institutions and practices. While these shifts are in part stimulated by social activism in the name of equity (Bryson, 1990), they are also the outcome of the ceaseless expansion of image markets. Today, the 'courting' of women viewers by commercial television sport, the persistent exhortations by the health and fitness industries for women to 'tone up', and the advanced professionalisation of several women's sports (notably tennis and golf) have all helped to intensify the involvement of women in sporting culture. As a result it is no longer possible to assert with the confidence of old that sport is incontestably a man's world.

While the male hold on sport as symbol and practice has been loosening, elite sport has, nonetheless, continued to be dominated by men (McKay, 1991; Kane and Disch, 1993). Indeed, images of male sports superstars (such as the recently retired basketballer Michael Jordan and his highly promoted 'successor', Shaquille O'Neal) have never been more pervasive. Vividly packaged sports and sports celebrities are continuously fanning out from the USA, where the application of modern marketing techniques to sports and sportsmen is most highly developed, into numerous other countries in a simultaneous if incomplete process of globalisation and Americanisation (Rowe, Lawrence, Miller and McKay, 1994). Paradoxically, however, it is at the American apogee of commodified male sporting superstardom that potential uncouplings of sport and "hegemonic masculinity" (Connell, 1987; 1990) are most likely to disturb the sports gender order.

The concept of hegemonic masculinity contains within it a two-fold axis of power. The first operates according to a male/female, masculine/feminine dualism in which the former exercises domination over the latter in a loosely defined framework of patriarchy. The second is activated within masculinity itself, whereby heterosexuality is asserted against homosexuality as the organising discourse of the sphere of the sexual[1]. As Miller (1990) and Pronger (1990a, 1990b) have pointed out, this second form of hierarchical differentiation is not easy to sustain with clarity in the experiential and iconic systems of sport.The strong element of homoeroticism within sports participation and spectatorship can, as a result, only be denied through an uneasy confinement of the male gaze to the nominally de-sexualised spheres of technique, camaraderie and emotion. In this paper I wish to point briefly to some current 'hot spots' in which this link between sport and hegemonic masculinity may be shown to be conspicuously problematic. Some recent controversies concerning male sexuality and elite American sport, and the rather more neglected area of the relationship of homosexual men to sport, are addressed in an attempt to discern current trends in the sport-masculinity nexus.

Sporting Masculinity in the Spotlight

The nature of sporting masculinity, and, in particular, its influence on sexuality and sexual conduct, has been under intense scrutiny in the early nineties. The United States — where celebrity, commodification and coverage meld into a sports-media complex of unprecedented scope — has been the principal ground on which this exploration of gender relations in sport has taken place. Two of the most exhaustively discussed instances have been the 1991 announcement that basketball hero and high-profile product endorser 'Magic' Johnson was HIV-positive and the imprisonment in 1992 of world champion boxer 'Iron Mike' Tyson (followed, in 1994, by the trial for murder of prominent sports celebrity 'OJ' Simpson).

Both cases have highlighted the ways in which elite male athletes commonly interact with women. The Johnson case produced a flurry of exposés concerning the 'promiscuity' of many elite male athletes. The most frequently presented picture was of male sports stars under siege from female sports 'groupies', with little choice but to 'accommodate' them and, by this means, to become exposed to a life-threatening virus. In this manner, the male sports star was constructed as the victim of ungovernable female sexuality (Crimp, 1993; King, 1993; Rowe, 1993 and 1994). The figure of the sports groupie appeared also in the Tyson trial as the defence described the nature of the 'contract' between sports 'superstud' and groupie, seeking unsuccessfully to persuade the court that Desiree Washington's allegations of sexual assault against Tyson stemmed from conflicting understandings of the protocols of 'groupiedom'. Elements in the media followed this defence line, adding that in the context of a moral panic about 'date rape' Tyson could not receive a fair trial (McKay, Rowe and Miller, 1994). The burden of sexual exploitation in professional sport was generally inverted in media discourse, with a largely sympathetic and male-dominated media stressing the unreasonable demands and temptations provided by female groupies. Only a few (mostly) female journalists (like Sally Jenkins, 1991) and sports stars (such as Martina Navratilova) questioned or criticised the behaviour of male 'sexual athletes' in capitalising on their celebrity, declaring that such sexual licence was unlikely to be extended to champion sportswomen. This position met with little sympathy in the context of a media-relayed 'body panic' (McKay, Rowe and Miller, 1994) which substantially reproduced the ideology of hegemonic masculinity through the stigmatisation of a marginalised and anonymous category of women — the sexually avaricious groupie.

The Johnson case did rather more than lay bare the extent of carnal activity among professional sportsmen. It also revealed the continuing male heterosexualist domination of sport and its direct lines of association with gender and sexuality-based inequalities in the wider society. Johnson (like the late tennis star, Arthur Ashe) was anxious to assert that he acquired the virus during heterosexual intercourse. On the *Arsenio Hall Show*, Johnson declared, to enthusiastic applause from the crowd on the set, that he was "far from being homosexual". As Douglas Crimp (1993: p. 259) notes:

> When the studio audience on the *Arsenio Hall Show* cheered so wildly, their homophobia was doubly displayed, for in their gloating that Magic was no fag, they could not but demonstrate that they would rather die than entertain the idea that he could be one. Had those "freaks" that Magic accommodated been men instead of women, Arsenio's loudly heterosexual audience *might* have wanted to heave a collective sigh of relief that they still aren't implicated in this terrible epidemic, as they've wanted to believe all along.

The dual elements of the ideology of hegemonic masculinity are evident here, first in the sympathetic media treatment of elite sportsmen at the expense of female sports 'groupies' and 'carping' female critics, and, second, in the resistance to any notion that male sports superstars might evince a form of masculinity that deviates from the approved heterosexual path. This concern to hold at bay the suggestion of male (and, to a significant extent, female) homosexuality is central to the currently dominant ideological formation of sport.

Sport and Gay Masculinity

Male homosexuality, which in differing degrees has gained official and public recognition in the last two decades in a number of cultural spheres (for example, in the spectacle of the urban gay Mardi Gras and in the institutionalised gaze of the art gallery), has been little in evidence in the realm of sport. Apart from the periodic presence of the Gay Games and the occasional 'coming out' of a sport star (such as the British soccer player Justin Fashanu), gayness and sport are seldom linked (unless within the realm of scandal). Surprisingly, in view of the preponderance of males in elite professional sport, it is lesbianism (for example, in women's tennis and, most recently, in women's cricket) that has attracted more media attention (of a usually disapproving kind — see, for example, Wells, 1991). This silence on the sexual resonances of often exclusively male cadres enjoying close physical contact can only be understood as the product of the repression of all but the most narrowly conceived pre- scriptions for male interaction. This is not to argue that male sport is in any straightforward way a veil for the expression of repressed male desire for other males. It is, however, a socially legitimate space in which men are licensed to behave in a manner which, according to Callaghan (1992: p. 21), is not in accord with the norms of:

> ...an Anglo-Saxon culture that prohibits the expression of feeling between men: [whereas] in other cultures kisses on the cheek (Russia) and holding hands (India) are everyday practices.

Sport's capacity to permit socially legitimate "feeling between men" does not, however, usually lead to greater tolerance of non-hegemonic masculinity. In fact, the outcome is likely to be the reverse. As Messner (1992: p. 151) discovered in interviewing former male athletes, the dominant form of locker room masculinity required, at least for public consumption, a consistent hostility to women and gay men:

> Homophobia and misogyny were the key bonding agents among male athletes, serving to construct a masculine personality that disparaged anything considered "feminine" in women, in other men, or in oneself.

The dissonance between playing sport and being gay cannot, however, be reduced to an essentialist notion that the pleasure of sport is reserved for heterosexual men. Rather, it is the institutionalised use of sport as a means of denying and disguising 'queerness' that places gay men in an often antagonistic relationship to sport. In school, for example, sport, especially in those forms which highlight hard physical contact and endurance, is commonly deployed to establish a heterosexually-founded group cohesion and to single out (both symbolically and in practice) an out-group of 'poofs' and 'girls' in routinised ceremonies of degradation. The dominant heterosexual ethos of sport may also be alienating and discomfiting for young gay men. Douglas Crimp (1993: p. 256), for example, recalls that:

> During my adolescence in the small town where I grew up, people meeting me for the first time would note my height and the size of my hands — big enough to palm a basketball — and say, "You must be a basketball player. " Admitting that I wasn't embarrassed me; it felt like divulging my sexuality. In fact I *did* play basketball throughout most of my childhood and adolescence, but being queer made me self-conscious in locker rooms, so I stayed away from organized sports. What I meant when I said I didn't play was only that I didn't turn out for the high school team. Like a lot of other queers, when I left my hometown and found out there were places where playing basketball wasn't the only measure of worth, I rarely played or watched a basketball game again.

For those gay men who display an aptitude and affection for sport, remaining in the closet is usually the easiest, if an inherently unsatisfactory, option (Messner, 1992). In public leisure sites such as parks and sports stadia, ritualistic displays of homophobia form part of the dynamic of group membership and the identification of 'otherness'. These formal and informal settings for the suppression of homosexuality are linked through the agency of a commercial mass media complex which requires that successful product endorsers and high-profile 'ambassadors of the game' are, as noted above, also conspicuous advertisements for heterosexuality.

The male heterosexual domination of sport has not, of course, gone un-challenged. Just as women (both 'straight' and 'gay') have sought to break the nexus between maleness and sport, gay men have begun to mobilise against the association of the 'sporting body' with a specific and oppressive form of masculinity. The conditioning and 'sculpting' of an athletic-looking male body is already an established part of the spectrum of gay male culture (Nixon, 1993). Working-out and body-building in gymnasia have become common practices for many gay men highly conscious of body image. Indeed, the normative prescription of body condition and shape — displayed in many 'cheesecake' presentations of the male form in the context of a homosexual gaze — has in some areas achieved the kind of force and uniformity more readily associated with fashion-generated images of women. For example, a recent issue of *Campaign*, an Australian magazine for gay men, contains, apart from several stylised images of muscular and hairless men, a "shopper's guide to hair removal"[2] (sandwiched between advertisements for hair removal and other aspects of "body care") which states:

> What we're talking about here is hair. The stuff that hides in pits and pubic regions, that colonises chests, backs and limbs, that shoots its follicles where no follicles should be found. Hair is the thing that rarely grows in the right place or at the right rate with the right colour and consistency.
>
> God gives it to us and we spend the rest of our lives removing it or rearranging it. (Bashford, 1992: p. 34)

An almost hairless body of a muscular young man wearing only a pair of swimming trunks and carrying a rugby football appears on the magazine's front page as part of a story on "The Rise of Gay Footy" (in this case rugby league), setting out to rebut the suggestion that "fags and footy don't mix" (Cuthbertson, 1992: p. 16). The article focuses on a gay touch football team, recounting some of its members' positive and negative experiences of sport, and concluding with an assertion of gay people's autonomy and collective identification through voluntary sporting activity:

> Like the men and women in other gay and lesbian activities and sports groups, these players are doing it their way, and doing it with pride. Watching this herd thunder elegantly across the field, watching their genuine love of the sport, you can see hard evidence of a gay community beyond the bars. (Cuthbertson, 1992: p. 20)

The deployment of sport to express pleasure and group cohesion among avowedly homosexual men is, in view of the earlier discussion of the role of sport in the reproduction of hegemonic masculinity, a clear example of the shaking of previously solid foundations binding sport to an hierarchical order of sexualities. It suggests that an ideological realignment of sport, power and sexuality is in process, but in a manner productive of manifest contradictions and acts of resistance.

Conclusion

In this brief paper I have tried to demonstrate that the linkage between sport and hegemonic masculinity is powerful and enduring, not least because of its symbolic potency in the articulation of a masculine identity founded on physical/symbolic coercion and exclusion. While it is important not to underestimate the depth and resilience of the more oppressive forms of sporting masculinity, it is equally necessary to appreciate the conditions of their potential transformation. These may be apprehended within the dialectic of reproduction itself. For example, just as sporting commercialism habitually draws on male heterosexual bonding through sport, it is also driven to extend its market reach to women and gay men. At the same time, determined efforts are being made by feminists and elements within the men's movement to thwart the hegemonically masculine monopolisation of sport. These moves, in turn, provoke the defence of male sporting territory by the established sports press (Rowe, 1993; 1994) and some of the more reactionary groupings who have sought to recover the mythical essence of masculinity (Bly, 1990).

Disruptions to the sports-masculinity formation may be represented as emanating both from above and below. At the most media-visible and professionalised level, the intermittent crises of male sporting celebrity provide ready vehicles for the exploration and possible modification of the culture of the sporting male. Meanwhile, sport is organised, practised and enjoyed in the arena of everyday life, far removed from the breathless manoeuvres of the sports media complex. In the middle ground, newly professionalising women's sports (such as netball) and 'de-professionalising' men's sports (such as lower division soccer) jockey for position in a sporting world where the liberal state has increasingly intervened, often in the name of gender equity (McKay, 1991). Under these circumstances of substantial change in the sporting domain and considerable flux outside it, sport is now a rather less reliable ally of hegemonic masculinity.

Notes

[1] While terms such as heterosexual/straight and homosexual/gay are used here, they do not represent an essentialist and dualistic view of human sexuality. They are applied as terms of convenience to those human subjects whose sexual preferences are expressed through reasonably consistent interaction and identification.

2 The same edition carries a shorter and much less prominent companion piece (Bashford, 1992: p. 37) about "bears", a vernacular term for men who retain their body hair and who are resistant to narrowly prescribed models of attractiveness:

> Not every gay man is attracted to smooth skin. Some like, and like to be, "bears". Ozbears is a Sydney club for hairy men and their admirers. According to their publicity, they are "saying to everyone that you don't need to be young and slim with every hair plucked from your body to be attractive to other guys".

Such sentiments clearly bear a close resemblance to those expressed by feminists in their critique of "The Beauty Myth" (Wolf, 1990).

References

Bashford, K. (1992) 'Blade runners', *Campaign*, 197 (August): pp. 34–38.

Blue, A. (1987) *Grace under pressure: The emergence of women in sport*. London: Sidgwick and Jackson.

Bly, R. (1990) *Iron John: A book about men*. Reading: Addison Wesley.

Bryson, L. (1990) 'Challenges to male hegemony in sport', in M. Messner and D. Sabo (eds) *Sport, men and the gender order: Critical feminist perspectives*. Champaign: Human Kinetics, pp. 173-184.

Callaghan, G. (1992) 'The greatest game of all?', *Campaign*, 197 (August): p. 21.

Connell, R. W. (1987) *Gender and power*. Sydney: Allen and Unwin.

Connell, R. W. (1990) 'An iron man: The body and some contradictions of hegemonic masculinity', in M. Messner and D. Sabo (eds) *Sport, men and the gender order: Critical feminist perspectives*. Champaign: Human Kinetics, pp. 83-95.

Crimp, D. (1993) 'Accommodating Magic' in M. Garber, J. Matlock and R. L. Walkowitz (eds) M*edia spectacles*. New York: Routledge, pp. 254-266.

Crook, S., Pakulski, J. and Waters, M. (1992) *Postmodernization: Change in advanced society*. London: Sage.

Cuthbertson, I. (1992) Footy Fanatics, *Campaign*, 197, August, pp. 16-20.

Fletcher, S. (1984) *Women first: The female tradition in English physical education 1880-1980*. London: Athlone Press.

Hargreaves, J. (1994) *Sporting females: Critical issues in the history and sociology of women's sports*. London: Routledge.

Hornby, N. (1992) *Fever pitch: A fan's life*. London: Victor Gollancz.

Howell, R. (ed) (1982) *Her story in sport: A historical anthology of women in sport*. New York: Leisure Press.

Jenkins, S. (1991) 'Where's the Magic?', *Sports Illustrated*, November 25: p. 152.

Kane, M. J. and Disch, L. J. (1993) 'Sexual violence and the reproduction of male power in the locker room: The "Lisa Olson incident", *Sociology of Sport Journal*, 10, 4: pp. 331-352.

King, S. (1993) 'The politics of the body and the body politic: Magic Johnson and the ideology of AIDS.' Paper presented at the Third International Conference of the Leisure Studies Association, "Leisure in Different Worlds", University of Loughborough, UK. Published in *Sociology of Sport Journal* 10, 3: pp. 270-285.

Lash, S. and Urry, J. (1994) *Economies of signs and space*. London: Sage.

McKay, J. (1991) *No pain, no gain? Sport and Australian culture*. Sydney: Prentice Hall.

McKay, J., Rowe, D. and Miller, T. (1994) 'Sport and postmodern bodies' (unpublished paper).

Messner, M. (1992) *Power at play: Sports and the problem of masculinity*. Boston: Beacon Press.

Messner, M. and Sabo, D. (eds) (1990) *Sport, men and the gender order: Critical feminist perspectives*. Champaign: Human Kinetics.

Miller, T. (1990) 'Sport, media and masculinity', in D. Rowe and G. Lawrence (eds) *Sport and leisure: Trends in Australian popular culture*. Sydney: Harcourt Brace Jovanovich, pp. 74-95.

————(1993) *The well-tempered self: Citizenship, culture and the postmodern subject*. Baltimore: John Hopkins University Press.

Nixon, S. (1993) 'Check out the beef! Masculinities, the body and contemporary men's magazines', in C. Brackenridge (ed) *Body matters: Leisure images and lifestyles*. LSA Publication No. 47. Eastbourne: Leisure Studies Association, pp. 73-78.

Pronger, B. (1990a) 'Gay jocks: A phenomenology of gay men in athletics', in M. Messner and D. Sabo (eds) *Sport, men and the gender order: Critical feminist perspectives*. Champaign: Human Kinetics, pp. 141-152.

————(1990) *The Arena of masculinity: Sports, homosexuality and the meaning of sex*. New York: St Martin's Press.

Rowe, D. (1993) 'Accommodating bodies: Celebrity, sexuality and "Tragic Magic"', in C. Brackenridge (ed) *Body matters: Leisure images and lifestyles*. LSA Publication No. 47. Eastbourne: Leisure Studies Association, pp. 276-282. Expanded and updated in *Journal of Sport and Social Issues* (1994) Vol. 18, No. 1: pp. 6–26.

Rowe, D., Lawrence, G., Miller, T. and McKay, J. (1994) 'Global sport? Core concern and peripheral vision', *Media, Culture and Society* (forthcoming).

Sabo, D. and Runfola, R. (1980) *Jock: Sports and male identity*. New Jersey, Prentice Hall.

Stell, M. K. (1991) *Half the race: A history of Australian women in sport*. Sydney: Angus and Robertson.

Ward, C. (1989) *Steaming in: Journal of a football fan*. London: Sports Pages.

Wells, J. (1991) 'Putting the squeeze on a Magic Model'. *The Australian*, November 28: p. 45.

Wolf, N. (1990) *The beauty myth: How images of beauty are used against women*. London: Chatto and Windus.

IDEOLOGIES OF PHYSICALITY, MASCULINITY AND FEMININITY: COMMENTS ON *ROY OF THE ROVERS* AND THE WOMEN'S FITNESS BOOM[1]

Alan Tomlinson
Chelsea School Research Centre, University of Brighton, UK

Men do, of course, inherit patriarchal identities, and reproduce these identities in their own lives. The language of patriarchy thus perpetuates the oppression of women. (Tolson, 1977: p. 141)

The embedding of masculinity in the body is very much a social process, full of tension and contradiction ... even physical masculinity is a historical, rather than a biological, fact ... constantly in process, constantly being constituted in actions and relations, constantly implicated in historical change. (Connell, 1983: p. 30)

Introduction

The theme of the social construction of femininity was prominent in social scientific periodicals of the early 1980s. Pieces noted how teenage girls inherit different social worlds to those of teenage boys, in terms of sexuality and the guarding of reputations (Lees, 1983; Lees, 1984). Analyses of television content revealed what any regular viewer was aware of — that "women are the main stars of about 14% of mid-evening programmes. Most women shown in television are under 30" (Durkin and Akhatar, 1983) and tend to be housewives or, if in paid work, secretaries or nurses. The researchers of this study also showed a clip of a Superman film to young children, and in answer to one question were told by the children that a Superwoman could never equal the hero's display of bravery, even if she could fly and was endowed with superpowers. Why not? The children confidently responded to this: "'Cos', in the

135

words of one boy, 'mans are stronger'" (Durkin and Akhatar, 1983). So even if the powers are supernaturally derived, the woman is still seen as inferior to the man. Femininity is something inextricably interwoven with, and often defined by, a masculine view of the innate superiority of the male.

The question of femininity was also covered in terms of the different contexts in which it is experienced and reproduced. Women's experience in different settings was studied, and, depending of course on the particular characteristics of one setting or another, such research reports showed how a sensibility to gender and inequality had yet to penetrate mainstream social institutions. Listen to one young British Army wife on her husband: "He's a typical male chauvinist pig, my husband ... and proud of it. He says women are a lower form of life. If they had any brains they'd be dangerous" (Chappell, 1983). Where it is acknowledged that girls do indeed have brains, there too, it has been widely claimed, one particular version of that brain is given strong emphasis. In schools, engineering is still seen as 'not nice' or 'not normal' for girls; cooking and sewing are the 'normal' activities for them (Steinberg, 1983)[2].

Not just the issue of femininity is raised in pieces such as these. For women's experience is so often defined by men — in the family, the school, the work-space, the place of leisure — that femininity is actively reproduced, within gender relations, by masculinity itself. Young men to whom the inclination to 'fuck well and often' (or at least to claim to do so) is a sign of status, will define as non-feminine any female who is similarly inclined. A lot of work on femininity helps us see not just what women experience, but also how men perceive both women and themselves. This latter perception is rooted in a negative identity learnt by males, in childhood: an identity in which masculinity is seen to comprise 'non-femininity'; and one in which men can be seen as learning to dread women, to actually go in fear of women, and all that is seen as feminine[3]. Studies of women's experience, then, are informative sources for an understanding of masculinity.

There is something more, though, that is necessary if the gender consciousness in critical intellectual work is to be at all complete: this is the study of how the subjective dimension of masculinity is reproduced. If work on femininity has shown us how 'becoming a woman' is a social and historical construction, then we should not ignore the need for work which shows how the process of 'becoming a man' takes place. Too often courses on gender have concentrated solely upon women's experience: this can reveal things about masculinity in the way I have just discussed. But we should not be afraid to look more closely at the processes whereby boys learn to become men in a male-dominated society. This might reveal an interesting set of contradictions, of discrepancies between the ideology of masculinity and the actual lived experience of being male.

In a contribution to the symposium at which this paper was first presented, Thelma McCormack referred to 'contradiction' as a vogue word, and asked why we might be interested in it. This paper is an attempt to show how certain views of a social actor in the world are not necessarily consonant with that actor's actions or everyday life. To see how these sorts of tensions between action and belief are worked through is to see ideology in formation. The "dominant symbols or forms of belief in a society"[4] may be subscribed to in consciousness whilst being far from characteristic of all aspects of everyday life. There will be, in any society, what Robin Williams once called "cultural fictions" (Williams, 1963)[5], which are values to which lip-service is paid but which do not match with or prescribe the limits of everyday action. This gap, this potential split between what we profess to believe and what we actually do, is a significant source of contradictions in our social existence. To identify such contradictions is to show that things are not always as they are said to be. To recognise contradictions between thought and action —between consciousness and practice —is also to see that cultural meanings are not fixed, not forever closed; it is to realise that such meanings are contestable and not inherently consensual.

If ideologies of gender are to be at all adequately understood then the processes whereby gender identities are constructed and experienced must be given detailed empirical consideration. To this end, I offer in this paper an analysis and some speculations. The analysis is of the image of masculinity worked within a boys' football (soccer) comic in Britain in the mid-1980s. The speculations concern ways in which a dominant masculinist ideology of sports might be challenged by alternative conceptions of physicality and physical activity. My argument is quite straightforward. I argue that in sports activities and in representations of sports activities (of which as an example I take boys' comics), contradictions inherent in an ideology of masculinity as lived in everyday life are transcended and resolved into idealised fantasies in which masculinity is conceived as an unproblematic, natural — and crucially — non-feminine state of affairs or condition; and that radically innovative forms of physicality which have the potential to redefine the spheres of the masculine as well as the feminine are all too easily appropriated by the market, and reworked in ways utterly congruent with the conception of masculinity which the form initially had the capacity to challenge.

In the following sections of the paper I do three things. First, I look at some questions concerning our understanding of masculinity and its deep-rootedness within sports. Second, I offer an interpretative reading of a British football comic. Finally, I consider some aspects of the women's fitness boom in the early 1980s, framed in some senses as a response to Angela McRobbie's reading of 'body boom' movies of that time, as presented in her contribution to the symposium at which this paper was first presented.[6]

"It's a man's world: sponsoring gender"

There is nothing particularly novel in the contention that modern sports have been bastions of maleness. Women may have found that their choices for leisure and sports broadened as did men's in, say, the middle and late 19th century in Britain. But the 'broadening' choice was broader for some than for others. Peter Bailey, reflecting upon the importance of a club atmosphere for "informal dealings in business and politics", went on to say that:

> All this suggests heavy male dominance, but the broadening choice of sports and outdoor activities provided increased recreational opportunities for the ladies as well. Games, parties and sports clubs provided cover for courtship and flirtation, and the constant surplus of women over men during this period accounts for female enthusiasm for the mixed sport of lawn tennis and croquet... The latter, we are told, offered "fresh air and flirtation in agreeable combination". (Bailey, 1978: p. 77)

It is hard to see this kind of 'broadening' choice as anything more than a form of pragmatism within traditional gender relations. The evocatively rich detail, though, in Bailey's study is not fully interpreted in terms of gender.

Garry Whannel highlights the gendered basis of sports culture. Sport, he argues, is:

> ...very central to being a 'real' man. To be good at sport is to be strong, virile and macho. To be bad at sport is to be inadequate as a man.... In Britain, sport culture is deeply embedded into traditional notions of masculinity. The stress on toughness, commitment, competitiveness,

aggression and courage in sport all fit into the traditional notion of 'being a man'. (Whannel, 1983: pp. 28–9 and p. 32)[7]

Whannel manages, in his study, to convey a real sense of both the class *and* the gender bases of modern sports. Recognising that women and working-class males also played sports, he stresses that "such involvement was always within the bounds of authority exercised by the men of the bourgeoisie" (Whannel, 1983: p. 53). Whannel's study simultaneously situated sports in the twin contexts of patriarchy and capitalism, recognising that both gender and class are key determinants in the evolution of modern sports. This is a vital point, and one which, if one reductionist fallacy or another is to be avoided, must be constantly kept in mind. The development of women's football developed in the context of male-dominated sport in a patriarchal society demonstrates this point well.

Women who developed women's football (soccer) in Britain initially met with little cooperation from the authorities within the Football Association itself. Ted Croker, the Secretary of the Football Association has said that:

> In the game generally women are far more involved now than they used to be. (Croker, 1983)

But when Croker stated that women were welcome within the world of football, he had a particular kind of help in mind:

> There are many secretaries now. Many clubs ... many well run clubs ... are handled by female secretaries. (Croker, 1983)

As far as the dominant male culture in the world of soccer is concerned, women can enter that world, but only on terms not of their own making. They must enter such worlds as useful workers, to make servicing contributions. Surveys showed that, where women's football developed, over one third of all players in 1978 were under 17 years of age; almost 2/3 of all players were under 20 years of age. Of players over the age of 16, only one in 7 or 8 were married; and only one in 14 was a mother (Bale, 1980). The game, then, was rooted in the years of adolescence — a game for girls *before* they become women? But regionally, too, in the growth of women's football in England and Wales, there are distinctions. Women's football was most entrenched in the South of England; and in rural and suburban areas. It was in the urban areas of the Midlands and the North (in England) — the working class centres of male football culture — that women's football prospered least. It is clear enough that although there is a general gender dimension to sports inequality (Croker clearly believes in the inherent superiority of the male), such inequality is manifested to varying degrees in different class contexts. A male element in a specifically *working class* culture may well be the primary constraint upon the growth of soccer for girls in Northern working class areas.

I make no claim in this paper for the priority of either gender or class, for the primacy of either patriarchy or capitalism. Instead, I approach sports as one sphere through which gender relations are reproduced in a class-ridden society. Too frequently definitions of what it is to be a man have been almost taken-for-granted, whilst the notion of femininity has been subjected to detailed investigation. Occasionally the notion of masculinity was presented as a problem to be explored[8]. But more often masculinity was taken to be the assumed backcloth against which femininity can be studied. Paul Willis has commented upon this in his work on male working class culture, pointing out that masculinist modes of sexism must never be seen as a 'natural' form of shop-floor life; rather, a central task has to be the critical comprehension of this relationship (Willis, 1979).

Sports are predominantly male, or so all British surveys of the late 1970s showed. In only two sports activities, in 1977, in a list of 31 sports featured in a national survey, were women more active than men — horse-riding and keep-fit/yoga. In most activities, the level of participation among men was considerably higher than that of women. In nearly one third of the activities, men's level of participation was at least five times as high as that of women — numbered among this one third were, not surprisingly, male team sports and mainstream working class sports (Veal, 1979). In the half a dozen or so years since the 1977 survey, it was argued, there was a "substantial increase in the level of sports participation in this country" (Veal, 1983). Running and cycling were identified as 'booms', and keep fit/yoga were seen to be still growing — one of the few predominantly female activities. But there was little indication that increased participation in physical activity meant that sports were becoming less male-dominated. The increase in sports participation is clearly, in many sports, also an increase in male participation. In this sense, sport continues to be a mere enclave, for some women, in empires of masculinity.

Images of masculinity in sports are further worked upon by outside agencies which enter the world of sports as sponsors. It is in ways such as these that our consciousness is directed towards particular conceptions of male and female within the world of sports. The key industries involved in sponsorship in Britain in the late 1970s/early 1980s were the tobacco, alcohol and life insurance industries. Nobody in the business world believed that this was a consequence of the love of the outdoor life of company executives. Indeed, the world of business is sometimes its own best analyst:

> Organisations engage in sponsorship in order to gain access to the media as an alternative to taking paid-for advertising space. There can be no doubt that sponsorship is fundamentally a reward-seeking commercial activity rather than an exercise in altruism. (Cranfield School of Management, 1977)

There is, unsurprisingly, an increasing interest in sports sponsorship by the tobacco industry when cigarette advertising is banned on television. The market's interest in sports is a consequence of the state of the market for the particular commodity involved, and is quite simply a form of indirect advertising. But what is of most interest, for the purposes of this paper, is the way in which the market, in the form of the sponsor, works within and then upon a traditional notion of gender identities. Tobacco firms have involved themselves as sponsors of most male-dominated sports. But they work too within a sense of class-specific and gender-specific sports. The cigarette manufacturer which sponsors male working class sports such as darts, angling, bowls, snooker and speedway is aiming for different markets than is the manufacturer which sponsors cricket, equestrianism, women's golf, tennis and table tennis. The latter is associating a more up-market product — the Lambert and Butler cigarette — with a range of specifically middle and upper class sports activities in which women are relatively well-represented. The Embassy company, on the contrary, sticks exclusively to the working class world of men. Marlboro, with its quarter-century background in reproducing images of masculinity, sponsors darts, motor cycling and motor racing. Drawing upon its North American 'B' movie cowboy motif, the Marlboro world reaches out to a world of the ruggedly classless male.

Women's squash was sponsored in the early 1980s by food, sportswear and tights manufacturers; gymnastics (mostly a girls' activity) by, among others, manufacturers of milk, soft drinks and sanitary towels (Sports Council, 1981). All of this cannot but work to perpetuate distinctive gender stereotypes in sport, a point not even raised in Britain's most sustained and extensive investigation into sports sponsorship (CCPR, 1983). Estimates of how much sponsorship money flowed into sports in Britain in the 1980s put the figure, at the point of estimate, at £60million. Much of this money served to reinforce deep-rooted prejudices of gender in both the world of sports and the wider social relations in which sports are embedded.

This section has indicated just how deeply embedded are the codes of gender, and in particular, a code of masculinity, in modern sports. Evidence of sports participation in Britain is evidence of gender inequality and male-dominance. Perceptions of masculinity are worked upon by forms of indirect advertising in the world of sports. There are variations in terms of class which are important too. But the main point to emphasise is: that sports, particularly top-level performance sports, in our modern consciousness, are primarily defined as male activities and, where they are not, as the specifically non-male — the feminine. How this continues to be the case is a major question. What are the processes, within our everyday culture, which reproduce a sense of the world of sports as a primarily masculine one? It is in response to this question that I offer the analysis in the following section.

"They're always scoring goals and it's always the same"

[Alys, aged 8, on casting aside a copy of *Roy of the Rovers*]

Parodying a classic text in the field of popular cultural analysis, this section might be subtitled 'How to Read *Roy of the Rovers*'. In their analysis of imperialist ideology in the Disney comic, Dorfman and Mattelart noted that the emphases in comic strip story-telling are often made at the expense of other possible emphases. Disney's stories are told in terms of avoidances just as much as in terms of issues which are actually dealt with. Thus the Disney comic strips avoid the realities of sex and children, producing parent-less, sex-less narratives — Disney's characters are 'eunuchs' who "live in an eternal foreplay with their impossible virgins" (Dorfman and Mattelart, 1975: p. 39). My critical analysis of masculinist ideology in a comic strip soccer magazine in contemporary Britain adopts a comparable approach, focusing on three major questions: how do particular types of ideological motifs recur within and across narratives?; how do such narrative constructions rest upon particular kinds of avoidances or absences or exclusions?; and how do these narrative constructions, often caricaturing one social category or another, relate to the everyday lives of the young people who read them?

I have used some copies of *Roy of the Rovers* in my teaching, and before revealing to a class that the session would involve looking at comics, I have sometimes asked them what the phrase ('Roy of the Rovers') meant to them. In one class made up of 15 or so adults, all the eight men, aged between 30 and 70, could offer a 'definition' of the term. Only one of the seven women (aged between 30 and 50), had the slightest idea what it meant. The men gave as definitions phrases like 'heroic performance', 'last-minute heroism', 'super-human achievement', 'skills which can win matches from out of the blue at the last minute'. The one woman to whom the phrase had any meaning at all was the mother of a young son, from whom she had received a sense of 'Roy of the Rovers' as some kind of 'special football hero'. It is therefore important to recognise the fact that in Britain the phrase 'Roy of the Rovers' can generate this almost exclusively male-rooted sense of male heroism in sports.

It has been suggested that the 'Roy of the Rovers' adventure or romance is a version of the giant-killing myth, in which a team of Davids humbles one of "the tournament's Goliaths" (Wren-Lewis and Clarke, 1983: p. 130). Although there is an interesting giant-killer motif in some of the stories in the comic, the 'Roy of the Rovers' romance is also the romance of the *immortality of the overdog,* not the momentary triumph of the underdog — in the eponymous comic strip, at least. The David/Goliath theme is just one version of the 'Roy of the Rovers' romance. Exceptional goal-scoring by anyone is referred to by players, sports commentators and fans as 'real Roy of the Rovers stuff'. The meaning of the term now resonates far beyond the comic text with which I am primarily concerned. But what it implies, generally, is the reaffirmation of a supra-ordinary male heroism — the continued triumph of the dominant, whatever respective odds or challenges have to be faced.

Roy of the Rovers started life as a weekly comic devoted to soccer adventure tales in September 1976. 'Roy' is Roy Race, a star soccer player with Melchester Rovers. He first appeared, as a comic strip hero, in the first issue of the comic *Tiger,* on September 11, 1954. In season 1983–84 Roy was still going strong, as a player-manager, still able to score heroic one-man goals *and* to contribute to overall team moves and scores in an unselfish fashion. By the middle of the 1980s Roy Race had featured in the weekly life of readers for over 30 years. He had, like all popular cultural heroes in fictional forms, performed miracles of chronology as well as of sports performance. In 1983 he was still characterised by an eternal youthfulness. He was a sporting Peter Pan, never needing to grow

up. His face had become a little fuller; he may have become burdened by the
pressures and obligations of club management and marriage respectively, but he
weathered all this well (**Illustration A**) — not just to survive, but to survive as
the legendary hero of a big-selling weekly.

Illustration A: **from *The Sunday Times*, 9 Sept. 1984: illustrations to
Mick Brown, 'Wallop! Goal! Roy's still over the moon
at 30'.**

Many things happened to Roy in this 30 year spell at the top. First of all,
ironically, as he aged he played more active football. In earlier years he was as
much an adventure hero off-pitch as on. Later his heroism was mostly on field.
He has also been "married, separated, shot, fathered three children, fallen into a
coma and starred with Sharron Davies and Suzanne Dando in a Christmas panto.
It's tough at the top" (Brown, 1984: p. 5). (Sharron and Suzanne were Britain's
contemporary 'sexy' superstars, from the worlds of swimming and gymnastics
respectively). For 13 years Roy's team went unbeaten, but in 1967 a more
realistic emphasis introduced the notion of defeat, and consequently, the element
of restoration, into the Melchester narrative. In a more contemporary world Roy
is given his fair share of problems: family, age, defeat. But his main protagonists
were still the unsportsmanlike hard-men of the football world: hatchetmen, often
from foreign lands.

The comic in its mid-80s form was made up of nine stories, a 'Roy Race Talk-In', a quiz, soccer jokes, and a team chart through which to keep tabs on your favourite real-life team. It was produced by IPC Magazines as one of a number of 'boys' adventure titles'. The comic was not categorised as a sports magazine, but an adventure comic, along with comics on war and science fiction. According to circulation figures for January-June 1983, *Roy of the Rovers* was selling 101,972 copies each week. The sports magazine *Shoot*, a feature and documentary weekly on soccer, was selling 176,753 weekly. Soccer and sports stories also featured in several other of IPC's weekly comics. Although *Roy of the Rovers* was not one of IPC's highest selling weeklies, for a *one-sport* comic its sales were huge. IPC magazines also produced a *Roy of the Rovers* Annual, for the Christmas-present market. This ran for many years, from well before Roy himself had his own comic. But in the early 1980s the Annual abandoned its focus upon sporting activities beyond just soccer. Earlier editions of the Annual included more prose/photo features, on a variety of sports, than comic strip narratives. The 1984 and 1985 Annuals were almost totally made up of extra-long comic strip stories — a bumper edition, really, of the weekly comic. It is likely that the success of the 'magazine format' (as in *Shoot*) polarised the forms: the comic-strip publication is precisely that, making few concessions to the non-visual, or to the exploration of the 'real world' in features. All the stories are about soccer.

What image of maleness and sport was being produced in this re-presentation of Britain's national game?

Three concerns are covered in this interpretation of the comic: first, recurrent motifs in the narrative; second, significant absences; and third, text/reader relations. With some reference to others among IPC's comic listings, I will look at how six recurrent motifs within stories construct particular types of meanings.

First, stories in the comic strip are both rooted in the experience of its young readership, yet simultaneously rendered timeless. The *cyclical/ever-recurring* nature of the sports season or calendar offers the sense that if you don't triumph this time, then there's always the next match, tournament or season.

A second motif, that of *mobility,* emphasises that with hard work or real determination, as well as talent, the young sportsman can 'go all the way' to Illustration B: "Goalkeeper!", *Roy of the Rovers* (18 Feb. 1984)Illustration B: "Goalkeeper!", *Roy of the Rovers* (18 Feb. 1984)the top (**see Illustration B "Goal-keeper!" and Illustration C "The Apprentices"**).

Illustration B: "**Goalkeeper!**", *Roy of the Rovers* (**18 Feb. 1984**)

Illustration C: "The Apprentices", *Roy of the Rovers* (3 March 1984)

Illustration D: "Tommy's Troubles", *Roy of the Rovers* (3 March 1984)

A *David and Goliath* fantasy is present, as a third motif implying that the little bag of bones can beat, outwit and humiliate the bigger bully figure (**see Illustration D "Tommy's Troubles"**). The bully, Bert, and his cronies are humiliated by Tommy Barnes, the determined 'Skinny' and the bespectacled 'Ginger'. Magic is sometimes central to this theme. Simon Benson has an accident and, with an implant, becomes a 'Bionic Boy' (*Roy of the Rovers*, 18 August, 1984). In a comic in which *Roy of the Rovers* previously featured (*Searcher*), 'Billy's Boots' were endowed with the skilful qualities of a great player of the past. Billy Dane was to bring his magic to later editions of *Roy of the Rovers*, keeping alive the legendary prowess of the owner of the boots, 'Dead Shot Keen'.

Fourth, the theme of *restoration* is a fairly prominent one. As mentioned earlier, this is a regular theme embodied in the sporting 'comeback'. If Melchester lose, there's always the next game, competition, or season. More supranormally, restoration works very much in the fashion of the classical fairy-tale motif. Mysterious individuals with hidden pasts, or para-normal influences emanating from great figures of the past, remind the young reader that his heroes are historically rooted ones. A man wanders into a football club with haunting and as yet imprecise memories 'from his past' (see **Illustration E "Who is Arrow?"**). Here, history is magically recycled as the basis of a 'natural' order of things in the here and now — a mysterious yet almost natural inheritance.

Fifth, the motif of *eternal but responsible youthfulness* reminds us that we can stay young and dominant even when ageing, most particularly if we can groom an appropriate type of successor. In the early 1980s Roy Race, as player-manager of his new Walford club, is clearly the model for Rob Richards, the new young golden-haired clone of Roy himself (see **Illustration F "This is Rob Richards..."**). Here, should the 'Roy of the Rovers' image lose some credibility through time, a ready-made substitute could be slotted in smoothly to take Roy's place.

Sixth, the embodiment of the male hero is widely cast. Physicality in the male protagonist is not narrowly conceived. The muscle-bound hero, the fat misfit, the skinny waif — these are all presented as capable of male heroism or stardom.

In these motifs, around one or more of which just about all the stories revolve, we see some of the ideological work which a particular 'telling of the story' can do.

Beyond the narrative motifs, my second concern in this interpretation of the comic's meaning is with how a story can be told and given a particular

Illustration E: "Who is Arrow?", *Roy of the Rovers* (17 Dec. 1983)

Illustration F: "This is Rob Richards", *Roy of the Rovers* **(3 March 1984)**

ideological direction by the decision to *leave out* particular elements, or to present them in a highly specific way. To see how this is done, it is illuminating to concentrate upon questions of work, and of women. I will spend most time on the latter.

The work involved in sustaining life as a professional sportsman is given a particular gloss. Roy and his men of Melchester are rarely depicted hard at work, despite the mobility motif. When they are, it is usually to highlight some personal drama. A training session, for instance, might be the place where a recalcitrant member of the squad — whose refractoriness is usually based in entrenched jealousy of Roy Race's talents and skills — attempts to undermine Roy's authority. Systematic and sustained physical work, though, is not presented as the prerequisite for the glories in the public arena. This gives the top-level action — the main focus of the Roy narratives — a quality of effortlessness. New generations of readers receive the impression that success comes easily. In training sessions it is only clashes of personality that prevent the smooth flow of preparation: pain, resentment, tedium, boredom, physical exploitation — these are rarely featured. Interestingly, in popularity charts of stories in *Roy of the Rovers* (based on readers' own votes) the two least popular stories/items were (late in 1983) 'The Apprentices' and 'The Best of Roy the Rovers'. The latter (old stories of Roy in the past) may be diachronically confusing for a readership in the here and now; and in 'The Apprentices', the very centrality of work (about young professionals whose job is mainly work and whose success is never glamorous, with perhaps the sole exception of Rob Richards) threatens the glamour and romance which is at the heart of the Roy of the Rovers stories. The Roy of the Rovers myth works around a romance of physicality in which physical decay does not set in, and injuries are easily overcome. Physicality as labour — sport as work — is significant in its very absence.

But it is in their presentation of the place and the role of women that such comics ply most effectively their ideological trade. Usually, women are simply absent or unobtrusively in the background. But they are also given some central spaces, and it is in such spaces that images of female-ness are evoked in such a way as to reaffirm the desirability of being male. The background is one of servicing. Melchester's secretary is a woman, presented in part as a career woman; representing, though, concessions made, in the world of masculine sports, which work towards the retention of male hegemony. Also, players have wives and mothers, working away invisibly in the background, providing the domestic services which are an important basis from which our sports heroes launch themselves on their adventures.

When women are given roles within the centre of the narrative, two major types are featured. First there is the female ogre, the tyrannical and sometimes physically gigantic termagant with threatening powers over a potentially demasculinised client group. A strange, absurd character called Kevin Mouse ('Mighty Mouse') is constantly threatened by the Matron in the hospital in which he is a footballing medical student — a matron of enormous proportions going by the name of Mad Annie (see **Illustration G**).

Illustration G:
'Mad Annie' from
"Mighty Mouse",
Roy of the Rovers
(24 September 1983)

Second, there is the interfering battle-axe of a wife or mother, the female who for one reason or another lets slip the smooth servicing role. Roy Race himself has been threatened by this type in the shape of what is seen as the fussing interference of his wife (see **Illustration H** overleaf).

Illustration H: *Roy of the Rovers*   (17 September 1983)

In both those cases the ideological effect is the same. The smooth reproduction of male success in sport is threatened by women abandoning their appropriate and 'natural' position in the social order. Mouse's livelihood and game are constantly threatened by Mad Annie's intention to replace him and her strategy to keep him off the playing field. Roy's game is suffering because of his 'unreasonable' wife. Once away from Mad Annie, Mouse's squeak turns into the lion's roar. Once Mrs. Race is no longer a nagging presence in Roy Race's life, Roy starts finding the net again.

My third and final major concern in looking at *Roy of the Rovers* is with how the construction within the text might relate to the everyday lives of young people. Comic strip heroes are not confined within the pages of the comic itself. They are picked up, like the stars of soap operas, and used in everyday life and other genres. In one of D. C. Thomson and Co.'s adventure comics *Victor and Buddy* there appeared a long established footballing hero called Leslie Thomson, striker with Darbury Rangers. Despite the physical disability of a limp, Leslie ('Limp-Along Leslie', No. 1180, Oct. 1, 1983) can round up stray rams on the remote farming land, and a scene or two later burst through the country's top soccer defences. Terry Venables, in his soccer novel *They Used to Play on Grass* (co-written with Gordon Williams, Hodder and Stoughton, 1971) calls a slow-moving, physically disabled club hireling 'Limp-Along Leslie'. When I interviewed Colin Welland, screenwriter of the movie "Chariots of Fire", about sporting heroes, one of his comments referred to another couple of long established athletic heroes, Alf Tupper and The Great Wilson. Tupper, the Tough of the Track, still featuring in 'Victor and Buddy" in the wake of the Marathon craze (see 'The Tough on the Marathon Trail', *Victor*, No. 1180, Sept. 15, 1984), usually triumphed upon the basis of a diet of fish and chips, a totally unstructured training schedule, and a very deep-rooted aversion to the 'toffs' in established sport. The Great Wilson was a mysterious reincarnation of a past athletic champion, a pure spirit undiluted by the crises of the contemporary world. Welland's heroes — two comic strip characters embodying the mythical timelessness of the male romance of physicality.

Textual constructions, then, live on in the consciousness of the readers. They fuel and refuel conceptions of masculinity, of male heroism, operating inter-textually and across the boundaries of textual representation and lived experiences. They become in a real sense themselves lived. Welland and I smiled indulgently in a shared male conspiracy of romance at the mention of such names. Welland said simply, after we had spent some time talking about Harold Abrahams (one of the athletic heroes of *Chariots of Fire*): "The Tough of the Track and the Great Wilson — they were our heroes".

Some very simple points must be made here. Boys constituted 88% of the readership of *Roy of the Rovers* in 1982, and many continued to read the comic *through* their mid-adolescent years. IPC's figures to 1982 showed this unambiguously: 57% of the readership was within the age band 11–14, but 9% were 7–8 and 18% were aged 9–10; 15–16 year olds made up 6%, and 10% of the readership was made up of 17–19 year olds. There was clearly a drop-out rate, but comics circulated among brothers, sisters, school-friends. And one in six of these male readers was of or beyond school-leaving age. It is doubtful that *any* comic for girls would have followed this pattern. *Bunty* was a long established comic for pre-pubescent girls. *Jackie* targeted mid-adolescent girls (McRobbie, 1977; Dunne, 1982). Work on these two comics has shown how an assertive physicality in pre-pubescence is superseded by an emphasis on girls' main work — the construction of themselves as objects of potential consumption by men. A brand new comic in the British market in early 1985 (*Nikki*) combined elements of both *Bunty* and *Jackie* and demonstrated that the ideology of adolescent femininity could be successfully marketed for even younger markets. The girls' comic market looks as if it is cunningly plotted by a team of developmental psychologists, subtly sensitive to the crises of femininity and sexuality of the adolescent female. *Roy of the Rovers*, read fervently by boys from 7–19, embodied no such dilemma of gender identity. Being male, surviving with an unquestioned maleness, achieving male heroism — the message was that this was normal enough for the boy-soon-to-become-man.

This pattern of readership was exclusive to *Roy of the Rovers*. IPC's rival 'Boys adventure' comic, *Victor*, had a readership which faded at 13/14, and which, astonishingly, rose again at 17/19. It is almost as if boys of 13/16 think that they have grown up or become adult, before recognising that the essence of masculinity is not growing up at all. The magazine/feature soccer publication *Shoot* lost its readership dramatically at 17/19. Pseudo-realism is displaced again by fantasy, by idealised fictional heroes. Similarly, the specialist science-fiction comic *2000 AD* was taken up again by 17–19 year olds, after a mid-adolescent fall in readership. As I have said elsewhere, sport and space offer similar sets of possibilities within the masculinist landscape (Tomlinson, 1982: p. 120). Not

growing up, the constant sense of masculinity as adventure and glory —
these are the key elements in the representation of sporting and adventure in
boys' comics.

How is such an ideology of masculinity lived? Reviewing a novel concerned
with the mid-life crisis of masculinity, Polly Toynbee (1983: p. 10) has
speculated on the hero's dilemma:

> Fantasy pictures of childhood heroes worry him, especially Jack
> Hawkins on the bridge of The Cruel Sea. How can you be a man without
> standing on the deck of a destroyer? Those brave noble creatures who
> showed few personal emotions but the male passions of manhood and
> comradeship were no use to a boy as models in ordinary life. What is left
> of manhood once the right to dominate has been removed?

What is actually left, of course, is the myth of manhood, operating powerfully
as an ideology in ordinary life. How many fictitious sexual male conquests have
been boasted about at Boy Scout camp, in school playgrounds, in College
fraternities? How many polls of sexual activity give respondents (both male and
female) a chance to, however anonymously, declare a scale of lived sexuality
which is closer to fantasy than their actual experience? Idealised images, as
Toynbee implies, are not of obvious use in ordinary life. But ordinary life is a
complex multi-layered process: we strike bargains with our idealised conceptions
of what-life-should-be-like. We read the world and ourselves sometimes in terms
of the textual representations with which we are familiar. It is not possible simply
to separate ordinary life from myth. *Roy of the Rovers* tells boys and youths that
life is a game and that male dominance is sometimes problematic but can be
taken-for-granted. Young people's own dilemmas of self-identity, sexuality and
so on, might carry a different message. But such 'experienced' differences do not
necessarily overcome the myth. They might in fact be smoothed over by the
constantly reiterated potency of the myth itself.

For in the end *Roy of the Rovers* offers a smoother than smooth path to male
glory. In a move towards the participatory, readers are asked in to the text, to
evaluate stories and so to produce charts of popularity. In similar adventure
comics this constitution of the reader's own potentially heroic subjectivity has
been taken to its limit. The bubbles of dialogue in the picture strips leave the
name of the protagonist unwritten — simply write in your own name! Also, in
the way in which real life sports stars are invited into the text, Roy is presented

Illustration I: "Roy Race and Sharron Davies...",
                        Roy of the Rovers (24 December 1983)

Illustration J: "Rovers New Chairman",
                        Roy of the Rovers (18 August, 1984)

as a form of pseudo-reality. Look, for instance, at **Illustration I** ("Roy Race and Sharron Davies...") and **Illustration J** ("Rovers New Chairman"). If you can mingle intimately with Sharron Davies, and become a close colleague of the legendary England cricketer Geoff Boycott, life away from the comic can be lived as a relatively dull and routine existence, a life which really only *comes to life* in the glory-seeking pages of the weekly fantasy.

The Roy Race narrative over time, has offered the post-war generation of British male soccer fans a remarkable romance. What is clear enough, though, is that the relation between representation in the text and aspects of the everyday life of young males is a symbiotic one. The *Roy of the Rovers* text offered a weekly recipe of dramatic heroic achievement (not infrequently against the odds); thus idealising as normal what only rarely happens in everyday life itself[9].

"Invading men's spaces": fitness, fashion and femininity

Angela McRobbie has argued that in the early 1980s there was an interesting shift, an "ideological reworking", as she called it, in some representations of female physicality in films. In *Flash-dance* and *Fame*, for instance, females are centrally featured as ambitious achievers. Although the female figure might be implicated in a relatively traditional romance, she does not represent an inertia. Rather, McRobbie argued, she signifies action, an image of femininity not as passive but as active (McRobbie, 1984).

Certainly the boom in women's physicality at the time encouraged women to adopt a more physically assertive profile, and films like *Fame* and *Flashdance* were both reflective of *and* generative on this trend. The permanence of such trends is of course open to question. Mind, spirit and body were seen as vitally inter-linked in any pursuit of the 'healthy' when *Cosmopolitan* commented on the 'body boom' in August 1982. Just a couple of years on, London's *Time Out* could carry a front page lead-in shrieking "Aerobics is Dead: So What's Next?", and talk of dwindling attendances at exercise classes, the closure of health clubs, the bursting of the fitness boom (February 14-20, 1985, No. 756). Rumours of a Jane Fonda heart attack, the death of James Fixx (the male guru of running), medical scares on injury-ignorance, the levelling out of a newish market — many factors may have contributed to the halting of the growth.

But women continued to *look* more assertive in terms of fitness, and groups of mothers collecting children outside schools were certainly wearing sports equipment and displaying a sports style. Without doubt the body boom had radical and challenging dimensions in terms of women's experience; but such potentially radical cultural practices can be shorn of their radicalism by particular ideological forces.

Three radical dimensions of the body boom revolve around three freedoms: freedom of space, freedom of physical expression, and the freedom to support/ co-operate. Keep-fit classes in schools, clubs and church-halls gave women their most 'legitimate' (in the eyes of their male spouses in particular) space since bingo. Physically, too, the boom offered, in the work-out and the class, a freedom of the body which has not been widely available to women before. This has its novelty value to the male voyeur. At one high-school in England in the early 1980s, this physical freedom was so novel that the Principal (male) of the college always happened to be 'passing by' when the class of female students and staff were working out uninhibitedly. And the third freedom, of co-operation, is a freedom to re-constitute physicality as a co-operative mutually reaffirming activity; not in the nature of the regimented physical jerks of the fitness crazes of past eras, but more in line with an era of individualism expressed in a collective context.

What did going to the work-out or the keep-fit class actually mean? Early on in the boom, one 35 year old member of an all female keep-fit class in a small town in Sussex could say that "everyone is just a woman in a leotard, no-one appears different", and the wearing of such an outfit could be seen as a great equaliser (Driscoll, 1981: p. 25). But clearly this is not so much the case once a great range of leotards really hits the market. This woman was one of a class in the winter of 1980-81, few of whom established new social patterns of friendship away from or around the class. As another observer of a women's keep-fit class (Webb, 1983) has noted: "Exercise classes obviously provide a convenient, relatively easy and widely available way [of exercising]. It requires little commitment, no special equipment and no previous experience. It is therefore less likely to be disruptive of typical gender roles in the home".[10] In her study of women's leisure activities in the new town of Milton Keynes from the summer of 1980 onwards, Rosemary Deem found that this non-intrusion of activities such as swimming, badminton and keep-fit into women's family obligations marked them as limited possibilities for any genuinely expanded female involvement in sport (Deem, 1982: p. 41) It is important, then, to note the constrained nature of the time and space which is taken by women for such activities. For many women, they are fitted into an already hectic schedule of domestic and profession obligations.

Three processes, most of all, worked to render the boom as ideologically reproductive as much as challenging. First, the commodification of the practice brought it into the mainstream of consumer relations. Swish clubs spring up; Roger Daltry (of the rock group 'Who') opens his 'Fitness Factory' in Brighton, and not surprisingly church-halls begin to look a little less attractive even to the most committed participants. One London club had no difficulty, during 1983, in finding 1,800 members willing to pay £350 a week (cited in 'The Money Programme', 20 November 1982, BBC2). New magazines and publications spring up, giving every photogenic super-sportsperson, however geriatric, the chance to launch him/herself into a lucrative new career. Look at the titles of some of these: *Workout,* for young adults; *Cosmopolitan*'s 'Zest'; *New Health*; *Fitness.* Even the tabloid Sunday papers get in on the act — the *News of the World*'s 'Sunday' covers up soccer superstar George Best's rather fleshy frame with an over-full working-out outfit, and pops him on the cover with his current girl friend, both presented as Get-Fit-Fast experts (Feb. 19, 1984). With this commercial dimension, female physicality begins simply to be shaped for sale, marketed as merchandise. *Any* emphasis becomes acceptable if it sells. A major theme, for instance, in *Fitness* magazine was 'fitness for sex', 'sexual exercises for women'. This becomes just a further example of the exploitative use of the female and the female body.

Secondly, as forms of documentation develop, women's physicality becomes the object of male attention again. Men film and watch women working out. The fit woman becomes the object of a far-from-disinterested male attention. Home videos, female fitness specialists on breakfast television: here the female space is reconstituted as a publicly available one, easily accessible to the male voyeur.

Third, a form of liberated sexuality of the female, very much fostered by a sense of physical assertiveness, shares with more traditional notions of the female the obsession with being 'equipped' for the male. This contributes in turn to a *male* perception of explicit female physicality as a statement of availability. As fitness becomes fashion the figure of the fit female can fuel male fantasy, often prompting a defence mechanism: she's available, but do I really want her?[11] This is, of course, a misreading of aspects of women's experience, an insecure response by men to their feeling of being threatened. But such responses are the stuff of the re-entry of the ideologically dominant.

It is not enough, then, to see a new kind of physically active female-ness just in its own terms. It must be situated within wider relations of patriarchy, within a context of deep-rooted and often persisting male domination. It is then that we can begin to see how ideologies of gender work. Two photographs, one from *New Health* (Illustration K), one from *Cosmopolitan*'s 'Zest' (Illustration L), will finish this section.

Illustration K:　　*New Health*　(March 1984) Vol. 1, No. 4
　　　　　　　　　　　　(a Haymarket publication)

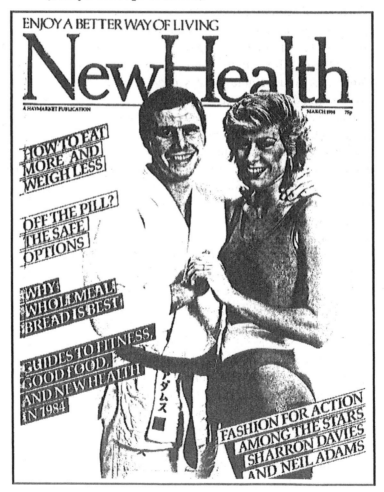

Yes, Sharron Davies — making sure that nothing in the fitness boom passes her by. Featuring in outlets straddling fantasy and fashion, across *Roy of the Rovers* and *Cosmopolitan*, she is surely evidence that the cultural space created by the development in female physicality is scarcely resistant to a "language of patriarchy" which "perpetuates the oppression of women" (Willis, 1982).

Illustration L   **"Sharron's sleek swimsuit'** *Cosmopolitan's Zest* **2nd issue (May, 1984). Picture courtesy of Cosmopolitan/©National Magazine Company**

Gender ideologies and cultural reproduction

Paul Willis has discussed how ideology works in three stages. First, ideology(ies) can be defining forces; second, they can be altered by responses to them based on alternative interpretations in 'social sub-regions'; third, there is so often a rebirth of ideology (Willis, 1982: p. 124). Women, born into a gender-specific culture, can create spaces of a radical kind — the keep-fit arena — which are challenging regarding traditional conceptions of gender. But, lacking a "counter-definitional force" (Willis, 1982: p. 130) of their own, women can so easily — however unintentionally — collude in the reassertion of ideology. The power of men, the prescience of the market, the nature of the media, all conspire to re-situate female physicality along traditional lines. When *Jane Fonda's Workout* could stay on the U.S. best seller list for 176 weeks, selling 1.8 million copies, and 270,000 video-cassettes could be sold at $60 each (and this only up to Feb. 1984) (Scobie, 1984: p. 33), then any counter-definitions at the grassroots were soon swamped by the major defining force: the female body as commodity in patriarchal capitalist relations. Stuart Hall has argued that 'popular and demo-cratic elements in daily life', such as the 'current craze for body maintenance', are important and potentially transformative elements of contemporary con-sciousness (Hall, 1984). This is certainly the case in any groundswell of participation in which the innovative practices are not fully commodified. Turned into marketable acquisitions, the meaning of such practices inevitably changes.

How, in sport and physical activity, do significant attempts at freedom and, in a sense, demystification, in the end contribute to the reproduction of dominant relations? They do so because the subjectivities which we develop, as males and females, continue to be framed within terms of traditional conceptions of gender. However much these conceptions might be doubted, modified or whatever in our personal lives and everyday experiences, wider determining forces constantly work to reaffirm our traditional subjectivities.

No cultural form or practice can or will be wholly comprehensible without a consideration of its conditions of production, its inner workings as a relatively autonomous phenomenon, and its impact at the level of everyday life. Sport is no exception to this. It is conceived, funded, staged for various reasons and motives; it is a spectacle in itself, as a match, as a lived narrative especially in, say, a media representation of it; and it is generative of everyday interactions, conversations and popular memory. Sports have been produced as gendered practices within patriarchal relations which are clearly to the fore in, for example, forms of sponsorship. In texts, particular representations of sport can continue to reaffirm conceptions of gender. In everyday life certain more challenging conceptions can be generated. What the particular outcome will be in terms of how values are either sustained or modified, or in terms of how gender-ideology is reproduced, will vary from case to case.

But Sharron Davies is a key figure in this case. 'Sexuality for sale' is her unstated but un-missable message for female proponents of the fitness boom and for the male followers of the Roy Race story. In the series of compromises which she represents it becomes clear how certain conceptions of femininity can contribute to the reproduction of relations of male domination. Abbey Hoffman, the director of Sport-Canada, commented thus on the fitness boom: "It is just as insidious as any other marketing technique. And unfortunately, the majority of people cannot attain the look"[12]. This is a recognition of the ideological derivation of gendered bodily relations, and a reflection upon the capacity of capitalist-patriarchal social relations to absorb and sometimes incorporate the most potentially challenging of cultural initiatives.

To see how innovative conceptions of femininity can be absorbed into the dominant culture of consumerism and body-image, whilst conceptions of masculinity have been relatively untrammelled by idealised conceptions of physicality, is to see ideology at work, reproducing gender ideologies within the sphere of sporting images and bodily practices.

Acknowledgements

For permission to use the illustrations, thanks are due as follows:

Sharron Davies illustrations:

Illustration K: Haymarket Publications and *Here's Health.*

Illustration L: *Cosmopolitan/*©The National Magazine Company.

Roy of the Rovers **illustrations:**

Permission for the use of illustrations from *Roy of the Rovers* was sought from IPC Magazines. Customer Enquiries there could find no trace of the title, and passed me on, in January 1995, to Fleetway Editions, where the new title of *Roy of the Rovers Monthly* (launched in Autumn 1993) is located. Enquiries to Fleetwood, concerning permissions for use of illustrations from the earlier title, received no response.

Afterword

A talk from which this paper developed was given in 1983 (see note 1) and the paper written-up soon afterwards. Looking back, I am pleased at the pertinence, ten years on, of both the moment of analysis and the analysis itself. There has, of course, been an explosion in work on masculinity since this paper was written. I am happy nevertheless to publish the piece ten years after it was written because, though unpublished, it has been widely circulated and cited; and for some years it was scheduled to appear in a book based upon the 1983 symposium which did not, in the end, appear. Committed to that collection, the piece could not be made available elsewhere. The CSRC event and this consequent collection provided an opportunity to make this piece available in an appropriate context of exchange, debate and reflection.

Notes

1   A version of this paper was originally presented to an International Interdisciplinary Symposium on 'Gender, Leisure and Cultural Production' at Queen's University, Kingston, Ontario, Canada (30 September—2 October, 1983). I would like to thank Rick Gruneau for encouraging me to produce this piece, and for guiding me to some of the sources cited.

2   There is, of course a wide literature on how schooling reproduces gender identities. For a summary of this literature as it stood in the early 1980s see Madelaine MacDonald (1981).

3   I have summarised, here, the main points in the early work of Ruth Hartley and the feminist work of Nancy Chodorow, as presented in Madelaine MacDonald (1981), pp. 9-16.

4   This is Anthony Giddens' definition of ideology in *Sociology — a brief but critical introduction*, Macmillan, 1982, p. 51.

5   Williams points out that there are different categories of 'cultural fiction' — pp. 391-95. I am not looking to find evidence for the relevance of any particular one. But it is important to see that consciousness-action tensions which do involve gaps between beliefs and conduct are the raw data of ideological processes.

6   Since published as 'Dance and social fantasy', in A. McRobbie and M. Niva (eds) (1984) *Gender and generation*, London: Macmillan.

7   See too, p. 62 (on the media), p. 14 and p. 30 (on the challenge women have

mounted to male dominance in sports) and p.7 (on sport as a form of feminist attack).

[8] See the provocative collection of quotes, comments and images drawn together by Patricia Holland in 'Manpower!', *New Socialist* No. 13, September/October 1983, pp. 52-4.

[9] The romance faded in 1993 when falling sales halted production. But a special monthly was launched a few months later after much protest from *Roy of the Rovers* enthusiasts. Many of the protesters were adult males regretting the loss of one of their post-War myths.

[10] See, too, Driscoll (1981: p. 19) — a 32 year old housewife with two children: "I find the keep-fit just right, an hour and a half. By the time I've got the meal ready and wash up I virtually race out and then when I come back I have to turn round and start to do baby's bottles and things like that. It's getting towards ten o'clock then and I'm just beginning to fade".

[11] The best example that comes to mind of this male reaction is documented in Prendergast (1975).

[12] Quoted in 'Fitness emphasis marketing ploy', in 'Living', *The Citizen*, Ottowa, October 15, 1983. Many thanks to Denise McConney for sending me this clip.

References

Bailey, P. (1978) *Leisure and class in Victorian England — rational recreation and the contest for control 1830-1885*. London: Routledge and Kegan Paul.

Bale, J. (1980) 'Women's football in England and Wales: a social-geographic perspective', *Physical Education Review*, Vol. 3, No. 2: pp. 137–45.

Brown, M. (1984) 'Wallop! Goal! Roy's still over the moon at 30', *The Sunday Times*, 9 September.

CCPR (1983) The Howell Report: committee of enquiry into sports sponsorship. London: Central Council for Physical Recreation (November).

Chappell, H. (1983) 'Married to the Army', *New Society*, Vol. 66, No. 1098 (1 Dec.): pp. 354–57.

Connell, R. W. (1983) 'Men's bodies', in *Which way is up? Essays on sex, class and culture*. London: Allen and Unwin.

Coward, R. (1984) *Female desire: women's sexuality today*. London: Paladin.

Cranfield School of Management (1977) *Sponsorship in the U.K.* (August), quoted in The Sports Council (1981) *A report on the allocation of monies by companies towards sponsorship of sport in the U.K.*, Information Series No. 6. London: The Sports Council, p. ix.

Croker, T. (1983) Interview with Diane Leonard in 'Women and sport', Open University BBC television programme, Course U221 ('The Changing Experience of Women').

Deem, R. (1982) 'Women, leisure and inequality', *Leisure Studies* Vol. 1, No. 1 (January).

Dorfman, A. and A. Mattelart (1975) *How to read Donald Duck: imperialist ideology in the Disney Comics.* New York: International General.

Driscoll, E. (1981) 'The educational significance of Adult Further Education keep-fit classes', B.Ed. Degree Linking Study, Brighton Polytechnic/University of Sussex.

Dunne, M. (1982) 'An introduction to some of the images of sport in girls' comics and magazines' in *Sporting fictions*, Centre for Contemporary Cultural Studies/ Department of Physical Education, University of Birmingham, England (September).

Durkin, K. and P. Akhatar (1983) 'Television, sex-roles and children', *New Society* (7 April) Vol. 64, No. 1064: pp. 10–11.

Giddens, A. (1982) *Sociology — a brief but critical introduction.* London: Macmillan.

Hall, S. (1984) 'The culture gap', *Marxism Today* (January): pp. 188–22.

Holland, P. (1983) 'Manpower!', *New Socialist* No. 13 (September/October): pp. 52–54.

Lees, S. (1983) 'How boys slag off girls', *New Society* 13 (October).

———(1984) 'Nice girls don't', *New Socialist* No. 16, (March/April): pp. 16-21.

MacDonald, M. (1981) *Class, gender and education*, Units 10-11, in Block 4 of Open University Course E353 ('Society, Education and the State') The Open University: pp. 15-30.

McRobbie, A. (1977) *Jackie: an ideology of adolescent femininity*, Stencilled Occasional Paper, Women Series SP No. 53, Centre for Contemporary Cultural Studies, University of Birmingham, England.

———(1984) 'Dance and social fantasy', in A. McRobbie and M. Niva (eds) *Gender and generation.* London: Macmillan.

McRobbie, A. and M. Niva (eds) (1984) *Gender and generation.* London: Macmillan.

Prendergast, S. (1975) 'Stoolball: the pursuit of vertigo?', *Women's Studies International Quarterly*, Pergamon Press, Vol. 1: pp. 15–26.

Scobie, W. (1984) 'Fonda-aerobics and a political flutter', *Observer Business* (26 February): p. 33.

Sports Council (1981) *A report on the allocation of monies by companies towards sponsorship of sport in the U.K.*, Information Series No. 6, London: The Sports Council.

Steinberg, J. (1983) 'Nice girls do biology', *New Society*, Vol. 63, No. 1061: pp. 429–30.

Tolson, A. (1977) *The limits of masculinity*. London: Tavistock.

Tomlinson, A. (1982) 'Sports fiction as critique: The novelistic challenge to the ideology of masculinity', in *Sporting fictions*. Centre for Contemporary Cultural Studies/Department of Physical Education, University of Birmingham (September).

Toynbee, P. (1983) 'Caught between an old and a new mythology about the nature of men and women', a review of Peter Prince's novel, *The Good Father*, in *The Guardian*, September 26.

Veal, A. J. (1979) *Sport and recreation in England and Wales: an analysis of adult participation patterns in 1977*, University of Birmingham Centre for Urban and Regional Studies Research Memorandum 74, (July).

Veal, A. J. (1983) *People in sport and outdoor recreation — 1980*, North London Polytechnic, England, 1983.

Webb, I. (1983) 'Body talk', unpublished paper, December 1983.

Whannel, G. (1983) *Blowing the whistle: the politics of sport*. London: Pluto Press.

Williams, R. (1963) *American society — a sociological interpretation* (Second Edition, Revised). New York: Alfred A. Knopf.

Willis, P. (1979) 'Shop-floor culture, masculinity and the wage form' in John Clarke, Chas Critcher and Richard Johnson (eds) *Working class culture — studies in history and theory*. London: Hutchinson.

Willis, P. (1982) 'Women in sport in ideology', in Jennifer Hargreaves (ed) *Sport, culture and ideology*. London: Routledge and Kegan Paul.

Wren-Lewis, J. and A. Clarke (1983) 'The World Cup — a political football', *Theory, Culture and Society — explorations in critical social science*, Vol. 1, No. 3.

IV.

POLICY AND ACTION

FACILITY MANAGEMENT: CASE STUDIES IN POLICY AND PATRIARCHY

Carolyn Carr and Anita White
West Sussex Institute of Higher Education

Alan Tomlinson
University of Brighton

Introduction

In recent years, women's* participation in sport and recreation has received increasing attention from policy makers and providers, particularly among those operating in the public sector of sport and recreation. One of the principal examples of the attention given to women's participation in sport and recreation has been at the national level, where the quasi-non-governmental organisation, the Sports Council, has recognised women as a 'target group' since 1982.

The Sports Council (1988) has attempted to quantify national trends in women's participation in indoor and outdoor sport and recreation by utilising General Household Survey data. The Sports Council estimated that between 1983 and 1988 approximately one million additional women participated in indoor sport and recreation, and that during the same period the numbers of women participating in outdoor sport and recreation fell by about 100,000 (Sports Council, 1988: p. 26). More recently the Sports Council estimated that the gap between men's and women's participation rates is continuing to narrow, with the main reason for this being the popularity of what was termed indoor keep fit and aerobics activities among women (Sports Council, 1993). It is estimated that women comprise 60% of those who participate in indoor sports

---

* The term 'women' is used for brevity throughout this chapter, and includes young women and girls of school age, as well as adult women. Issues particularly relevant to young women and girls will be discussed as appropriate in the text.

only, but just 6.7% of participants in outdoor team games (Sports Council, 1992). Whilst these data have provided some indication of national trends in women's sport and recreation participation, it should be borne in mind that such national statistics provide only a broad overview of general participation patterns. The General Household Survey does not explore issues which may influence the statistical patterns which emerge from the survey data, such as women's lifestyles and the meanings women attach to their sport and recreation participation.

The limitations of national quantitative data on understanding women's participation in sport and recreation suggest that localised, qualitative studies are required in order to gain a more in-depth understanding of the patterns suggested by the national data.

During the 1980s public sector sport and recreation provision was in part characterised by facility provision, and by sports development initiatives, through which emphasis was given to promoting sport and recreation among particular 'target' groups, and to developing people's involvement in sport at foundation, participation, performance, and excellence levels. In considering the relationship between facility development and the development of sport among women, it is generally acknowledged that the provision of indoor sport and recreation facilities played a significant role in facilitating increases in women's participation in indoor sport and recreation during the 1980s. Whilst research that has been conducted at the local level (e.g. Taylorson and Halfpenny, 1991; Roberts, 1989) has supported this, there has been little discussion and research on the impact of the provision of outdoor facilities on women's participation in outdoor sport and recreation.

The purpose of the research on which this chapter is based was to contribute to an understanding of the impact of the provision of outdoor artificial turf pitches on women's participation in sport and recreation, by investigating the issue at the local level. The research focused on an analysis of the interface between the policies and practices of the agencies and agents involved in the provision and operation of the artificial turf pitches, and the dynamics of women's participation.

Artificial Turf Pitches — The Context

Artificial turf pitches are flexible and adaptable multi-use facilities which enable greater intensity of use than traditional grass pitches, and which are generally considered to facilitate the quality of participation through providing a truer playing surface (Davies, 1983). Since artificial turf pitches are more expensive to install than traditional surfaces, they tend to be provided in densely populated areas where intensive use of space is required, and where land values are high. The investment required to provide pitches is often seen within the context of offsetting the costs of regular maintenance, and under use of traditional surfaces. According to the Sports Council (1993), there are now over 280 artificial turf pitches in England, the large majority of which have been provided by local authorities, although others have been provided by voluntary and company sports clubs, and schools. A key feature in the provision of many artificial turf pitches has been partnership between a number of agencies; the Sports Council has been a central agency in this respect, often providing grants to both offset the capital costs of provision, which tend to range from £200,000 to £500,000, and to provide a catalyst for an injection of funds from other agencies.

Although artificial turf pitches are used for a variety of sports such as lacrosse, tennis, netball, and American Football, they tend to primarily be used for hockey and soccer. According to Dunnett (1990), artificial turf pitches have altered the technical nature of the game of hockey, and are regarded as being central to the future development of the sport. Nearly all international matches are played on artificial surfaces, and this is a requirement for English National League, Cup, and County Championship games for both men's and women's hockey. The *Playing Pitch Strategy* (Sports Council, 1991), the most recent Sports Council publication focusing on playing pitches, emphasised the growing importance of artificial turf pitches in hockey by highlighting the role they play in meeting the competitive needs of the sport. In the case of soccer the picture is different, with considerable debate continuing on the role of artificial surfaces in the sport. Whilst artificial turf pitches are used widely for training, particularly at the local level, the Football League imposed a ban from the start of the 1991/92 season for First and Second Division Clubs, and from 1995/96 for Third and Fourth Division Clubs (or as they were from the 1993/94 season onwards, Second and Third Division Clubs); by 1994 Preston North End, the sole remaining League club still playing on an artificial surface, had reverted to a natural turf pitch.

The Sports Council, the principal agency responsible for formulating national sport and recreation policy in England, made specific reference to the role of artificial turf pitches in sport and recreation provision in *Into the 90s — a*

Strategy for Sport (Sports Council, 1988). The strategy was based on two central themes, the promotion of mass participation, particularly among two target groups, women and young people, and the promotion of performance and excellence. One mechanism by which the Sports Council attempts to promote its objectives is through financial assistance for the provision of new sports facilities. The strategy suggested that one means of promoting mass participation objectives is through encouraging the provision of new artificial turf pitches, with the Sports Council specifically seeking to support planning strategies which "identify where new artificial surfaces can help enhance the sporting experience, attract new participants, especially women, and meet the volume of demand generated in dense urban areas where grass pitches are in short supply" (1988, p. 65). In contrast, it is interesting to note that the *Playing Pitch Strategy* (1991) did not specifically refer to women in relation to artificial turf pitches. Instead it stated that artificial turf pitches have a particular role to play in locations where high volumes of use for all sports can be guaranteed or developed, in areas where land values are high, and in dense urban areas where there is a shortage of natural grass pitches. The 1993 Sports Council strategy, *Sport in the Nineties — New Horizons*, differed from its predecessors in that it did not set out detailed policies, programmes and priorities. Instead the strategy identified a vision for the future of sport and outlined five strategic themes, including advocacy, education and training, and service provision, which were seen as helping towards realising the vision of equality and quality of sporting opportunity. Whilst there was no specific reference to the provision of artificial turf pitches as helping to achieve the vision for sport, the importance of appropriate facility provision to the future of sport permeated the principal strategic themes.

The artificial turf pitch strategy of the South East Council for Sport and Recreation was stated in *Prospect for the Eighties* (Sports Council, 1982), the regional recreation strategy for London and the South East. The regional strategy stated that "a minimum of another 49 intensive use pitches are required in the region" (p. 12). Provision of artificial turf pitches was stated as being one solution to providing adequate playing fields, with the estimate being that the provision of 49 pitches would accommodate an extra 1,470 games, and therefore 37,000 players each week; provision in relation to user issues was only referred to in terms of this quantification of participation. In the South East Council for Sport and Recreation (1986) review of *Prospect for the Eighties*, when targets were revised for the second half of the eighties, one of the three themes for sports grounds was "to provide a network of floodlit, intensive use pitches in strategic locations in the region" (p. 3). Whilst there was recognition that facility provision and participation in sport were "two sides of the same coin" (p. 4), there was little to suggest that the relationship between facility development and sports development had been considered in any depth or detail in order to inform the strategy review process.

Artificial Turf Pitches — The Theoretical and Research Context

Whilst artificial turf pitches have received some prominence in Sports Council strategies on sport and recreation, and in the strategies of the Regional Councils for Sport and Recreation, and a large number have been provided in recent years through considerable capital investment, there has been a paucity of research on the impact of such provision. Previous research and discussion of artificial turf pitches has largely focused on technical issues such as surface selection, playing characteristics, maintenance and durability (e.g. Roberts, 1985; Tipp, 1986). The most recent example of this was the Sports Council publication *Artificial Turf Pitches for Hockey* (1990), which provided a guide to technical aspects of artificial turf pitches, including planning, design, and construction, but did not include any consideration of management and user issues.

One of the few commentators to discuss non-technical issues in relation to artificial turf pitches is Milner (1991) in the North American context. Milner suggested that technological advances in the quality of surfaces have not only benefited elite level sport, but also the opportunities for mass participation. Milner suggested that synthetic turf has met its objectives of providing surfaces which can be used for more hours than grass, and which are 'user friendly'. Milner estimated that artificial turf could be used for 3,500 hours per year, as opposed to grass which he considered to be limited to approximately 200 hours per year as a quality surface. Milner suggested that the principal reasons for these patterns included artificial turf requiring less maintenance, and being more durable than grass, and being a surface that could be used in climatic conditions where participation on grass would not be possible. Although Milner is one of the few to consider mass participation issues in relation to technological developments in the provision of artificial turf pitches, his work was somewhat descriptive and lacked in-depth critical analysis.

Previous empirical work which has incorporated some consideration of management and user issues in relation to artificial turf pitches has been largely quantitative, such as a statistical analysis of the use of artificial turf pitches in Islington and Hackney by Birch (1975), and a more recent 'costs-in-use' project on different types of natural and synthetic pitches by Nottinghamshire County Council and the Sports Council (1990). Although there has been a paucity of research on management and user issues in relation to artificial turf pitches, two recent projects, one for the Southern Region of the Sports Council (1992), and the other by the West Midlands Region of the Sports Council (1992), did incorporate management and user issues as a central focus of analysis.

The Sports Council (Southern Region) project centred on a survey of the characteristics of artificial turf pitch users, and the factors which influenced their usage. Six artificial turf pitches within the Bracknell Forest Borough were studied, having been selected on the basis that they were considered to provide a cross-section of management structures. The research involved interviewing the managers of the artificial turf pitches about programming objectives and user patterns, conducting interview surveys with nearly six hundred artificial turf pitch users, and distributing postal questionnaires to officials from local clubs who both did and did not use the pitches. The research found that despite the relatively generous levels of artificial turf pitch provision in the catchment area, and no active marketing by the managers of the pitches, the levels of demand were high. Hockey and football club use dominated participation on the pitches, with virtually all the pitches being "fully booked during the periods of peak demand at evenings and weekends during the winter months" (1992: p. 2). In terms of women's participation, it was found that women accounted for just under one-third of all users, and slightly more than half of the hockey users; no women used the artificial turf pitches for football. The research recommended that in order to maximise and optimise use of the pitches, managers should take a more proactive approach to programming, for example through delivering introductory sessions to attract young people to participate.

The Sports Council (West Midlands Region) study focused on an analysis of the dynamics of sports development on synthetic turf pitches in Birmingham, with the primary objective being to examine management and usage within the context of the Sports Council's sports development continuum, (that is taking part in sport at foundation, participation, performance, and excellence levels). The research involved interviewing the artificial turf pitch managers, conducting interview surveys with over eight hundred pitch users at nine pitches, and administering postal questionnaires to physical education teachers, hockey clubs, and relevant governing bodies. The research found that management policies towards usage of the artificial turf pitches emphasised firstly, maximising use of the pitches by providing a range of activities, and a balanced programme between community and club use, and secondly, giving priority during peak times to clubs and organisations with a commitment to developing their sport. On average, 70% of peak usage was for football, and 20% for hockey, with club use dominating. Whilst there was no gender analysis in terms of the total usage, a user survey over a one month period revealed that women constituted 10% of all users.

These projects on artificial turf pitches provide some valuable insights into artificial turf pitch management and user issues. However, management tended to be explored only in terms of the management functions of promoting and programming the pitches, whilst a consideration of the dynamics of women's use of the pitches formed only a small part of the research agenda. Further, the 'administrative' approaches of the research projects meant they lacked a theoretical underpinning, and stopped short of a full critical analysis which could have explored the relationship between policy formulation, facility provision and management, and the use of the artificial turf pitches.

The Project Case-studies

The case-studies reported in this chapter add to previous empirical work on artificial turf pitches by focusing specifically on the dynamics of women's participation, and the ways in which management policies and practices impact on women's use.

The research utilised a case study approach. Three artificial turf pitches which had received a capital grant from the Sports Council (South East Region), or a grant administered by the Sports Council on behalf of another organisation, were investigated. The locations of the three pitches were within a radius of thirty miles along a 'coastal strip'. Each location had been identified as a priority area for the provision of an artificial turf pitch in the South East Council for Sport and Recreation (1986) strategy review, with one being a priority from the original 1982 strategy, and the other two new priorities.

Specifically, the research sought to explore the values and ideologies underpinning the management of artificial turf pitches; the nature of the connection between the ideologies underpinning the management of artificial turf pitches and women's participation; and how different management structures impact on women's use of artificial turf pitches. The research was also intended to have some practical application by facilitating the development of recommendations for the management of artificial turf pitches, particularly in relation to women's use.

Case Study 1

Case study 1 was a dual-use artificial turf pitch situated on a County Council school site. Provision of the facility was initiated by a voluntary men's hockey and cricket club, which funded the facility in partnership with the Sports Council region, the County Council and the District Council. The facility was primarily managed by a voluntary Management Committee (a Sub-Committee of the club Management Committee), and a part-time paid pitch manager. The period of analysis was November 6th 1988 — November 4th 1989.

An initial approach about the research was made to the Chair of the Management Committee by the Non-Affiliated Users' Representative, who was also the research supervisor. This approach resulted in the Chair of the Management Committee inviting the researcher to attend a Management Committee meeting, and present an outline of the project. The researcher subsequently attended the next scheduled meeting, and introduced the research as a Sports Council-supported monitoring and evaluation project. The presentation was well received by the Management Committee, and all members expressed support for the project, and agreed to provide their full co-operation.

Case Study 2

Case study 2 was an artificial turf pitch situated on the site of a previous 'red gras' facility at a local authority Leisure Centre. The facility was provided by the Borough Council in partnership with the Sports Council region, who provided a grant which they administered on behalf of the Football Trust. The pitch was managed by the Borough Council, and came under the direct management of the Leisure Centre Manager. The period of analysis was September 11th 1989 — September 10th 1990.

The initial approach about the research was made by letter to the Borough Council Leisure Services Officer, whose Secretary contacted the researcher on his behalf to arrange a meeting with the researcher, the research supervisor, and the Manager of the Leisure Centre where the pitch was sited. At the meeting both the researcher and the research supervisor outlined the research as a Sports Council-supported monitoring and evaluation project. The assistance that would be required was discussed, and both the Borough Council Leisure Services Officer and the Leisure Centre Manager offered their full support and co-operation.

Case Study 3

Case study 3 was a dual-use artificial turf pitch situated on the site of a previous 'red gras' facility at a Community School Sports Centre. The pitch was provided by the Borough Council in partnership with the County Council and the Sports Council region through a grant administered on behalf of the Football Trust. As in case study 2, the pitch was managed by the Borough Council, and came under the direct management of the Sports Centre Manager. The period of analysis was November 16th 1990 — November 15th 1991.

The initial approach about the research was made by letter to the Borough Council Director of Leisure Services, who informed the researcher by letter that both he and the Sports Centre Manager, with whom he had discussed the research, would give their full co-operation. The reply also advised the researcher to contact the Sports Centre Manager to discuss the research further, and a meeting was subsequently arranged by telephone. At the meeting the research was introduced as a Sports Council-supported monitoring and evaluation project. Some time was spent discussing the areas in which assistance would be required from the Sports Centre Manager, who reiterated that he would give his full co-operation to the project.

In each case study, the researcher was pleased with the outcome of the initial approaches, with those contacted seemingly willing to give their support and co-operation to the research. The 'hidden agenda' of the gender focus of the research was not discussed during the initial approaches about gaining access to the case studies for research purposes, nor was it discussed during any other stage of the research. Whilst the way in which the research was introduced to those involved in the case studies raised an ethical issue for the researcher, it was felt that to have revealed the gender focus of the research would have been extremely detrimental to the research process[1].

Procedure

A range of qualitative and quantitative research techniques were employed. This enabled fieldwork data to be gathered and analysed from a range of sources, specifically Interviews, Booking Records, Management Meetings, Staff Interactions, and Pitch Publicity Materials.

Interpreting the Case Studies

This section identifies and discusses three central issues which emerged from the fieldwork case studies in relation to the management and women's use of the artificial turf pitches. These issues are: Policy Process; Management Practices; Women's Participation.

Policy Process

One of the principal emergent themes from the fieldwork case studies was that of policy process, with management having been conceptualised within the research as policy formulation, policy implementation, and policy evaluation. The following section will identify and discuss the interconnection between these three aspects of policy in terms of inter- and intra-agency issues and practices.

Provision of the artificial turf pitches in each case study was initiated at the local level, by a voluntary men's hockey club in case study 1, and by the Borough Councils in case studies 2 and 3. In each case study the South East Region of the Sports Council grant-aided the provision of the pitch, in case study 1 directly, and in case studies 2 and 3 through a grant administered on behalf of the Football Trust. From the perspective of the two Sports Council Regional Officers, the principal reason for the Sports Council supporting the schemes was to further the Sports Council's own strategy objectives, both for the provision of artificial turf pitches, and in case studies 1 and 3, for supporting dual-use schemes. This suggests that the Sports Council's priority in grant-aiding each pitch was based on a 'facility approach' to sport and recreation provision, in which the priority was to get a facility on-the-ground, rather than on participation objectives. The Sports Council region's artificial turf pitch strategy (stated in *A Review of Prospect for the Eighties*, 1986) gave no indication of there being Sports Council objectives in supporting schemes for pitches, beyond actually providing pitches in identified locations.

The Sports Council region's apparent absence of participation objectives for the provision of the artificial turf pitches, beyond getting facilities on-the-ground, seemed to be reinforced through intra-agency analysis. The two Regional Officers of the Sports Council had differing perceptions of artificial turf pitches as sport and recreation spaces. The Regional Officer in case study 3 discussed pitch use only in the context of school use in the day, and local club matches and training during public access times. His perception was that artificial turf pitches were unlikely to play a particular role in sports development. In contrast, the Regional Officer in case studies 1 and 2 discussed user issues beyond hockey and football, stating that artificial turf pitches have been identified as good 'Sport for All' facilities. He "hoped" the pitches would play a role in furthering Sports Council participation objectives, particularly in terms of promoting use among the target groups of women and young people. There was no indication that he or the South East Region of the Sports Council had developed a strategy to realise these 'hopes' in practice, for example through ensuring that sports development objectives informed the artificial turf pitch management practices at the local level.

Within the context of a paucity of Sports Council (South East Region) policies and objectives for the provision of the artificial turf pitches, beyond actually providing the facilities, it is perhaps not surprising that the agents at the local level did not perceive that there were any particular stipulations or guidelines in terms of what the Sports Council wanted to see from the provision, and subsequent use of the pitches. In case studies 2 and 3 the Borough Officers' and the Pitch Managers' perceptions were that the Sports Council's support for the pitches was primarily based on furthering the facility aspects of its own regional strategy. No agent at the local level in case studies 2 and 3 referred to Sports Council participation objectives as being objectives in grant-aiding the schemes. In case study 1, the Chair of the voluntary Management Committee seemed to be aware of the Regional Officer's hopes that the pitch would further participation objectives, when he stated that he recognised that the Sports Council was looking for increases in "youth participation and ladies". However, the Chair indicated that there had not been any strategic approach to further these objectives in practice through incorporating them as pitch policies. In fact, in discussing community use and target group participation in the context of pitch provision, the Chair did so in terms of the benefits it had for the Sports Council's support for the scheme, rather than in terms of a genuine commitment to community use issues. This suggests that a 'false alliance' was formed in order to facilitate actual pitch provision; as the Non-Affiliated User's Representative on the Management Committee indicated, although the Management Committee made reference to the Sports Council's objectives being incorporated as pitch objectives during the negotiations for provision of the pitch, this did not happen in practice once the pitch had been provided.

Having indicated that the South East Region of the Sports Council did not make explicit policies and objectives in relation to its support for the provision of the pitches, beyond furthering its own strategy of providing pitches in strategic locations, and for supporting dual-use schemes, it was not surprising that there was no transference of policy from the regional state level, to management at the local level. Thus it can be assumed that local agents and agencies were largely autonomous in terms of formulating policies for the management and use of the artificial turf pitches.

In case study 1, policy formulation clearly did not form a central part of the management of the artificial turf pitch at the local level. Members of the Management Committee were not aware of management policies, and there was no evidence to suggest that policies and objectives guided practice in service delivery. In case study 2, intra-agency differences were evident. Whilst the Leisure Services Officer indicated that one of his principal management functions was to set policies and then "let the on-site management get on with it", the on-site Manager did not seem to be aware of any specific policies for the management of the artificial turf pitches. In case study 3, although the Borough Council was one of the principal funding agencies for the pitch, it did not play any role in policy formulation, with the Sports Centre Manager being autonomous in this respect. The Manager explained that policies were based on priority access for the school in the daytime, and for club bookings at weekends and in the evenings.

One interesting feature in all three case studies was the lack of influence on pitch provision and policies of the District or Borough Council Committees, who merely seemed to give their 'stamp of approval' to Leisure Officers, and in case study 1 to the proposals of a voluntary hockey club. In the case of the latter for example, the Chair of the Recreation and Amenities Committee stated there were no criteria for support of the scheme other than the general "worth" of the project. It is interesting to observe here Tomlinson's (1987) consideration of the relationship between the state and the voluntary sector.

Tomlinson's discussions centred on the interface between the state and the voluntary sector in the inner city context, which he saw as being characterised by the voluntary sector increasingly being used by the state apparatus as a mechanism of social control. It is interesting to contrast Tomlinson's perceptions of the interface between the state and the voluntary sector in the inner city context, with the findings from this research. In case study 1, the state agencies who contributed economic resources to the provision of the artificial turf pitch lacked clear policies in providing the pitch. These state agencies were largely powerless in terms of influencing the subsequent management and use of the pitches, with the voluntary sector men's hockey club which initiated provision of the pitch having control in this respect. The implications of this for women's use will be discussed in due course.

In all three case studies it emerged that whilst the power to formulate policies did in fact reside with providers and managers at the local level, with some agents having more influence than others, in practice there was a lack of clear policies relating to the provision and operation of the artificial turf pitches. Even when clear policies were stated, as in the case of the Leisure Services Officer in case study 2, there was no indication that they guided practice in any strategic sense since the on-site Manager did not appear to share them. Only in case study 3 did the policies, autonomously established by the Sports Centre Manager, appear to guide practice, but they were based purely on priority access issues.

The findings from the case studies in relation to policy formulation suggest that in order to gain an insight into sport and recreation policy, it is necessary to conduct analysis at a number of levels, through considering inter and intra-agency interactions and practices. Consideration will now be given to the research findings in relation to the work of Henry (1993), Bramham (1991), and Coalter, Long and Duffield (1986), who have discussed ideological approaches to sport and leisure policy at the national and local state levels respectively.

In a discussion paper on the organisation of sport in Britain, Bramham identified what he considered to be four major changes in the ideologies underpinning the national state approach to sports policy and provision over the last two decades. In a recent text on the politics of leisure policy, Henry provided a discussion of the nature of political ideologies, and their implications for contemporary leisure policy. Whilst both Bramham and Henry have provided useful frameworks for understanding national state approaches to sports policy, neither discussed in any sustained way the ways in which national state policies are translated into practice at the local level. The findings of this research suggest that it is important to analyse the interrelationships between the state agencies, in order to reveal who has the power to control to what extent policies are implemented at the local level. One example of this in the current research is the issue of women's use of the artificial turf pitches. It is suggested that the Sports Council's strategy for sport for the period 1988–1993 was partly underpinned by an ideology of anti-managerialism (Bramham, 1991), by emphasising the promotion of 'target' group participation in sport and recreation through community recreation approaches. Whilst the strategy stated that the provision of artificial turf pitches should be encouraged in part to increase women's participation in sport and recreation, this 'policy' did not get incorporated as a specific aim for the provision of the case studies' artificial turf pitches by the regional state or local state providing agencies. In the case of the former, the South East Region of the Sports Council emphasised 'facility' rather than 'people' aims in pitch provision. Whilst community recreation and welfare-oriented values, such as promoting women's participation, were held by some agents involved in policy formulation at the local level, they lacked the power to ensure these values guided practice.

Coalter, Long and Duffield (1986), in contrast to Bramham and Henry, conducted a critical analysis of leisure policy at the local state level. They suggested that local authorities tended to have a relatively greater degree of autonomy over leisure policy formulation and implementation compared with other policy areas, which was likely to lead to variations in values and practices between local authorities. The case studies' fieldwork provided support for this on one level, in that the local authorities seemed to have the power to decide what sports facilities and services were provided (within the context of capital constraints). However, the local authorities differed in the extent to which they influenced policies relating to actual service delivery, depending upon whether they were merely a providing agency through grant-aiding pitch provision, or whether they had a management as well as a providing role. In case study 3 for example, whilst the Borough Council invested considerable capital in the provision of the pitch, the Borough agents had no input into policy formulation, since the Manager of the Sports Centre where the pitch was sited had control in this respect. Whilst Coalter, Long and Duffield analysed leisure policies within the local authority context, this research suggests that to gain a fuller under-standing of leisure policy formulation and implementation, it is necessary to explore both the local authority context, as well as the on-site management of facilities and services, and the dynamics of the connections between leisure departments and facility managers.

Coalter, Long and Duffield identified three ideological approaches to leisure policy in the local authority context: managerialist, professional, and political partisanship. These approaches will be considered in relation to the agents operating at the local authority level within this research, as well as those involved in direct facility management (i.e. members of the Management Committee in case study 1, and the Pitch Managers in case studies 2 and 3). A managerialist ideology appeared to predominate in all three case studies, since it was the prevailing ideological position among those who had most power and influence over the pitches. The dominant members of the Management Committee, and the three Pitch Managers, discussed meeting financial targets (with there being no similar reference to user targets), and placed emphasis on cost-effectiveness, and maximising income irrespective from which sectors of the community the income was generated. One particular example of this was provided by the Pitch Manager in case study 1, who explained that during the initial operation of the pitch he had wanted to be seen to be generating income, and therefore had made the decision to primarily target men's sports groups, "because there are so many of them about". It is suggested that such a managerialist ideology is imbued with patriarchy through emphasising the generation of income from male groups; this has the effect of reinforcing inequities in participation between men and women. The managerialist ideology may well also be indicative of current trends in leisure services, and other aspects of local authority service delivery, in which increasing emphasis is being placed on cost-effectiveness and accountability.

Whilst the professional ideology, based on a welfare-oriented view of leisure policy and practice, appeared to underpin the values of some case study agents, such as the Director of Leisure Services in case study 3, and the Non-Affiliated Users' Representative in case study 1, their personal agendas tended not to permeate policy formulation and implementation since their role in relation to these aspects of management was peripheral. In terms of a political partisanship ideological position, this appeared to be a feature of the local state in case study 1, in which the Chair of the Recreation and Amenities Committee stated that the Council did not support the idea of having a District Sports Development Officer since this would impose on people's freedom to choose their own sporting activity. This can be interpreted as being allied to a 'conservative' ideology of state provision, and can also be seen to be imbued with patriarchy by failing to recognise that material and cultural factors constrain women's 'freedom' to choose their sports participation.

No interviewees referred to the formulation of specific policies for women's use of the artificial turf pitches during discussion of the policy formulation process. Whilst women's participation was on the personal agendas of some agents involved in the pitch provision process, particularly those who had a professional ideology of leisure policy and practice, they tended to lack power and influence in terms of policy formulation. Examples of this included the two women members of the Management Committee in case study 1. Whilst they had a great deal of personal commitment to women's sport, and were members of the Management Committee which controlled policy formulation and service delivery, they had minimal power to influence the policy process, since the men's hockey club owned and controlled the pitch.

Whilst Coalter, Long and Duffield's (1986) research provided a useful framework for analysing the ideological positions of those responsible for policy formulation at the local state and pitch management levels, it has been shown that Coalter *et al.* did not consider the ways in which managerialist, professional and political partisanship ideologies may be imbued with patriarchal ideologies. The case studies' findings on policy formulation support the argument that a great deal more theoretically informed research is needed into the relationship between gender relations and leisure policy, to further understand women's sport and leisure participation (e.g. Yule, 1992).

It is interesting to contrast the lack of policies on women's participation in relation to public access with practices in the education setting. Although the focus of this research was on women's use in the public sector, policy formulation within the education sector emerged as an issue in case studies 1 and 3, where the pitches were located at school sites. In case study 3, there was a mixed physical education curriculum; boys and girls participated separately in extra-curricular activities, where practices were in operation to facilitate equality of access between them. In case study 1, where physical education for boys and girls was taught separately, an agreement was reached during the provision of the artificial turf pitch on equal access between the Boys' and the Girls' Schools. The Head of Girls' Physical Education, who was also a member of the Management Committee, played an important role in facilitating girls' access to the pitch. She negotiated access with the Head of Boys' Physical Education, and was particularly proactive in encouraging girls' hockey participation for both curriculum and extra-curricular activities. Whilst equality in terms of the amount of time allocated for use of the artificial turf pitch by boys and girls appeared to be more formalised and accepted in the statutory education sector than in the public community sphere, additional research would be required to explore this further (see for example Scraton's 1987, 1988 work which revealed that in practice power relations and patriarchal ideologies permeated the decision-making processes and practices in girls' physical education).

Within the context of a lack of policies guiding artificial turf pitch management practices, it is not surprising that formal policy evaluation did not emerge as a feature of the management process at any level within the management framework. In all three case studies it was evident that little formal policy evaluation occurred, with evaluation tending only to be discussed informally in terms of agents' reflections on the first year of operation of the respective pitches. Policy evaluation will now be discussed in more detail.

The funding agencies conducted little formal evaluation or monitoring of the artificial turf pitches. The principal exception to this was that the Sports Council region funded a researcher to monitor the first year of operation of the artificial turf pitch in case study 1. Whilst the monitoring was valuable in terms of highlighting issues in relation to the management and the use of the artificial turf pitch, it was conducted within the context of there not being any stated objectives or targets to evaluate, and with the funding agency lacking any power to ensure that recommendations for the future management of the pitch would be implemented. As the Sports Council Regional Officer in case studies 1 and 2 stated, the money was granted for the facility and not for its use, and once the facility was on-the-ground the Sports Council was limited in its power to make stipulations about the management and the use. During informal evaluation of the pitches, he reinforced the Sports Council's priority of providing a pitch to satisfy the Sports Council's regional strategy; he doubted that the pitches had done much to further the Sports Council's participation objectives. Similarly, the other principal funding agencies, the County Council in case studies 1 and 3, and the Borough or District Councils in all three case studies, did not conduct any formal evaluation of the artificial turf pitches once they had been provided. These findings reinforce the ways in which the on-site Managers, and the

Management Committee in case study 1, had a great deal of autonomy over policy, not having to formulate objectives or targets which would be evaluated by the providing agencies.

In terms of those who had a direct role in the management of the artificial turf pitches, policy evaluation did not form part of their management function, largely because policies had not been formulated. No formal evaluation was conducted in any of the case studies beyond an evaluation of the financial targets, and in case study 3 quantitative hours of use. Informal evaluations among those at the local level tended to focus on the facilities themselves, with the Chair of the Management Committee in case study 1 stating that the original aim of providing "an artificial turf pitch for the [City] hockey club" had been achieved. In case study 2, the Leisure Services Officer, who had been the only agent who had discussed policies being formulated for the operation of the pitch, made some evaluation of the impact on football and hockey, which was purely based on his own perceptions. In all three case studies, an evaluation of the use of the pitches was not discussed in any depth or detail beyond the benefits to football and hockey. The exception to this was the Director of Leisure in case study 3, who held welfare-oriented values towards use of the pitch, and discussed the contribution of the pitch to furthering the Borough's general sports development objectives.

The research findings in relation to policy evaluation reflect the issues raised in Knox's (1991) discussion paper. Knox's statement that there has been minimal policy evaluation in public leisure was certainly reflected in this research, where none of the public agencies involved in the provision and operation of the artificial turf pitches conducted any formal evaluation. Knox suggested that one difficulty in conducting policy evaluation within the public sector was that leisure managers are often not clear about leisure objectives. Within this research, the findings on policy formulation revealed a paucity of clear policies and objectives underpinning the provision of the pitches, and the subsequent service delivery. This research would certainly endorse Knox's conclusions that firstly, there is a clear need to identify objectives for public sector leisure services; secondly, performance indicators should be developed which do not only focus on measures of the economy and efficiency, but take some account of the quality of service and customer perceptions; and thirdly, policy evaluation and monitoring should be an on-going process within the public sector.

Whilst Knox's conclusions would appear to be pertinent, the three foci for evaluation must be considered within the context of who has the power to identify policy objectives and the criteria for performance indicators, and from what ideological positions policy formulation and evaluation are conducted. Within this research, those who had the power over policy formulation and implementation tended to share a managerialist ideology, thus being primarily concerned with getting a facility on-the-ground, and with cost-effectiveness issues based on maximising income irrespective from which sector of the community the income was generated. The ideologies of those who controlled the artificial turf pitches were not characterised by welfare-oriented values. As a result performance indicators in terms of sports development issues within the context of a sports development continuum, and target group use, did not permeate policy formulation or management practices.

In summary, although management was conceptualised as policy formulation, policy implementation (in the form of service delivery), and policy evaluation, the findings from the case studies suggest that the conceptualisation of management did not reflect the reality of the management process. Policies and objectives for the provision and use of the artificial turf pitches were not formulated at any level of the management structure. The research did not explore whether those operating at the local state and facility management levels established policies for other aspects of their sport and recreation provision, or whether the lack of policies relating to the artificial turf pitches was indicative of the general approach to facility provision and operation. Clearly, if the lack of policies was a general feature of sport and leisure provision within the three Boroughs, this has significant implications for service delivery. The local authorities featured in this study either failed to take a strategic approach to the pitches beyond 'traditional' use, (as in case studies 1 and 2), or had a strategic vision but lacked the power to ensure this permeated management practices (as in case study 3).

Management Practices

The second issue to be considered which emerged from the fieldwork case studies is that of management practices. The discussions will focus particularly on those who had most power and influence over the facilities, i.e. in case study 1 the Management Committee and the Pitch Manager who had responsibility for, and control over service delivery, and in case studies 2 and 3 the Leisure

Centre and Sports Centre Managers respectively. The findings revealed that the three Pitch Managers, and the most influential figures on the Management Committee in case study 1, adopted a traditional method of facility-oriented service delivery. The findings will be discussed in relation to the work of Bramham (1991), and Henry and Bramham (1986).

In a discussion of state approaches to sports policy, Bramham suggested that the latter half of the 1970s was characterised by an anti-managerialist ideology. This ideology was said to have emerged in response to the failure of public sector leisure services to attract some sections of the community, a failure which was considered to have in part derived from the traditional management approaches and methods employed at the local level. Whilst the latter part of the 1970s, and into the 1980s, did see community recreation approaches emerging in response to the inequalities in sport and recreation participation, Bramham did not consider the extent to which anti-managerialist ideologies which underpinned community recreation approaches permeated facility-based provision, as well as people-based initiatives. The findings from this research suggest that those involved in the management of the artificial turf pitches were aware of community recreation approaches, and in case studies 2 and 3 were operating in Boroughs which had community recreation initiatives in the form of an Action Sport team and sports development officers. However, an anti-managerialist or community recreation ideology did not permeate policies or management practices in relation to the development of the artificial turf pitches. Instead, the managers adopted a traditional method of facility-oriented service delivery, which was characterised by centralised decision-making, reactive programming, and a consistent failure to attract large numbers of users from some sectors of the community, such as women (Henry and Bramham, 1986). These issues will be discussed in relation to the findings from the case studies.

A facility-oriented approach to the artificial turf pitches was demonstrated in a number of ways. It has already been indicated that during the provision and the policy formulation processes, agents placed a great deal of emphasis on actual facility provision, with far less consideration being given to user issues. In case study 1, the Chair of the Management Committee explained that the primary aim was to provide a good quality facility for the men's hockey club to further its playing ambitions, whilst in case studies 2 and 3 emphasis was given to upgrading the existing 'red grass' pitches, and to improving the quality of sports facilities in the Boroughs. The facility-based approach was perhaps most clearly evident in case study 2, in which the Leisure Services Officer seemed to prioritise providing the best facility to "create the best synthetic pitch in the country", and thus bring status to both the Borough, and it could be suggested, to himself. Clearly the prevailing ideology among those who had most control over the provision of the pitches was facility-oriented rather than people- or welfare-oriented, with user issues rarely having been discussed as part of the rationale for the provision of the pitches.

In terms of centralised decision-making, all key decisions in relation to the provision of the pitch and policy formulation in case studies 2 and 3 were made by representatives of the local state and the Pitch Managers; there was no indication of there having been consultation with user groups. In terms of decisions on policy implementation and service delivery, it was apparent in case studies 2 and 3 that the Leisure Centre Manager and the Sports Centre Manager respectively had a great deal of power and autonomy in the decision-making process. This resulted in the ideological positions of the two Pitch Managers underpinning the management practices. In case study 1, representatives of the Boys' and Girls' Schools, the women's hockey club, and the non-affiliated users sat on the voluntary Management Committee. In theory these representatives put the case for the agencies they represented during the decision-making process. Whilst management decisions tended to be characterised by a process of discussion and negotiation (which explains why there was more fieldwork data on the management process in case study 1 relative to case studies 2 and 3), in practice members of the Management Committee associated with the men's hockey club had most power and influence over decisions. Examples of how this operated included the appointment of the first Pitch Manager, and the debate about his successor. These findings reinforce Talbot's (1988) assertion that provision for sport and recreation within the voluntary sector is based on an ideology of 'consumer control'. Whilst this will be discussed further in relation to women's use of the artificial turf pitches, it is interesting to note that the consumers within the voluntary sector who had power over the artificial turf pitch in case study 1 were members of the men's hockey club, who assumed ownership of the pitch.

Pitch programming in all three case studies was characterised by a reactive approach, which was based on allowing regular access by sports clubs to predominate, and minimal proactive encouragement of participation. In case study 1 the majority of the Management Committee perceived their role in a reactive, problem-solving context. One example of this was the Boys' School Representative who evidently felt that the main management function had been in terms of the provision of the pitch, and not the subsequent service delivery: "the management side of it has lessened obviously — I mean the main thing was the installation of the pitch". In case study 2, the Leisure Centre Manager relied on use being generated from existing 'red gras' demand. He saw little point in promotional work since the pitch was being used, albeit primarily at peak times, and because he felt it would never "sell" during the day. The only proactive approach to programming appeared to be through experimenting with Astro-bowls. In case study 3 the pattern was similar, with club bookings taking priority during the winter; although there was some indication that the Sports Centre Manager took a slightly more proactive approach to programming during the summer, for example by organising courses on the pitch, he still defined the pitch primarily in terms of football and hockey activities, organising courses only in these two sports. In all three case studies the programming approach appeared to be based on enabling club football and hockey bookings to dominate, with the prevailing ideology being to maximise use, largely irrespective of the user, in order to generate income.

Some members of the Management Committee in case study 1 explained that the lack of a proactive community recreation approach derived from the fact that firstly, the Management Committee was a voluntary group, which could not be expected to take a more active role itself, and secondly, that there was a lack of a supporting infrastructure within the District or County which could take on a promotional role. Whilst both of these factors may have influenced the profile of community use in case study 1, the fieldwork suggested that community use was not of particular concern to those associated with the men's hockey club, whose priority was to secure 'ownership' of a quality facility for their own use.

The patterns of community use on the artificial turf pitches certainly reflect the management approach to programming, with the pitches predominantly being used by a small sector of the community, i.e. adult men who played football, and men and women hockey players. It can be suggested that these groups were easy targets as pitch users, since they were likely to form the networks known to the Pitch Managers. Whilst there were of course other sectors of the community who did use the pitches, such as junior football players, and in case study 2 most likely the 'older' section of the community through Astro-bowls, their use was minimal in comparison to that of the dominant groups. Whilst voluntary sector sports clubs have tended to be dominated by high user groups, i.e. white middle class men (Hargreaves, 1986), the dominance of football on the pitches and in male working class culture (e.g. Whannel, 1983) suggests that the artificial turf pitches may well have been used by men from all social classes. The demographics of the catchment areas of the three pitches suggest this would have been most likely in case study 3, although only a preliminary interpretation can be made in this respect since an analysis of the social class of pitch users did not form part of the research process. An in-depth consideration of women's participation is presented in the next section.

Women's Participation

The third theme from the fieldwork case studies in relation to women's use is that of promoting women's participation. This will be considered in terms of the ways in which management ideologies shaped policies and practices in this respect.

It has already been indicated that management in the three case studies did not actively promote women's use of the artificial turf pitches. The only policy established for promoting women's use in the public access context was the differential pricing policy in case study 1, although the fact that the majority of the Management Committee and the Pitch Manager did not refer to it when asked about management policies suggests it was not an issue that was particularly central to their management agendas. The pricing policy derived from a proposal from the Non-Affiliated Users' Representative on the Management Committee, who stated that whilst she was pleased the policy proposal had been accepted, she felt this had not resulted from any great commitment to women's use among members of the Management Committee, but that it was a "small concession that it wouldn't hurt them to make". Certainly the pricing policy appeared to have minimal impact on promoting women's participation, with the values behind the policy not being shared by some male members of the Management Committee. During the interviews, some of them questioned whether the policy was sexist, or went against the notion of equal opportunities. The implication of the findings in relation to this specific policy is that even when policies are established for promoting women's sport, the ideological position of those responsible for policy formulation may not be based on a genuine commitment to the policy aims. Instead agents who have control may

198

allow concessions to subordinate groups such as women, as long as such concessions would not threaten the established social relations in terms of the dominance of male user groups.

There were no case studies' examples of management policies which may have promoted women's use of the pitches. Other specific examples of ways in which women's use had been promoted were based on individual resourcefulness, particularly among women who were strongly committed to women's sport, such as the Girls' School and Women's Club Representative in case study 1, who encouraged county women's hockey teams to use the pitches.

In discussing what could be done to promote women's use, the consensus among those with most control over the artificial turf pitches was that nothing could be done, or that women's use could only be promoted through specific sports, particularly hockey, netball and stoolball. These suggestions were clearly underpinned by ideologies based on stereotypical notions about women's sport, and reflect the findings of Glyptis, Kay and Murray (1985), who revealed that Action Sport staff in the West Midlands held stereotypical definitions of 'acceptable' behaviour for women, and about what women wanted from sport. One criticism of Glyptis *et al.*'s research was that it failed to consider the findings in terms of gender relations and patriarchal ideologies. Within this research, although it has been stated that the managers of the artificial turf pitches defined them as spaces for football activity, only the Non-Affiliated Users' Representative in case study 1 referred to women's football development as a way of promoting women's use of the pitches. The Head of Physical Education in case study 3 felt that developing tennis (another traditional 'women's' activity) on the pitch would promote women's use, but she lacked power in the decision-making process. In the case of tennis development, the Sports Centre Manager in case study 3 decided tennis provision would not be extended for financial reasons. In summary, whilst women's use of the artificial turf pitches was an important issue for some agents involved in the management process, their value-orientation was not shared by those who had most power and control over the pitches. The managers' approaches to the artificial turf pitches were based on a managerialist ideology. Such an ideology is imbued with patriarchy through emphasising income generation and cost-effectiveness in service delivery. Such an ideology is likely to reinforce inequities in participation, for example through the pitches being promoted to traditionally high user groups, and through a paucity of provisions to meet the needs of women users.

Patriarchal ideologies emerged in a variety of ways to influence the managers' approaches to women's use of the artificial turf pitches. Perhaps the most overt illustration of the ways in which patriarchal ideologies shaped service delivery was in case study 2. The Leisure Centre Manager made it clear that promoting women's participation in sport and recreation was not a specific aim of the pitch. In discussing what could be done to promote women's use, his approach was clearly underpinned by a traditional ideological position based on 'appropriate' activities for women. Examples of this included his statements that:

> ...[women] don't really want to go out and put a divided skirt on, and go and run around with a hockey stick, which is about all they can do out there, or maybe develop five-a-side football. ...They much prefer to be inside with a pretty leotard on ...and taking part in a[n aerobics] session, playing a bit of badminton."

It was evident in all three case studies that there were unlikely to be specific initiatives targeted at women, with the response of the Boys' School Representative on the Management Committee in case study 1 being indicative of the reactive approach to women's use:

> I can't help feeling that if women wanted to do it, or were motivated to do that sort of thing, they'd get up and get on with it ... I don't think they are discriminated against in any way at all. I haven't heard of scores of women actually queuing up to say 'look, hang on, we are not getting a fair crack at the whip'.

These specific examples of attitudes to women's participation on the artificial turf pitches reflected Talbot's (1988) argument that rather than recognising that constraints on women's participation derive from management structures and practices, managers imply that it is the target group which must change its behaviour. In this research, the 'blame' for women's user patterns appeared to be apportioned to women themselves, for not wanting to get involved in the types of activities that 'occur' on artificial turf pitches, and for not making more effort themselves. Such an ideology implies that women are 'free' to choose their own sports involvement, and fails to recognise the ways in which women's participation is influenced by cultural relations and economic constraints.

The findings in terms of managers' perceptions of promoting women's use of the artificial turf pitches reinforce Talbot's (1984) assertion that decisions by providers of sport and recreation about what is 'offered' to women are based on perceptions of gender-appropriate behaviour, which is both socially learned and reinforced. The findings reflect the work of both Deem (1986a, 1986b), and Scraton (1988), who have researched and discussed the ways in which provision for women is shaped by patriarchal ideologies about appropriate physical behaviour for women.

In a consideration of public sector leisure provision, Deem suggested that leisure provision for women is shaped by patriarchal ideologies about the roles of women, and what types of behaviour are appropriate for women. This was certainly reflected in the range of activities that were discussed in terms of ways of promoting women's use, with suggestions mainly focusing on traditional 'women's' sports. The findings also lend support to Deem's argument that provision largely consists of what men think women need, and is "frequently based on stereotyped notions of femininity" (1986a: p.144). The most obvious example of this was the Leisure Centre Manager in case study 2, who held stereotypical definitions of the types of activities in which women 'prefer' to participate.

Scraton's research on girls' physical education revealed that those in decision-making positions hold an ideology of the physical, which sets limitations on female activity and physical contact, and which permeates girls' physical education programmes. Similarly in this research, those in the decision-making positions held ideologies of women's participation in sport and recreation, based on patriarchal ideologies of appropriate behaviour for women, which permeated the ways in which the artificial turf pitches were defined as sports spaces for women.

Allison's (1993) recent claim that academic writing within 'sports feminism' has tended to "concentrate on banalities like the existence of structural male power in sport" (p. 13) trivialises a major issue ion contemporary sport — the question of the means whereby male power is reproduced. At the heart of the patriarchal profile of contemporary sport lies not just physical power or prowess, as Allison claims, but institutional power embedded in the managerial and administrative structures of the developmental and providing agencies of sport. On the basis of this study of three innovative examples of facility provision, it is evident that the policy process, management practices, and approaches to women's participation remain powerfully patriarchal.

Policy and Practice Implications

The policy and practice implications outlined are based on effecting change in sport and recreation policy processes and management practices, with a view to creating social conditions which would facilitate women's sport and recreation through promoting their use of artificial turf pitches. The implications are stated within the context of recognising that if their implicit commitment to change is to be shared by all those involved in the management of sport and recreation opportunities, more fundamental change is likely to be required. Such change would focus on transforming the existing male-dominated and -defined structures and ideologies, rather than on making superficial changes to the conditions under which sport and recreation operates. Nevertheless, it is suggested that the changes recommended in the policy and practice implications could impact on existing trends, and would help to promote women's use of artificial turf pitches.

The policy and practice implications are stated in terms of the three management levels identified and analysed within the research, and are as follows:

National/Regional state agencies should:

- develop clear policies which identify objectives for the management and use of artificial turf pitches, which are based on sports development considerations.
- ensure such policies permeate practices at local level, through having an input into policy formulation and policy evaluation processes.
- build into grant agreements evaluation and monitoring procedures, and should be able to input into policy processes if evaluation findings are not satisfactory.
- prioritise support for the provision of artificial turf pitches in locations where use by 'target' groups, including women, will be promoted.
- develop strategies for getting more women into management positions, and for ensuring that women in such positions have an input into the decision-making process.

Local state agencies should:

- develop clear policies which identify objectives for the management and use of artificial turf pitches.

- ensure such policies permeate practices at facility management level, through having an input into service delivery policies, objectives, and evaluation.
- prioritise support for the provision of artificial turf pitches in locations where facility managers are committed to, and competent in developing use by 'target' groups, including women.
- develop strategies for getting more women into local state and facility management positions, and for ensuring that women in such positions have an input into the decision-making process.

Facility Management should:

- be committed to, and competent in developing women's use of artificial turf pitches.
- define artificial turf pitch 'spaces' as multi-purpose, sports development facilities, and develop policies and practices for maximising their use in this respect.
- take a strategic, proactive approach to promoting women's use of artificial turf pitches, perhaps by working in partnership with those operating in sports development infrastructures.
- give greater priority to providing support facilities to meet the needs of women users, such as child care provision and accessible, clean changing facilities.

Note

[1] The full case studies are presented in C. Carr (1993) M. Phil. Thesis 'The Policy Game: Women's Use and the Management of Artificial Turf Pitches', Chapter Five, 'Fieldwork Case Studies', University of Southampton.

References

Allison, L. (1993) 'The changing context of sporting life', in L. Allison (ed) *The changing politics of sport*. Manchester: Manchester University Press: pp. 1–14.

Birch, P. (1975) *Thirty games a week — a study of the use of artificial grass pitches in Islington and Hackney.* London: The Sports Council and the Greater London and South East Regional Sports Council.

Bramham, P. (1991) 'Explanations of the organisation of sport in British Society', *International Review for the Sociology of Sport* Vol. 26, No. 3: pp. 139–151.

Coalter, C., Long J. , and Duffield B. (1986) *Rationale for public sector investment in leisure*. London: The Sports Council and Economic & Social Research Council.

Davies, J. (1983) Management Considerations — The Management and Use of Artificial Outdoor Surfaces for Sport, Seminar Report. Reading: The Sports Council Southern Region.

Deem, R. (1986a) *All work and no play? The sociology of women and leisure.* Milton Keynes: Open University.

————(1986b) 'The politics of women's leisure', in F. Coalter (ed) *The politics of leisure,* LSA Publication No. 24. Eastbourne: Leisure Studies Association, pp. 68–81.

Dunnett, R. (1990) 'Below the surface', *Sport and Leisure* (January/February): pp. 35–37.

Glyptis S., Kay, T., and Murray, M. (1985) *Working with women and girls — the attitudes of staff of the Action Sport West Midlands Scheme.* Birmingham: The Sports Council West Midlands Region.

Hargreaves, J. (1986) *Sport, power and culture: A social and historical analysis of popular sports in Britain.* Cambridge: Polity Press.

Henry, I. (1993) *The politics of leisure policy.* London: Macmillan Press.

Henry, I. and Bramham, P . (1986) 'Leisure, the local state and social order', *Leisure Studies* Vol. 5, No. 2: pp. 189-210.

Knox, C. (1991) 'Policy evaluation in leisure services — the Northern Ireland case', *Leisure Studies*, Vol. 10, No. 2: pp. 105-118.

Milner, E. (1991) Technology in Service to 'Sport for All'. Unpublished paper presented at World University Games, Sheffield.

Nottinghamshire County Council/The Sports Council (1990) Cost in Use of Artificial Pitches, Seminar Report, Nottingham: Nottinghamshire County Council.

Roberts, K. (1989) *Community response to leisure centre provision in Belfast.* London: The Sports Council.

Roberts, J. (1985) *Artificial grass surfaces — for soccer, hockey and multi-games areas.* London: The Sports Council.

Scraton, S. (1988) Shaping Up to Womanhood: A Study of the Relationship between Gender and Girls' Physical Education in a City-Based Local Education Authority. PhD Thesis, The School of Education, The Open University.

South East Council for Sport and Recreation (1986) *Prospect for the eighties — a review,* Summary Document. London: South East Council for Sport and Recreation.

Sports Council (1988) *Sport in the community — into the 90s. A strategy for sport 1988-1993.* London: The Sports Council.

———(1990) *Artificial turf pitches for hockey.* London: The Sports Council.

———(1991) *The playing pitch strategy and guide to assessing playing pitch requirements and developing local policy.* London: The Sports Council.

———(1992) *Women and sport consultation document.* London: The Sports Council.

———(1993) *Sport in the nineties — new horizons.* London: The Sports Council.

Sports Council, Greater London and South-East East Council for Sport and Recreation (1982) *Prospect for the eighties — A regional recreation strategy.* London: Greater London and South East Council for Sport and Recreation.

Sports Council, Southern Region (1992) *Artificial turf pitches in Bracknell Forest.* Reading: The Sports Council Southern Region.

Sports Council, West Midlands Region (1992) Sports Development on Synthetic Turf Pitches in Birmingham Summary. Unpublished research.

Talbot, M. (1984) 'Women and sport: A gender contradiction in terms?', in A. Tomlinson (ed) *Leisure and social relations*, LSA Publication No. 25. Eastbourne: Leisure Studies Association: pp. 56–72.

———(1988) 'Their own worst enemy? Women and leisure provision', in E. Wimbush *et al.* (eds) *Relative freedoms — women and leisure.* Milton Keynes: Open University: pp. 161–176.

Taylorson, D. and Halfpenny, P. (1991) *Women and sport in the North West.* Centre for Applied Social Research, Manchester: University of Manchester.

Tipp, G. (1986) 'Artificial grass surfaces for sport-clubs in the community', *Recreation Management Workshop Report.* London: The Sports Council.

Tomlinson, M. (1987) 'State intervention in voluntary sport: the inner city policy context', *Leisure Studies* Vol. 6, No. 3: pp. 329–345.

Whannel, G. (1983) *Blowing the whistle: the politics of sport.* London: Pluto Press.

Yule J. (1992) 'Gender and leisure policy', *Leisure Studies* Vol. 11, No. 2: pp. 157–173.

TOWARDS GENDER EQUITY IN SPORT: AN UPDATE ON SPORTS COUNCIL POLICY DEVELOPMENT

Anita White
Head of Development
The Sports Council, London, UK

Introduction

This paper takes the opportunity to review some of the main policy development in the Sports Council over the first four years of the 1990s. The paper is organised in three parts. First, I will discuss the 'target group' approach to 'Sport for All' and explain the shift towards a 'Sports Equity' approach in Sports Council policies and programmes. Second, I will outline the recently developed policy for Women and Sport which uses a Sports Equity approach. Third, I will discuss policy implementation in the current social and economic climate.

From Target Groups to Sport Equity

The so called 'target group' approach was the cornerstone of much sports development work during the 1970s and 1980s. Sports development workers were employed to do outreach work in the community to increase participation among targeted groups; women, people with disabilities, black and ethnic minorities, the old, the young and the unemployed. Appraisal of this approach has revealed a number of strengths and weaknesses.

Three main strengths of the approach were identified. The needs of targeted groups were highlighted, and resources (human and financial) were specifically allocated to generate increased participation. The focus on these groups heightened awareness of the barriers to participation experienced by women, the elderly, people with disabilities and black and ethnic minorities (Sports Council, 1991).

However the approach also had a number of disadvantages or weaknesses. The groups identified were not homogenous and often too large and too diverse to use as a basis for realistic planning of strategies and programmes. For example, the category of "people with disabilities" includes a multitude of different kinds of physical and mental disability: the needs of blind people and paraplegics are very different.

Members of some groups resented the stigma of being 'targeted' and labelled as disadvantaged or deprived. Targeting is a marketing concept. The assumption was that ways needed to be found to sell the product of sport to the target market. It was usually assumed that there was nothing wrong with the product, the problem lay with the target market. Consequently there was often insufficient attention given to the ways that the structures and institutions of sport itself might need to change to accommodate the target market rather than the other way round.

However the biggest problem with the approach was that it tended to be purely participation based. People were encouraged to participate, but opportunities to progress from casual participation to improved performance and sustained involvement were not available — the facilities, coaches, and club structures needed to develop performance were not in place.

It is also well known that opportunities to achieve excellence are also not equally available to all. For example the costs of training and preparation at top level are often beyond the means of people on low incomes. Women are disadvantaged in most competitions including the Olympic and Commonwealth Games competitions by the fewer number of events open to them in comparison with events open to men. The increasing commercialisation of top level sport has served to exaggerate and exacerbate inequities. Mainstream, popular sports get good media coverage and are further popularised with a few top level sportspeople achieving star status and therefore the potential to acquire considerable sponsorship while the majority of competitors struggle to make ends meet (British Olympic Association, 1993). Sports for people with disabilities and women's sport do not, on the whole, enjoy equitable media coverage or financial support.

The target group approach also failed to address issues to do with the structure and culture of organisations and institutions concerned with sports provision. Most of these sports organisations, whether democratically elected or not, tend to be unrepresentative of the population of a whole. People from black and ethnic minorities, people with disabilities and women are usually few and far between. The effect of this unrepresentative nature of the boards, councils, committees and organisations that provide for sport is that their restricted experience makes it difficult for them to cater adequately for the needs of the whole population.

In view of these weaknesses, it was necessary to adopt an approach which addresses these issues, and which would permeate sporting practice in a more thorough and comprehensive way.

The approach advocated takes '*equity in sport*' as a goal. To achieve this goal there is a commitment to identifying inequities and taking special measures to redress the balance. Moreover, rather than focus just on participation, there is a commitment to equity principles permeating both the delivery of sport to clients at all levels of sports development and the structure and culture of organisations which provide for sport.

Sports Equity Permeation

The nature of sports equity permeating client delivery at all levels of sports development is represented diagrammatically in **Figure 1**.

The vertical axis represents the principles of Sport for All, encompassing equal opportunities, access, the identification of inequities and the need to take the affirmative action to redress inequities. Factors which currently determine inequity in sport — disability, gender, ethnicity, age and socio-economic status (SES) — are identified. The horizontal axis represents sports people (or the "client side" in local authority terms) at all levels of sports development.

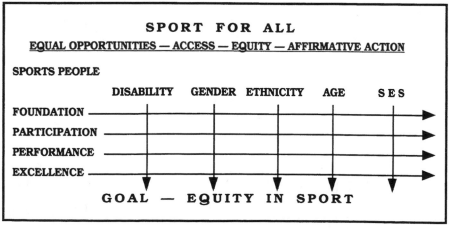

Figure 1:   **Sports Equity Permeation — Client Side**

On the client side, the aim should be to provide opportunities for everyone to participate and develop their full potential in sport. The Sports Council uses the sports development continuum (foundation — participation — performance — excellence) as a framework for planning all aspects of sport (Sports Council, 1993a). Sports Development needs to start at *foundation* level, with the acquisition of basic movement and sport skills and a positive attitude towards a healthy lifestyle. Schools are the main providers or deliverers at this level through the physical education curriculum, but local authorities also have an important role in play provision for youngsters of both pre-school and school age. At *participation* level local authorities play a major role both in supporting club sport and providing facilities where people can participate on a casual or informal basis. Moreover those authorities with active sports development units engaged in outreach work do a great deal to make sport and recreation participation accessible to sectors of the community which otherwise would not participate. For some, participation in sport is enough, but others wish to improve their *performance* and a few will reach publicly recognised standards of *excellence*. A sports equity approach aims to ensure that opportunities to perform and excel are available to all those who have the necessary desire and talent. Governing bodies of sport and voluntary clubs are the main providers at these levels although local authorities are increasingly becoming involved in performance work.

Taking the groups in society which often experience limited opportunities — people with disabilities, women, black and ethnic minorities, the elderly and people on low incomes — it is necessary to consider whether or not appropriate and equitable opportunities are accessible at *all* levels of the sports development continuum. For example, do holiday playschemes cater for youngsters with learning difficulties? Are coaching opportunities provided for women who have attended introductory sessions, but want to improve their performance? Are leisure centres welcoming to the elderly? Are we providing a quality service that caters for the needs of all, and is accessible to everyone in the community?

A sports equity approach also requires the permeation of equity principles on the *staff side* within sports organisations themselves, be they clubs, governing bodies or local authority leisure committees and departments. **Figure 2** illustrates this concept. Again the traditional areas of inequity are shown on the vertical axis. On the horizontal axis interfacing with these is a range of aspects of the organisational culture which could be considered.

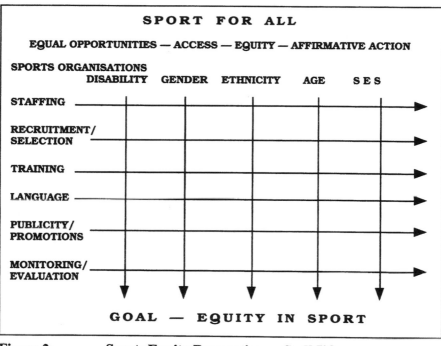

Figure 2:   **Sports Equity Permeation — Staff Side**

The first, *staffing*, includes matters such as representation and distribution of different social groups among employed staff (how many black people hold senior management positions?). *Selection and recruitment* procedures should reflect good equal opportunities procedures. Most local authorities have well articulated equal opportunities policies and practices in this area, but only a few governing bodies of sport have developed them. Understanding and implementing sports equity often requires raising awareness and acknowledging inequities within long established systems, in order to bring about attitude change. So staff *training* is a fundamental requirement. *Language, publicity and promotions* give strong messages about the values of an organisation through the language and publicity materials used — too often they serve to exclude certain groups rather than include all. Finally, organisations need to *monitor* and *evaluate* their own progress towards equity within their organisation against established targets.

So the achievement of sports equity requires the permeation of equity principles and considerations through both service delivery and organisational practices. In explaining the sports equity approach some examples of the issues that need to be considered to provide sports opportunities for all and ensure equity within organisational practices have been given. For sport and leisure providers to work effectively towards sports equity, these kinds of considerations need to become an integral part of the strategic planning process. The process should include the following stages:

1 *Consultation* with client groups and staff through the organisation.

2 *Information Gathering* to assess the current situation with regard to use of services by different groups, and to identify inequities and discriminatory practices.

3 *Development of Special Measures* to reduce inequities where they have been shown to exist and increase involvement in sport and recreation by under-represented groups.

4 *Implementation* of programmes to achieve set targets which might involve training of staff. Regular communication about equity goals and targets is important.

5 *Monitoring and Evaluation* to measure the success of special measures programmes against set targets, analysing the results, and setting new goals and targets.

Sports Council Policy for Women and Sport

Guided by the overall principles of sports development and sports equity, the Sports Council, in consultation with its partners, has recently developed a series of policies for specific populations; young people, women, people with disabilities and black and ethnic minorities. The Sports Council hopes that these policy documents will prove to be useful working documents for organisations concerned with the provision of sport to use in their strategic planning. Against a background of the current 'state of play' in each area of work a series of policy aims and objectives has been developed. These are necessarily broad in scope since we are trying to create policies to which all agencies concerned with the provision of sport can subscribe. Different agencies will have different parts to play in the overall implementation of the policies. The Sports Council's main role is to advocate the adoption of policies and to encourage other agencies, singly and in partnership, to work towards agreed policy objectives, identifying where gaps in provision exist and avoiding duplication of effort.

The Policy for Women and Sport has an overarching aim: to increase the involvement of women in sport at all levels and in all roles.

This aim recognises that in promoting sport for women we need to look beyond just increasing participation, to increasing women's involvement at *all* levels of the sports development continuum and in *all* the many and varied roles that are part of the sport system.

Six policy objectives are identified as crucial to the realisation of this aim.

The first three are concerned with sports development:

1   To encourage equality of opportunity for girls to acquire basic movement skills and to develop positive attitudes towards an active lifestyle.

2   To increase opportunities and reduce constraints to enable all women to participate in sport.

3   To increase opportunities and reduce constraints to enable women to improve their levels of performance and reach publicly recognised levels of excellence.

The next two are concerned with human resources:

4   To increase the numbers of women involved in the organisation of sport and encourage them to reach senior positions. This includes facility managers, sports development officers, sports leaders, administrators/executives, coaches, officials, physical and sport educators, sports scientists and women working within the field of sports medicine and the sports media.

5   To encourage all appropriate organisations to adopt gender equity policies and practices.

The final objective concerns communication.

6   To improve communication about women and sport and establish appropriate communication networks.

Policy Development Process

The policy on 'Women and Sport' was developed over a three-year period. In June 1990 an internal policy working group of Sports Council staff was set up. This group reviewed the current position regarding women and sport and considered a wide range of information, including published and unpublished research and expert opinion, to produce a position statement. From this a series of policy objectives was developed, aimed at reducing gender inequity through a comprehensive approach based on the concept of sports equity.

A draft paper was considered at a day seminar in December 1990 by a group of invited experts who represented the range of areas addressed and revisions and amendments were made in the light of their comments. A second draft was produced in February 1991 which was widely circulated for consideration by Sports Council staff in different regions and units and to people outside the Council who had particular expertise or might be involved in policy implementation. The Sports Council considered the policy in October 1991 and agreed wider dissemination and consultation with partners and key agencies was desirable.

In January 1992 a Consultation document was published and circulated to approximately 1600 governing bodies of sport, local authority leisure and recreation departments, youth agencies, and educational institutions (Sports Council, 1992). Consultees were asked to respond to the document by commenting on the accuracy of the position statement, signifying their level of agreement with the proposed policy aim and objectives and indicating the extent of their organisation's work in the field.

Responses to the Consultation document were analysed by Tess Kay and Lesley Randolf and a report produced for the Sports Council in August 1992 (Kay and Randolf, 1992). However, there was extensive support for the approach suggested and need for a comprehensive policy supported by a wide range of organisations. There was a major discrepancy between the expressed level of support for policy objectives and the extent to which organisations were taking action to further them, or planned to do so. Most of the work was taking place in connection with the Sports Development objectives (33%) reflecting the well-established nature of participation initiatives. Less was being done in connection with Human Resources (20%) and in relation to the Communication objectives (22%).

The aim and objectives were revised to reflect the responses of consultees and the revised policy was accepted by the Sports Council in December 1992. A series of 'frameworks for action' was drawn up to guide the policy implementation process and a one-day seminar was held in February 1993 with key agencies in the field to discuss the feasibility and appropriateness of this guidance. After further consultation, refinement and revision, the final version of the 'Women and Sport Policy and Frameworks for Action' was published by the Sports Council in November 1993 (Sports Council, 1993b).

Policy Implementation

If the policy development process seems somewhat tortuous, policy implementation is likely to be even more challenging. Achieving some kind of consensus on the current position and what needs to be done is one thing, bringing about substantial change towards gender equity in sport is quite another.

The national policy for women and sport requires more than 'academic acceptance'. It requires fundamental attitude changes among many men (and women) who have grown up with male definitions of sport and patriarchal value systems and accept them without question. For women to be empowered in the sports context means that men have to be prepared to relinquish the power base they have held for years. It is notoriously difficult to bring about cultural and organisational change in sports organisations, particularly voluntary ones.

Policy documents all too easily gather dust on shelves, and have little impact on what happens on the ground. There are many well documented analyses of the policy/practice interface, and the difficulties of translating policy into practice (Sports Council, 1993c; Carr, 1993; Fasting, 1993). In most local authorities there is a clear divide between sports development and facility management. There is little liaison between sports development teams and centre managers, and centre managers do not use sports development and sports equity principles as a framework for planning. For example the Centre for Leisure Research's study on the impact of Compulsory Competitive Tendering on Sport and Leisure Management (Sports Council, 1993c) describes policy specifications as "largely non-developmental". Although contract specifications often referred to particular user groups (three quarters referred to people with disabilities, young people, the unemployed and over 50s) very few set specific measurable throughput targets or suggested particular policy approaches such as concessionary charges or time allocations.

The key to success is the extent to which the various providers of sporting opportunities have 'ownership' of the policy, believe it is right for *them* and how well the policy fits with their other agenda priorities. Most organisations concerned with provision of sporting opportunities in the UK are feeling the effects of the economic recession. Many governing bodies of sport are under severe financial pressure with decline in the population's spending power and in people's preparedness to do voluntary work for sport. Survival is their prime concern. Gender equity is only relevant if it can be seen to increase their chances of survival.

Local authority leisure and recreation departments face many uncertainties with local government restructuring. Sport and leisure may find itself grouped with different partners in new departments. Where these partners share equity principles and objectives, for example education and social services, then these partnerships may prove conducive to the development of equity work. But in other cases restructuring may be less helpful.

With sport and leisure a discretionary service, it is always likely to suffer the effects of cuts more than services which are statutory. Within sport and leisure there may be a tendency to focus limited finances on facility maintenance. Existing buildings have to be maintained and run — sports development workers can be sacked. Yet it is in the field of outreach sports development work that most innovation has occurred and most progress been made towards sports equity. Despite the excellent record of sports development work in local authorities I believe it is under threat. We should do all we can to safeguard and preserve it, as it is something of which we, in the UK, can be proud, and it would be ironic if we saw its demise at a time when it is just becoming established and its worth recognised.

Most organisations which have some responsibility in providing sporting opportunities and 'delivering the policy' have major economic concerns. Meeting financial targets is of paramount importance, and if providing more equitability for women costs money, then it is likely to move to the bottom of the agenda. Many will say they subscribe to the principles of gender equity, but say it cannot be achieved within the current economic climate.

However to claim that the current economic climate prevents progress towards gender equity is to misunderstand the principle of equity. Working towards equity implies the redistribution of resources (including power) so that inequities are redressed. However limited the resources it is still necessary to examine their distribution and assess the effect they have on opportunities for men and women to participate in sport. Existing patterns of provision favour men, the evidence is unequivocal. All organisations concerned with the provision of sport should be prepared to critically examine their current practices and change them in such ways as are necessary to provide equally for girls and boys, women and men.

Conclusion

This paper has outlined policy development towards gender equity in sport which was led by the Sports Council from 1990–1993. It has explained the shift from a target group approach to a sports equity approach, outlined the Women and Sport policy, and discussed implementation issues. It remains to be seen to what extent sports organisations and institutions are prepared to make the necessary ideological, cultural and practical changes to achieve gender equity in sport.

References

British Olympic Association (1993) *The BOA Athlete Report 1993: "25 ways to put the Great back into sporting Britain"*. London: BOA.

Carr, C. (1993) The Policy Game: Management and Women's Use of Artificial Turf Pitches. Unpublished MPhil Thesis, University of Southampton.

Fasting, K. (1993) *Women and sport: Monitoring progress towards equality — A European Survey*. Oslo: The Norwegian Confederation of Sports.

Kay, T., and Randolf, L. (1992) Policy for Women and Sport: A Response to the Women and Sport Consultation Exercise. Unpublished, Loughborough University of Technology.

Sports Council (1991) *National demonstration projects: Major lessons and issues for Sports Development*. London: Sports Council.

———(1992) *Women and sport: A consultation document*. London: Sports Council.

———(1993a) *Sport in the nineties — new horizons*. London: Sports Council.

———(1993b) *Women and sport: Policy and frameworks for action*. London: Sports Council.

———(1993c) *Sport and leisure management: Compulsory competitive tendering national information survey report*. London: Sports Council.

FEMINIST ACTIVISM IN SPORT:
A COMPARATIVE STUDY OF WOMEN'S SPORT
ADVOCACY ORGANIZATIONS

M. Ann Hall
Department of Physical Education and Sport Studies
University of Alberta, Canada

In 1974 the American professional tennis player Billie Jean King took the prize money she had won as the year's best female athlete and donated it to start the Women's Sports Foundation. King and other top athletes including Donna de Varona, Micki King Hogue, and Wyomia Tyus met and sketched out their ideas of what a foundation advocating women's sports might hope to achieve. Then they set up a board of trustees including other well known athletes like Chris Evert, Kathrine Switzer, Sheila Young, Joan Joyce, Jane Blalock, and established a work space in the California office of King Enterprises (Halpert, 1989). The Women's Sports Foundation was the first of the advocacy organizations established explicitly to achieve a better deal for girls and women in sport.[1] Today, there are several organizations in various countries around the world with similar goals most of which were formed because of the initiative in the United States. Some of these organizations are modelled on the Women's Sports Foundation, and indeed have taken the same name, but most have evolved quite differently given the unique features of the sport systems in these countries.

The purpose of this chapter is to document, analyze and explain the differences in history, structure and function of organizations in different countries whose purpose is to advocate on behalf of sportswomen. Four in-depth case studies systematically examine organizations in the United States, Australia, Canada, and the United Kingdom which have emerged between 1974 and 1991: (a) the Women's Sports Foundation in the United States (WSF); (b) the Canadian Association for the Advancement of Women in Sport and Physical

Activity (CAAWS); (c) the Women's Sports Foundation in the United Kingdom (UK WSF); and (d) Womensport Australia.[2] Another goal of this study is to examine the extent to which these organizations see themselves as feminist, and as part of the larger women's movement within their country. In other words, to what extent are these organizations "pro-woman" in the sense of improving women's collective status, opportunities, power and self-esteem, as well as being political and socially transformational (Martin, 1990)? Yet another goal is to examine the ways in which these organizations negotiate their place within broader sport systems, both at the national and international levels, because they are each attempting to provide an alternative to traditional sport organizations. For those associations that have been in place for over a decade, it is important to assess the extent to which they have been able to maintain their political and advocacy functions.

Researching the Organizations

I first joined the WSF in the United States in 1974 through an advertisement placed in the original *womenSports* magazine which was published by Billie Jean King. I have kept a file since then but have remained at a distance from the organization until recently when a decision was made to do this study. Subsequently, I have collected an enormous number of documents such as newsletters, reports, annual reports, and the like. As well, I attended the 1993 annual conference on Long Island where I also visited their new offices in Eisenhower Park. At the same time, I interviewed a number of the WSF staff, consulted their archives, and took copious notes from my informal discussions and observations primarily at the conference. What is interesting is that a careful search of the literature has produced no academic studies of the WSF, nor is the WSF itself aware of any ongoing study of the organization.

With regard to the Canadian association, CAAWS, I am a founding member in that I was part of a small group which had been invited to a workshop at McMaster University in March, 1981 to discuss whether or not an organization to advance the cause of women's sport in Canada was needed. We voted unanimously that it was, and CAAWS was born. Although I have not been involved in the leadership of CAAWS, I have been a member since its inception, and have followed the organization again from a distance. One of my former graduate students, Janis Lawrence-Harper, undertook to write a "herstory" of CAAWS documenting their first ten years (Lawrence-Harper,

1991). With the addition of a theoretical frame-work and analysis, this subsequently became her completed master's thesis (Lawrence-Harper, 1993). For these projects, she interviewed twenty-three women from across the country who at one time had been either a volunteer director or paid staff member of the organization. Of the four organizations being compared here, CAAWS has certainly been studied the most either through student theses or academic papers (cf. Forbes, 1993; Lenskyj, 1991a, 1991b; Scott-Pawson, 1991; Theberge, 1983).

The Women's Sports Foundation in the United Kingdom came to my attention in 1984 when it was first founded. When I began the present study early in 1991, I was located in Australia for six months whereas my colleague Trevor Slack was on sabbatical leave in England. I asked him to assist me and he did so by conducting a number of interviews with several founders and leaders of the WSF (UK). He also collected a variety of documents, newsletters, reports, and the like. Subsequently, another of my graduate students, Brenda Grace, had also been a volunteer committee member with the UK WSF between 1988 and 1992, and is presently completing her thesis which is an organizational case study of the association.

As mentioned previously, I was teaching at the University of Western Australia between January and June, 1991. During this time, I familiarized myself with the various governmental and non-governmental organizations in Australia whose focus is women in sport. I attended conferences and meetings of some of these groups; in addition I conducted several informal and formal interviews with the founders and leaders in primarily two organizations: the Women's Sports Foundation of WA Inc and the Australian Association of Women's Sport and Recreation (SA Division). While I was in Australia, there were ongoing discussions between these two associations as well as women's sport organizations in the other states and territories, directed towards the formation of a coalition which later in 1991 became Womensport Australia Alliance (now shortened to Womensport Australia). I have followed the development of Womensport Australia through receiving their newsletter and keeping in touch with some of the principal players by means of electronic mail and fax.

Finally, in May 1994, I attended an international conference on women's sport in Brighton, England which was organized by the British Sports Council and supported by the International Olympic Committee. At the conference were some 300 delegates from over 85 countries representing governmental and non-governmental organizations, national Olympic Committees, international and national sport federations, and educational and research institutions. Here I met up again with several of my contacts in the various organizations under study, and I was able to up-date and amplify the information.

Analyzing Feminist Organizations

Feminist organizations in the modern Western women's movements have, according to Patricia Martin (1990), "proved to be extraordinarily prolific, creative, variegated, and tenacious" (p. 183). She developed ten dimensions that can be used to frame comparative research on feminist organizations in order to understand their structures, processes, and outcomes. These dimensions are: founding circumstances, feminist ideology, feminist values, feminist goals, feminist outcomes, structure, practices, members and membership, scope and scale, and external relations. She argues further that an organization is feminist if it meets any *one* of the following criteria: (a) has feminist ideology; (b) has feminist guiding values; (c) has feminist goals; (d) produces feminist outcomes; (e) was founded during the women's movement as part of the women's movement.

Although Martin's dimensions provide a useful framework for comparing organizations across cultures, her approach is more suited to a one-time snapshot of these organizations which makes it difficult to analyze (and compare) organizational change within these organizations. To overcome this problem, other theorists have suggested a biographical approach that highlights the fluidity of organizational life without predefining the transitions and stages through which an organization may pass (see, for example, Kimberly, 1987). Therefore, in order to take advantage of both these perspectives, they have been combined to provide a theoretical and comparative framework for the analysis of feminist organizations.[3]

Founding Context. It is concerned with the influence of the initial internal and external contexts, and with the ongoing influence of an organization's founding leaders. This replaces and expands Martin's founding circumstances.

Feminist Ideology and Values. Martin defines feminist ideology as officially endorsing beliefs associated with the women's movement (i.e., acknowledges that women are oppressed and disadvantaged as a group, sees this as rooted in social arrangements, and articulates beliefs that its correction, or elimination, requires social, political, and economic change). Feminist values stem from a political analysis of women's lived experience. They focus on: the primacy of interpersonal relationships; the empowerment and personal development of members; the building of self-esteem; and the promotion of enhanced knowledge, skills, and political awareness. It is important to identify the general and specific nature of this construct and an organization's commitment to the construct, and to plot any alterations or variations from an original organizational position.

Feminist Strategy. Three of Martin's dimensions have been grouped under this construct (feminist goals, feminist practices, and feminist outcomes) because each relates in some way to action. Feminist goals are defined by Martin as "action agendas" that an organization wishes to achieve and that it actually pursues. Practices are the strategies and tactics employed by the organization. Feminist outcomes are the consequences of organizational activities for members, for other organizations, or for all women. Briskin (1991) defines feminist strategy as a continuum with the strategy of mainstreaming at one end and disengagement at the other, and that optimal strategies for feminist organizations lie somewhere between the two ends of the continuum.

Structural Components. This construct comprises three of Martin's dimensions —structure, members and membership, scope and scale — because there are obvious relationships between them. Structure is an organization's normative internal arrangements, specifically the manner in which control or authority is organized, the way in which power is distributed, the way work is divided up and integrated, and the arrangements for decision making and conflict resolution. Membership concerns who is viewed as appropriate to belong; the rules and regulations of belonging; and how members are recruited, incorporated, socialized, and terminated, or how they voluntarily affiliate and leave. Scope refers to whether an organization is local versus national (or international). Scale refers to membership numbers, number and range of activities, number of clients served and services provided, and size of annual budget.

External Relations. These concern the nature, intensity, and content of an organization's ties to its environment or to individuals, groups, and organizations (including the state) beyond its boundary. The relationship between an organization and its environment is either one that centres power with the environment (e.g., controls an organization's resources), or locates power with members (e.g., completely self-sufficient).

Using this framework as a general guideline, a comparative analysis of the four women's sport advocacy organizations now follows.

Founding Contexts: Women's Sport Advocacy and the Women's Movement

The founding leaders of the WSF in the United States were well-known amateur and professional athletes led by Billie Jean King. The Foundation's first executive director was Eva Auchincloss, handpicked by King, and at the time assistant publisher of King's magazine, *womenSports*. They established the Foundation as a non-profit, membership-based organization with the goal of getting all women of all ages and skills involved in sport activities for their health, enjoyment and personal development. Certainly throughout the 1970s and 1980s, the WSF did not perceive itself as a feminist organization, nor has it been linked directly to the larger women's movement in the United States. Early issues of the original WSF newsletter, *Frontiers*, refer only a few times to attempts to connect with the larger women's movement. For example, in 1977 the WSF advised its members to contact the Women's Equity Action League which had set up a sports clearing house on matters relating to sex discrimination in sport. At the International Women's Year National Meeting in Houston in 1976, the Foundation was seeking support for a "sports resolution" that pinpointed areas where sports development for girls and women could be changed at the national level. However, as American sport historian Susan Cahn (1994, p. 252) argues, "women's efforts to attain the right to fully participate in sport, to enhance their strength and coordination, and to compete without psychological or institutional restrictions were consistent with the broad range of feminist activities designed to win for women the right to control and enjoy their own bodies."

The reasons for the WSF's reluctance to link with the broader, more politically oriented women's movement in the United States are quite straightforward. It did not wish to alienate the so-called "grassroots," the millions of girls and women for whom the goal was to improve their physical, mental and emotional well-being through sports and fitness participation; and it certainly did not wish to alienate its corporate sponsors who to this day provide virtually all its funding. They have not, until recently, attempted to connect with the larger women's movement because in their view, it has marginalized sport by seeing it as irrelevant and unimportant to the larger cause of women's rights.

However, according to some in the WSF, the women's movement in the United States seems to have finally "discovered women's sport." For example, the Feminist Majority Foundation founded by two former presidents of the National Organization of Women has a task force on women's sport; *Ms. Magazine* has recently run several feature articles on women's sport; and ironically the WSF has been called "radical feminists" by football coaches in an article in *USA Today* because of their stand on gender equity.

The circumstances surrounding the founding of CAAWS could not be more different. Compared to the United States, there is a very high degree of government involvement and funding in the Canadian sport system. In fact if you look back at the various conferences and workshops that preceded the founding of CAAWS, they were all government sponsored. In 1974, the first National Conference on Women in Sport was sponsored by Fitness and Amateur Sport (FAS), the branch of the federal government responsible for sport. Smaller workshops and conferences at both the municipal and provincial level broadened and diversified the settings in which the issues facing females in sport were addressed.[4] In 1980, at the Female Athlete Conference, co-sponsored by Simon Fraser University and FAS, delegates recommended the establishment of a "National Women's Sport Foundation to serve as a communication network and advocacy group across the country" (Popma, 1980:185). Finally, in March 1981, at a workshop funded by the new Women's Program of FAS, and attended by a small group of sport administrators, federal government representatives, athletes, coaches, university-based physical educators, and representatives from the major national feminist organizations, CAAWS was born.

From the very beginning, CAAWS saw itself as a feminist organization. Its first mission statement read: "CAAWS seeks to advance the position of women by defining, promoting and supporting a feminist perspective on sport and to improve the status of women in sport" (CAAWS Annual General Meeting Kit, 1982). The fact that CAAWS was at the same time openly feminist and government funded was not at all unusual given the politics of the state and the Canadian women's movement at the time. As Canadian political scientist Jill Vickers has pointed out, an operational code of the second-wave women's movement in Canada is the belief that change is possible and that state action is an acceptable way of achieving it. "Most Canadian feminists," she argues, "perceive the state more as a provider of services, including the service of regulation, than a reinforcer of patriarchal norms, and most seem to believe that services, whether child care or medicare, will help" (Vickers, 1992: p. 44–45). The founders of CAAWS and its subsequent leaders struggled hard to work out its relationship with the larger Canadian women's movement, and the feminist perspective that was the basis of its organizational philosophy. Also, the women's sport network in Canada is relatively small which has meant that a few key individuals, all with a strong sense of feminism, have remained influential in CAAWS since its inception or have returned at various points to provide leadership and energy.

The founding of the WSF in the United Kingdom is a little more difficult to pinpoint. Beginning in the early 1980s, a small group of women sport leaders situated in institutions of higher education (including Anita White, Celia Brackenridge, Margaret Talbot, and Sue Campbell) formed an informal network based on their shared concerns about women's sport. At one point they met with Derek Wyatt, an ex-England rugby player and journalist who was interested in a number of social issues around sport. He had visited the WSF in the United States, and the ad hoc group decided that the time was ripe to organize a similar association in the United Kingdom. They expanded their contacts to include top sportswomen, more women in higher education, sport journalists, and others. Celia Brackenridge, who had also visited the US WSF in the summer of 1984, offered to produce a working document outlining the mission, philosophy, goals, structure, etc., of the proposed organization. The group produced an information sheet to keep a record of their evolving ideas and to help spread the word about the new organization.

Interviews with many of these women show that although for the most part they shared feminist goals, most did not have a clear picture of the relationship between sport and feminism, nor were they connected to the larger women's movement. However, as they debated the issues around the formation of the WSF, and the group expanded, the minutes of these meetings (and the participants' recollections) reveal a good deal of tension between those with a more radical feminist analysis, who were pushing strongly for a women-only, lesbian-positive organization also sensitive to the needs of minority women, and the more apolitical sportswomen with little understanding or analysis of these important issues. I will return to a further discussion of these debates and tensions within the UK WSF later in the chapter.

Between the spring of 1984 and its first annual general meeting in October 1985, the WSF UK met as an ad-hoc working committee. Enthusiastic subcommittees working on the constitution, media, education, and sponsorship were formed to tackle various issues. On the issue of men in the organization, the group eventually voted that although they could not be members, they were welcome to make donations or provide assistance, which meant that it was no longer appropriate for Derek Wyatt to be actively involved. A proper organizing committee was formally elected at the AGM in London on October 19, 1985 marking the official beginning of the WSF in the United Kingdom.

The newest organization, Womensport Australia, formally established in 1991, is fundamentally an alliance of non-governmental associations in the various states and territories that constitute Australia. In 1990, the Women's Sport Promotion Unit of the Australian Sports Commission brought together representatives from the diverse women's sport and recreation groups across the country to examine the possibility of a national network. One of these groups, the Women's Sport Foundation of Western Australia, was headed by Dr. Lynn Embrey who had spent two years studying in the United States in the mid-1980s and had taken a good look at the WSF in the United States. Another group, the Australian Association of Women's Sport and Recreation (South Australia Division) was formed in 1986. Its founders wanted to "think big" in that eventually there would be a national association with branches in all states and territories. It was this group who were primarily responsible for obtaining a small project grant from the federal Office of the Status of Women. As an alliance the organization's leaders have had some difficulty in bringing together the various (and sometimes conflicting) philosophies of its member groups. For instance, the name by which the organization would be called sparked debate around the notion of elite, high-performance sport (including the increasing commodfication of top level women athletes) as opposed to the more egalitarian, non-competitive, recreational-based participation aimed at the "ordinary" woman. As well, there was debate over the concept of "foundation" (which some saw as too American) versus "alliance" (which some saw as too threatening). In the end, they chose Womensport Australia and under this is written "Sport and Physical Recreation for Women."

Of less concern were debates about whether or not the organization should be feminist. My interviews (and experience in Australia) indicate that as in most Western countries, there is considerable backlash against "feminism", and hence the understandable reluctance among many women to identify themselves as such. As a result, there has been some resistance to discuss how this relatively new organization should be feminist, and specifically how it should link with the larger women's movement in Australia. However, under new leadership, Womensport Australia now seems more willing to develop stronger networks with a range of national women's organizations (Womensport Australia, 1993).

Feminist Ideology and Values: Liberal to the Core

Feminist organizations either officially or unofficially endorse an ideology which can be classified according to type: liberal, radical, socialist, Marxist, lesbian, or other (Martin, 1990). Despite the cross-cultural differences, the organizations discussed here are officially liberal in the sense that their focus is on ensuring girls' and women's right to equal access to the sport and recreation opportunities that have long been available to boys and men. However, before discussing the organizations with respect to why they have followed a liberal path, I want to explore briefly the liberal versus radical feminist agendas in sport activism.

Liberal Versus Radical Feminist Agendas in Sport

Over the past decade there has been a subtle shift in the discourse of human rights in many Western societies from "equality" to "equity." This has occurred in most areas of organizational life including sport. Equality generally meant "equality of opportunity" and women (along with other disadvantaged groups) were identified as target groups. In sport, equal opportunity programs were designed to increase women's overall participation by opening up opportunities for them to enjoy equal access. The shift to equity signals a more comprehensive view where the focus is no longer exclusively on women (or any other group) but on a system, in this case sport, which needs to change to accommodate them.[5] As long time Canadian sport activist Bruce Kidd puts it: "Equality focuses on creating the same starting line for everyone; equity has the goal of providing everyone with the same finish line" (CAAWS, 1993, p. 4). Another way to state this is: "An athletics program is gender equitable when the men's program would be pleased to accept as its own the overall participation, opportunities and resources currently allocated to the women's program and vice versa" (*Athletics Administration*, April 1993, p. 22). For many sport organizations this would be seen as a "radical" departure from the past.

Whether the focus is on equality or equity, the fundamental philosophy underlying both is best described as liberal reformism. Sport feminists have worked hard especially over the last decade to ensure that more sports are now more accessible to more women than ever before. They have fought for, and sometimes won, "easier access and better facilities for women in sports, improved funding and rewards, equal rights with men under the law, top quality coaching on par with men, and an equivalent voice with men in decision-making" (Hargreaves, 1994: p. 27).

While liberal approaches to sport equity often seek to provide girls and women with the same opportunities and resources as boys and men, and remove the barriers and constraints to their participation, they do not always see as problematic the fundamental nature of male-defined sport with its emphasis on hierarchy, competitiveness and aggression. Liberal feminism in sport also tends to treat women as an homogenous category, not recognizing that there are enormous differences among us in background, class, race, ethnicity, age, disability and sexual preference which lead to very different expectations and experiences of sport.

A more radical feminist approach would adopt an unequivocal women-centred perspective which recognizes and celebrates differences among women, and at the same time seriously questions male-dominated and male-defined sport. It also recognizes the centrality of issues around sexuality in women's experiences of oppression. Women involved in sport advocacy work often fail to take up issues raised by their more radical feminist counterparts outside sport, such as sexual harassment and abuse, male violence against women, lesbian visibility, and the politics of difference. In practice, radical feminists have, as Helen Lenskyj, suggests "worked towards establishing autonomous clubs and leagues that are completely outside state-controlled amateur sport systems" (Lenskyj, 1991a: p. 132). These include the many women-only clubs and leagues, some openly lesbian or lesbian-positive, which are free to modify the rules and organize their play along explicitly feminist principles of participation, recreation, fun, and friendship. Examples in Canada include the Notso Amazon Softball League in Toronto and an outdoor group in Edmonton called Women of Outdoor Pleasure. Jennifer Hargreaves, a British sport sociologist, describes a netball club called Queens of the Castle which is situated in an inner-urban area of London with a predominantly working-class and black membership. Defying the strait-laced, schoolgirl image of British netball, the Queens of the Castle have created their own sport culture by encouraging non-conformist and flamboyant playing clothes, the open discussion and negotiation of all values and practices, a truly caring ethos and support network, and opposition to all forms of racial harassment. They have become successful at attracting y oung, urban, working-class women to a sport not noted for its egalitarianism (Hargreaves, 1994, pp. 250–51).

Liberal Statements of Philosophy

In the United States, most mass-membership and national feminist organizations are officially liberal feminist, and this is certainly true of the WSF, although it did not wish to be perceived as feminist at all. Their original statement of philosophy contained several key components, stating that the WSF: (a) "encourages all women to participate in sports because sports contribute to mental, emotional and physical well-being"; (b) "recognizes that participation at all levels of sports for one's health, enjoyment and personal development is essential for girls and women as well as boys and men"; (c) "encourages all *parents* to give girls opportunities to learn skills in both team and individual sports"; (d) "encourages all *women* to seek regular sport activities for themselves to keep active and fit, as well as to bring them personal enjoyment"; and (e) "recognizes the need for female sport models."[6]

There has been no fundamental change to the WSF mission statement throughout the years except for the addition of "fitness" to their agenda because of the remarkable growth and increasing importance of the fitness industry in the 1980s. They also acknowledged that women will likely be more attracted to sport through fitness activities. The current mission statement of the WSF reads:

> The Foundation is a network providing leadership, vision, resources and financial support to create an open environment for women's growth and development through sport and fitness activities. By encouraging participation in sport and fitness, the Foundation seeks to improve the physical, mental and emotional well-being of all females.

The similar structure of the amateur sport systems in the other three countries — primarily state-funded through national sport bodies — has in large measure been responsible for the liberal path that most feminist organizing has taken. Helen Lenskyj (1991a) argues that in the Canadian case, the tightly structured and hierarchical nature of the sport system allows for limited points of entry for feminist activists. The male sport community is the most vocal exponent of sport as a political neutral activity, and the high degree of government involvement in sport (and in the women's sport advocacy groups) means that it is sometimes difficult for these groups to criticize the hand that feeds them.

In the last few years, CAAWS has drifted away from its original mission which was:

> CAAWS defines, promotes, and supports a feminist perspective to advance the position of girls and women and to improve the quality of sport and physical activity.

In its latest promotional material there is no mention of feminism, and they announce that in 1992 a new vision for the organization was created. Their mission statement now reads:

> To ensure that girls and women in sport and physical activity have access to a complcte range of opportunities and choices and have equity as participants and leaders.

The new vision includes being recognized as the leading organization for girls and women in sport and physical activity in Canada; being inclusive and equitable in its philosophies and practice; providing expert advice, positive solutions and support to Canada's communities; and to operate with efficient and effective management, and a strong base of volunteers. It is the only organization studied that explicitly states its values:

> The way we achieve change is as important as the positive change we seek. We adhere to values of equity, inclusiveness, fairness, and respect. We value the spirit of cooperation, collaboration and recognition. The right to safety and confidentiality is a belief we hold. Empowerment is central to our process.

In 1990, CAAWS was one of several national women's organizations in Canada to lose all its operational funding from the Secretary of State Women's Program, and although it had some project money from the Women's Program in Sport Canada, it was forced to down-size drastically and rely on volunteer assistance. The organization struggled to survive only to be saved a year later by an agreement to move it into the mainstream of sport by establishing an office in the Canadian Sport, Fitness and Administration Centre in Ottawa, where all national and multi-sport organizations are located, and to provide it with substantial core and project funding through Sport Canada's Women's Program.

There is an important distinction to be made here between an organization that promotes *sport for women* versus one that advocates for *women in sport*. The former denotes a more radical feminist perspective in the sense that CAAWS is a women's organization that promotes its aims through sport; the latter represents a distinctly liberal approach which seeks to improve the lot of women already in sport through a sports organization for women. As an organization, CAAWS has struggled between these two visions for its entire existence. Its current focus on gender equity, its physical presence at the Centre, its visibility and work in the Canadian Sport Council, and its willingness to work with other national sport organizations means that its path is even more decidedly liberal now than ever before.

In the United Kingdom, the UK WSF's mission as stated in a 1992 publication read:

> The aim of the WSF is to promote the interests of all women in and through sport and to gain equal opportunities and options for women.

The phrase "in and through sport" was a deliberate effort on the part of those who wrote it to make the distinction discussed above, that is between an organization that strives to change sport for the betterment of women (a women's organization) versus getting more women into the existing sport system (a sport organization). However, the most recent publicity material from the WSF UK makes it clear that they now see themselves more as a sport organization "committed to improving and promoting opportunities for women in sport at every level" through an increased awareness of issues, supporting women to become involved, encouraging sport organizations to improve access, challenging instances of inequality, and raising the visibility of British sportswomen. Therefore, the more radical vision of the original founders of the WSF UK has been replaced by a much more liberal agenda. The reasons for this are discussed in the next section on the sexual politics within these organizations.

In Australia, it may be too early to tell what the primary focus of Womensport Australia will be although judging by both its mission statement, and a statement by the two co-presidents, it will be decidedly liberal (Womensport Australia, 1993). An earlier mission statement read as follows:

> Equality of opportunity for Australian women and girls to actively participate in Sport and Physical Recreation at the levels of intensity of their choice, so there is equity in outcomes.

What is interesting about this statement is that it makes an important distinction between the more liberal strategy of "equality of opportunity" versus the more radical strategy of seeking "equality of outcome." The statement has now been shortened to "facilitate full participation and equity for women in and through physical activity" and is guided by three basic principles: women will construct their own physical activity models; women will have decision-making roles in the administration of physical activity; women will have an equitable proportion of public, community and corporate resources.

Feminist Organizing and Sexual Politics

Even though these organizations are expressly liberal feminist, there are still struggles within them around differing ideological positions. The difference has primarily been between those who proclaim a liberal approach versus those who seek a more radical feminist agenda, and for the most part, the struggle has been around sexual politics. As was pointed out earlier, women involved in sport advocacy work have often been reluctant to take up issues like sexual harassment and abuse, raised by their more radical feminist counterparts outside sport.

Sexual politics and lesbian visibility have been viewed very differently in each of the four organizations considered here. They have been virtually ignored and suppressed when necessary in the WSF despite the fact that its founder Billie Jean King has acknowledged her bisexuality and seems comfortable with gay rights (King, 1982: pp. 26-28), and tennis player Martina Navratilova, who is openly lesbian and increasingly active in gay and lesbian politics, is a member of the WSF Board of Trustees. For example, at the 1983 New Agenda Conference, co-sponsored by the Women's Sport Foundation and the US Olympic Committee, and funded by a host of corporate sponsors, organizers agreed to table a resolution that dealt openly with lesbianism when these same corporate sponsors threatened to withdraw their funding if the word "lesbian" appeared in official conference documents (Cahn, 1994: pp. 267-68; Krebs, 1984). My interviews indicate that sexuality issues have been deliberately "kept under the rug" until the late 1980s, but in the past few years the WSF is quietly undertaking a number of initiatives. For example, they now have a non-discrimination statement which includes sexual orientation:

The Women's Sports Foundation seeks to encourage diversity and equal opportunity in sports and therefore does not discriminate in any of its programs or activities on the basis of race, age, religion, color, national origin, sex, handicapping condition or sexual orientation.

They took a firm stance in 1993 against the homophobic Amendment 2 (no protected status based on homosexual, lesbian or bisexual orientation) in Colorado when they dropped the city of Denver from the potential candidates to house the WSF offices. They have also incorporated homophobia discussion panels at some of their annual conferences, and they have held homophobia workshops for their staff. Finally, they are fully supportive of an independent film-maker who is currently making a documentary film about homophobia in women's sport. In sum, their approach is certainly not pro-active; it is quiet, educative, and liberal.

CAAWS, on the other hand, has at various times in its history been embroiled in sexual politics, and the debates have been both public and well documented (see Lawrence-Harper, 1991, 1993; Lenskyj, 1991a, 1991b). Throughout its existence, CAAWS has made a serious effort to be both anti-homophobic and lesbian-positive. In the mid-1980s, resolutions were passed at various annual general meetings: "CAAWS endorses the inclusion of sexual orientation in the Canadian Human Rights Code;" "CAAWS is opposed to discrimination against lesbians in sport and physical activity, and that CAAWS undertakes to support advocacy efforts to ensure lesbian equality of rights;" and "Given that there are lesbians with CAAWS, and homophobia within CAAWS, the Association needs to address these internal concerns." However, despite these well meaning resolutions and the workshops that produced them, lesbians in CAAWS have experienced difficulty in keeping the lesbian visibility and homophobia issues on the agenda. The membership and leadership have always been split between those who see sexuality as a private and personal concern versus those who see it as a political issue. For some, the organization was perceived to have an "image problem," as expressed through letters of concern to the CAAWS newsletter, whenever the lesbians in CAAWS became too visible. For others, and certainly those taking a more radical stance, the human rights and education strategies were insufficient because they were too liberal and they depoliticized sexuality. There has been relative silence on the issue for the past few years, and to some extent the state has played a role in enforcing this silence with the 1987 directive from the Secretary of State Women's

Program (which at the time was a major source of funding for CAAWS) that it would no longer fund proposals and groups whose primary purpose was "to promote a view on sexual orientation."

The UK WSF is yet a different story of sexual politics. An early membership brochure dating from the late 1980s included statements from members, one of which read: "Lots of people think all sportswomen are lesbians. Well, some of us are. So what?" It is easy to conclude that this reflected a deliberate effort on the part of the UK WSF to be openly lesbian-positive and anti-homophobic when in fact this issue met with continued debate and resistance within the organization. Information obtained through interviews suggests that originally the UK WSF was seen as "an organization for dykes" although in reality the early membership was split on the advisability of making the organization unequivocally lesbian-positive. Those who were against such a move believed that sexuality was a private and not an organizational issue, whereas those who were pushing such a step were well versed in radical feminist politics.

Several events dramatically changed the organization. The first was that in 1990 the WSF UK was officially recognized by the British Sports Council and was eligible for government funding. Coupled with the 1988 Local Government Act which introduced Clause 28 prohibiting the promotion of homosexuality using public money, this meant that it was extremely difficult for groups like the WSF to declare openly that it supported lesbianism. Debate took place within the organization, but clearly those who argued that it was inappropriate and highly damaging for the WSF to be associated with lesbianism won the day. Then in 1992, the Tambrands corporation contributed $100,000 to sponsor the Tampax/WSF Sports Awards for Girls and Young Women the goal of which was to celebrate young women's (age 11-19) achievements in sport as well as reduce the drop-out rate of teenagers from sport. Motivated by the fear of losing funding from the Sports Council, and certainly their corporate sponsor, all public discussions about lesbian visibility have ceased, and the issue has been depoliticized. The latest membership brochure does not have a single reference to lesbian visibility.

Womensport Australia, to my knowledge, has not begun to deal with these issues at least not publicly. However, an incident occurred in early 1994 which has provoked considerable debate and controversy. A leading player with the Australian national cricket team alleged that she was dropped from the team because of sexual politics, which the governing sport body strongly denied.[7] As a heterosexual, she claimed that selections to the team were made on the basis of sexuality, not ability. She also attempted to file a complaint with the state anti-discrimination board which could not deal with her allegations under present legislation. The ensuing uproar has, as one account suggested, "given everyone an excuse to explore the sexual behaviour of women cricketers and, to a wider degree, that of women in other sports" (Wilson, 1994). The controversy has been devastating to women's cricket in Australia, and to some degree women's sport in general. Women athletes, whether they are straight or gay, have no way of effectively countering the innuendo unless they publicly declare their sexuality. The negative public reaction, especially in the media, also points out why Australian women's sport organizations have been very reticent to deal openly with lesbianism and homophobia as well as the dangers of not doing so. Like most women's sport communities, it is polarized around these difficult issues, and Womensport Australia will need to negotiate its role in the continuing debates very carefully.

Feminist Strategy: Achieving Gender Equity

Sport itself has been stubbornly resistant to feminism, liberal or otherwise, and it remains a highly conservative institution. Gender issues are mostly non-issues for the vast majority of individuals, both male and female, in mixed sport organizations. Even when women admit that many of their problems are organizationally based (e.g., unconscious discrimination, the success of male networks, women's lack of awareness of positions), they, along with men, are often opposed to the idea of a gender equity policy or program in their organization on the grounds that equal opportunity already exists.[8] Often, the only way significant change occurs is that the funding of national sport organizations through public money be tied to their commitment to equity and accessibility.

Individuals supporting or working in women's sport advocacy organizations understand these problems and find satisfaction through attempting to bring about change, although as was discussed in the previous section, there often have been disagreements over the degree and nature of this change. Regardless, each of these organizations now have liberal feminist agendas in that they are each working towards gender equity within the sports system of their respective countries. They are all focused on similar projects which are probably best articulated by the WSF in the United States — education, opportunity, recognition, and advocacy — although obviously the situations in each country do vary.

Through their *education* programs, the WSF[9] works to improve public understanding of the benefits of sports and fitness for girls and women of all ages through conferences, publications, research, public service announcements, videotapes, and an information service for the public. Foundation grants provide *opportunities* for girls and women to discover and fulfil their athletic and leadership potential. Specifically the Travel and Training Fund provides grants to aspiring athletes and teams to reach their goals, and an internship program with special emphasis on minority women provides opportunities for them to gain valuable experience and exposure to a variety of sports careers. The Foundation *advocates* changes in policies, laws and social patterns that discourage female sports participation. Events include a special day in Washington each year designed to educate the nation's leaders about the needs and achievements of girls and women in sports. Foundation staff monitor legislation, Title IX (sex discrimination) enforcement, and policies at organizations that govern sports, in addition to providing information to individuals experiencing discrimination. Finally, the Foundation *recognizes* and honours outstanding individuals for their athletic achievements and contributions to women's sports. The Community Awards and Grants program provides groups in local communities with a way to honour girls and women in all areas of sport. This program is a vehicle that brings together youth-serving groups, sports groups, coaches and administrators, business and professional leaders to promote women's sports in their area. Many of the Foundation's national awards are presented at a popular yearly gala in New York City.

In Canada, CAAWS[10] lists the following as its strategies for the 1990s:

> The movement for gender equity is not intended to dis-enfranchise men; rather it is a long overdue process to bring women to an equitable level. CAAWS' strategy for change is based on strong and vibrant partnerships.

> CAAWS works in close collaboration with Sport Canada.

> CAAWS operates in a positive "focus-on-solutions" manner.

> CAAWS takes a service intensive approach and emphasizes sport community education and consultation.

> CAAWS works toward change on many fronts, both within and outside the sport community. Because CAAWS doesn't know all the answers — we don't even know the questions — we approach change from a multi-faceted point of view in order to enhance the likelihood of success.

This is part of the "new vision" discussed earlier, and it also reflects the fact that CAAWS now sees itself as part of the Canadian sport community, and much less so as a feminist organization linked to the women's movement. For 1993-94, it lists goals in the following specific areas: gender equity and leadership, research, communication, partnership and liaison, and community initiatives. To meet these goals, CAAWS develops educational materials (e.g., *Towards Gender Equity for Women in Sport: A Handbook for National Sport Organizations*); provides consultation and hands-on support to sport organizations, designs seminars and workshops; publishes research reports (available studies include female participation rates in major games, self-esteem and sport, sexual harassment, gender equity and the law, girls on boys' teams, eating disorders and sport, pay equity and sport); publishes a regular newsletter called *Action Bulletin*; hosts the annual Breakthrough Awards honouring individuals and organizations; handles increasing media inquiries; and liaises regularly with relevant organizations and groups, as well as many other activities.

The UK WSF[11] lists the following as its objectives:

> To involve women from all walks of life and with as many varied opinions as possible in a network to facilitate the achievements of the group's aim. There will be no discrimination on any grounds whatsoever, and special consideration will be given to women who face particular difficulties.

> To serve as a source of information for this women's sporting world, with a register of all groups and individuals who take part and are interested in women's sport.

> To liaise with relevant agencies in sport for information and advice and with the appropriate commercial and public organisations for financial support and publicity.

> To develop and distribute promotional and informative literature and establish a library/research centre for women's sporting achievements and interests.

> To promote and support research into the factors which affect women's participation in sport.

> To establish a charter identifying the rights of women in sport and lobby for changes in legislation to make provision for women's needs in sport.

It works towards accomplishing these goals through developing resource materials and information packs (e.g., *Good Practice Guide to Promoting Women's Sport for Governing Bodies*); establishing and supporting regional groups and networks around the country; organizing career seminars to raise women's awareness about the range of employment opportunities in sport and recreation; press and publicity projects to increase the quality and quantity of women's sports coverage in the media; the Women Friendly Sports Centre Scheme designed to increase women's access to sport and recreation facilities; and the Tampax/WSF Awards for Girls and Young Women.

As the newest organization, and the only one which is a coalition of already established women's sport advocacy groups, Womensport Australia is in the process of working out its role and strategy.[12] The most recent (July 1994) lists its aims as follows:

> Provide a platform for women's sport and recreation groups to communicate and share their common problems and solutions.
>
> Act as a united group to inform and lobby legislators and decision makers to include sport and recreation issues on agendas at both state and federal levels.
>
> Make public comment about issues facing women in sport and recreation.
>
> Provide support to members in their actions to address inequitable practices.

The implementation strategies it plans to use at the national level are to lobby for equal representation on the Australian Sports Commission Board, to support member organizations developing gender equity plans, and to continue to promote physical activity as an item for discussion on the feminist agenda. At the local or state level, it wants to compile a resource directory of women's sport and recreation boards and committees, continue information sharing and networking, and support member initiatives and activities.

Structural Components: The Need to Rationalize

Throughout their organizational life, women's sport advocacy groups have undergone changes similar to most sport organizations in Western countries. Organizations that once showed low levels of specialization, little in the way of formalized operating procedures, and consensual decision-making with control by volunteers now show high levels of specialization and formalization with most decision-making in the hands of professionals (Hall *et al.*, 1991). The "kitchen table administration" of earlier days has now been replaced by a more corporate style of management if the organization is funded primarily by the private sector, or a professional bureaucracy if funded by the state. In some cases, organizations now exhibit high levels of bureaucratization where control of the organization is decentralized to the level of the professional staff, not the volunteer board as has traditionally been the situation in amateur sport organizations. Not all amateur sport organizations have adopted this design, and some have openly resisted it, but those which are funded by the state, including women sport advocacy organizations, have had little choice but to rationalize their structure and operations.

The largest and most rationalized organization is the WSF in the United States. The day-to-day operations of the WSF are run by a professional staff of about ten including an Executive Director, Communications and Advocacy Director, Special Projects Director, and so forth. Governance of the Foundation is by a volunteer Board of Trustees who are leaders in women's sports. They include athletes, coaches, administrators, business people, academics and others who support women's sports. The Board usually comprises about 25 individuals who choose and elect their members, and who each contribute $1,000 in dues. A 200-member Board of Advisors provides expertise in areas such as sports psychology, sociology of sport, administration, marketing, exercise physiology, sports medicine, and others. The Board is divided into four councils: coaches, athletes, organizations, and public at large. Members include anyone with an interest in women's sports. A donation of $25.00 or more automatically makes the donor a voting member of the Foundation (there are now over 2,500). In addition, subscribers to *Women's Sports and Fitness* magazine, approximately 200,000, are associate members of the Foundation. The collective membership of all organizations represented on the Advisory Board, such as the LPGA, National Softball Coaches Association, Girl Scouts of America, totals over 50 million.

The other three organizations are very small in comparison, not so rationalized, and do not have nearly the same resources (see next section) to hire staff, nor can they draw on the same membership base. CAAWS is governed by an elected Board of Directors comprised of about ten individuals who represent the various provinces or regions of Canada. The geographical size of Canada makes it expensive for the Board to meet in one place so that a smaller Executive

Committee really runs the organization in conjunction with the paid Executive Director who, along with one or two staff, is situated in an office in Ottawa. Membership in the organization has been small at the best of times (around 200) and at present there is no membership fee — one simply gets on a mailing list which now comprises some 2,500 individuals and groups.

Both the WSF UK and Womensport Australia are governed and run in a similar fashion. The WSF UK is managed by an elected Executive Committee comprised of officer positions and regional representatives. Membership is open to any individual and group willing to pay the membership fees. Womensport Australia, because it is a national umbrella organization for other women's sport advocacy groups, is governed by an Executive Committee with consultation among representatives from state organizations, although it is still working out its relationship to the other state organizations and vice versa. Womensport Australia is able to hire a part-time Executive officer and has recently moved its national office from Adelaide to Canberra in order to improve relations with the Australian Sports Commission's Women and Sport Unit and the Office of the Status of Women.

Within their internal structures, these organizations have not paid much attention to feminist process and tools which have certainly been issues in other women's groups. By 'feminist process' what is usually meant is a more caring and nurturing environment involving consensus decision-making, rotating leadership positions, and particular tools used during meetings such as time keepers, vibes watchers, note takers, and the like. For a specific period, between 1987 and 1989, the CAAWS Board of Directors experimented with these processes and others in an attempt to make themselves more cognizant and aware of their feminist roots. However, like most groups, they discovered that these efforts took considerable time and demanded commitment, and as well they were often resisted by those who were more task oriented and wished "to get some work done" (Lawrence-Harper, 1993: pp. 77-78). Consequently, and also as a result of increased pressure from their funding sources to become more professionalised, they abandoned their attempts to utilize specific feminist processes. Similarly, the WSF UK, in the very early stages, made some attempt to engage feminist processes specifically at meetings where co-chairs were the norm and a conscious attempt was made to involved everyone in attendance. However, like CAAWS, it found that this took a good deal of time, effort, and commitment on the part of the participants.

External Relations: Corporate versus State Sponsorship

The four organizations vary considerably with regard to their external environment, and more specifically their resource dependence. Interest group organizations like these have really only two choices when it comes to resources — the private sector or the state —and some are able to seek funding from both sources. In the example here, two of the organizations represent the extremes of the continuum with the other two somewhere in between. In the United States where sport is funded entirely by the private sector, so too is the WSF, whereas in Canada where the state plays a much larger role in the funding of sport, CAAWS is almost entirely dependent on government monies. The situation in Britain and Australia is more mixed.

The WSF in the United States was established as a charitable, non-profit organization which from the beginning raised funds through the private sector, either in the form of memberships, donations, sale of products, or grants from foundations and corporations. As early as 1979, it produced a quarterly corporate newsletter called *Business and Women's Sports* which provided information on the interrelationship between women's sports and business. The contributions of the earliest sponsors of women's sport (e.g., Colgate, Philip Morris, Avon, Bonne Bell, American Athletic Division, Kodak, and Coca Cola) were lauded, and at the same time, it provided ideas on how corporations could become involved with women's sports such as sponsoring teams and events, awards and scholarship programs, film documentaries, product endorsements, and the like. Through their corporate newsletter, the WSF argued that "perceptive business people know that the dramatic growth of women's sports means big business," and that both advertising and promotional targets may best be met through an identity with women's sports.

The WSF's relationship with the corporate sector has not changed over the past twenty years except that the stakes are higher now and there is much more money involved. Today, WSF funding is approximately 90 percent corporate based (total revenue in 1991 was $1.3 million), and although it has numerous corporate benefactors, its two major sponsors are Sudafed and Reebok. In fact, in 1993, when it took Reebok on board, it was in the position of making a choice between two athletic shoe giants — Nike and Reebok. It chose Reebok because of its identification with fitness and the ordinary athlete as compared to the superstar image of Nike. Nonetheless, it would like to increase its individual benefactors with less reliance on the corporate sector.

Another example of the WSF's willingness to seek corporate friends is how it came to be located in a huge, rambling, tudor style mansion which sits in the middle of 940 acres of beautiful parkland in Nassau County on Long Island, New York. When the rent for their executive offices became too prohibited in downtown Manhattan, they decided to relocate by putting out a call for proposals from all over the United States. Ten cities made formal bids and they narrowed the list to five, one of which was Colorado Springs which they dropped following the passage of anti-gay legislation in Colorado. In the end, it came down to a bidding war between Dallas in Texas and the Nassau County Sports Commission with the latter offering rent-free space for 20 years, free office equipment, and free architectural planning and construction of the long awaited International Women's Sports Hall of Fame.

The WSF has zealously sought to protect the name "Women's Sports Foundation." Now that other countries are establishing similar organizations sometimes with almost identical names, the WSF is seeking to prevent this from happening unless certain conditions are met. For example, it has made an agreement with the Women's Sports Foundation Japan to allow it to use its logo and name for a nominal consideration on the condition they continue to promote and encourage the development and participation of women in sport and fitness.[13] It has recently advised the WSF UK that a similar arrangement should be made otherwise it may seek a legal remedy. Whether or not the WSF has the legal right to do this is one matter, but it is also doubtful whether or not they can control the use of their name given the increasing proliferation of women's sport advocacy groups around the world.

For the first couple of years of its existence, the WSF UK was totally self-financed drawing on memberships, fees for services, and t-shirt sales which obviously produced minimal income. From 1987 to 1991, it set up an office in the London Women's Centre with support from the London and South East Region of the Sports Council and the London Borough Grants Unit which enabled it to at least provide services for women in the London area. With funding uncertain from year to year, it applied for and received recognition from the Sports Council in 1990. Although this has benefitted the WSF with funding for a National Development Worker (the present one is funded through to 1996), it has not provided the necessary core funding for the organization to become financially stable. This has been a problem in the past, and it will certainly be one in the future. As for support from the private or corporate sector, in 1992 the Tambrands corporation sponsored the Tampax/WSF Sports Awards for Girls and Young Women. The scheme, which amounted to £50,000 a year, unfortunately lasted only two years and for marketing reasons was not renewed. The report of the first year of the current national development project makes very little mention of how the WSF UK intends to expand its resource base (Women's Sport Foundation, 1994) beyond its present reliance on the Sports Council, although I do know that they are seeking another corporate sponsor.

Funding for Womensport Australia comes from the Office of the Status of Women through the National Agenda for Women Grants Program. It initially provided a small projects grant ($10,000) in 1991 which allowed for representatives from various state organizations to meet and form the new organization. Since then, it has provided a yearly grant ($40,000) to allow Womensport Australia to establish a national office (now located in Canberra) and to hire a part-time Executive Officer. With the move to Canberra, they are now able to work more closely with the Office of the Status of Women, and more importantly, with the Women and Sport Unit o f the Australian Sports Commission. Womensport Australia has not yet been in a position to seek sponsorship from the corporate sector; however, in conjunction with the government's Women and Sport Unit, they are helping to conduct and facilitate marketing seminars which help women to market and "package" their sport more professionally to attract media interest and sponsors (Womensport Australia, 1994). What is interesting about the situation in Australia is that because some of the groups which comprise Womensport Australia are considerably older and more established, they have access to much more funding. For example, in 1992/93 the Women's Sport Foundation of Western Australia had an income of over $400,000 about half of which came from government sources (Annual Report, 1993). This has enabled them to hire staff, expand their programs into the far-flung regions of Western Australia, and to undertake several new initiatives such as the "Links to Leadership" courses designed to assist girls and young women in realizing their leadership potential. It remains to be seen just how Womensport Australia will be able to acquire the equivalent potential in resources.

In Canada, throughout CAAWS' existence it has been entirely dependent on government sources for its funding aside from a very small amount of income from members' fees and the sale of publications.[14] In fact, government funding was critical to its formation in 1981 when Sport Canada's Women's Program initiated and partially funded the workshop out of which CAAWS was born. From 1982 until 1985, it continued to receive project monies from the Women's Program even though concern was expressed by some in the leadership of CAAWS that it was becoming increasingly difficult to criticize Sport Canada without losing its major source of funding. In 1984, CAAWS applied for and was successful in securing core or operational funding from the Secretary of State Women's Program, the federal government department whose responsibility it is to promote the organizational development of women's groups in order to increase their effectiveness in working towards equality of women. Along with project money from both Sport Canada and Fitness Canada, CAAWS' annual budget had grown to $120,000 by 1990 despite warnings from some that it was becoming too reliant on the state for funding. The money from the Secretary of State did not come without strings — the organization was required to establish a national office, incorporate itself, increase it regional representation, and justify the need for an executive director, all of which it attempted to do.

Disaster struck in 1990 when CAAWS lost all its funding from the Secretary of State Women's Program primarily because the Program itself had suffered substantial budget cuts and had to make hard decisions as to which groups would continue to receive funding. In CAAWS' case, they maintained that the organization had failed to comply with funding regulations and that it was not sensitive enough to issues of difference. CAAWS was forced to downsize drastically and rely again on volunteer assistance. The organization struggled to survive only to be saved a year later by an agreement to move it into the mainstream of sport by establishing an office in the Canadian Sport, Fitness and Administration Centre in Ottawa, where all national and multi-sport organizations are located, and to provide it with substantial core and project funding (over $250,000) through Sport Canada's Women's Program. The situation is much the same today although CAAWS never knows from one year to the next whether or not it will receive funding. The federal government is re-examining its financial commitment to all its social programs including sport, and CAAWS is certainly a vulnerable organization.

Conclusion: Politicizing Women's Sport (and Women in Sport)

Sportswomen have generally been resistant to taking an overtly political stance on women's issues and on issues of discrimination. As Jennifer Hargreaves suggests, the politicization of women's sports is unusual because sportswomen tend to see sports in an insular way and often claim there is no connection between participation and politics (Hargreaves, 1994, p. 254). Nor have the politics and practice of feminism been recognized as particularly important nor relevant. By politics we both mean the struggle to define and control women's sport: its meanings and values, the structures required, and the debates over policy. Feminist practice in sport, when it does occur, varies between liberal reformism to a more controversial radicalism thus producing the inevitable tensions between the two approaches. Where governments have made women's sport a priority, their programs and policies have been overwhelmingly liberal but with a welcome shift from a focus on equality to equity over the past decade. When women's sport advocacy groups, such as the organizations studied here, become more dependent for funding on either the state or the private sector, they focus more on a liberal gender equity framework for change and are less willing, often resistant, to engage in radical cultural politics. This effectively depoliticizes the issues surrounding women in sport (homophobia is a good example), and makes it difficult for those interested in pursuing more radically defined issues and change to be effective. Male-defined sport can be, and often is, challenged and resisted but primarily at the local level far removed from state-controlled amateur sport systems.

There is a very long road ahead before any form of radical cultural politics is recognized as being both viable and necessary to future change in women's sport. As I was finishing this chapter, I attended an international conference on women's sport organized by the British Sports Council and supported by the International Olympic Committee. At the conference were some 300 delegates from over 85 countries representing governmental and non-governmental organizations, national Olympic Committees, international and national sport federations, and educational and research institutions. The conference specifically addressed the issue of "how to accelerate the process of change that would redress the imbalances women face in their participation and involvement in sport," and it approved a declaration with the overriding aim "to develop a sporting culture that enables and values full involvement of women in every aspect of sport" (The Brighton Declaration on Women and Sport, 1994). Thematic workshops addressed the continuing problems that plague women's sport: the lack of women in sports administration, development of women coaches, and gender bias in physical education and research. Issue seminars focused on the usual topics: equal opportunity legislation, integration versus separation, cross-cultural differences, challenging sexism, marketing strategies, working in a male environment, and admittedly a few more controversial topics such as women's sport in Muslim cultures, sexual harassment, homophobia, and integrating women athletes with disabilities. Skills seminars provided information on mentoring, networking, advocacy and lobbying, community sports leadership, dealing with the media, and gender awareness training. Delegates agreed to establish and develop an International Women in Sport Strategy which they hope will be endorsed and supported by governmental and non-governmental organizations involved in sport development on all continents, and enable model programmes and successful developments to be shared among nations and sporting federations. There was general agreement that strong, international women and sport networks are needed for mutual support, for exchanging knowledge, skills and "good practice," and for sharing resources.

A new organization, Womensport International, was also announced at the conference. It aspires to be an umbrella group which will seek positive change for girls and women in sport and physical activity by facilitating global networking and communication. Given the fact that the founders of Womensport International wish the organization to be global in scope and outlook, and to connect a vast array of differing cultures, it is no wonder that notions of politicization and radical cultural struggle are absent from its vision. However, it must take on board this more radical perspective or become just like every other women's sport advocacy association, some of which have made significant gains in bringing more girls and women into sport, but sport itself remains as male-dominated and as male-defined as always. This is not necessarily meaningful progress.

Acknowledgements

I am grateful to the University of Alberta for research monies for this project through its Support for the Advancement of Scholarship Fund. My colleague Trevor Slack, and graduate students Brenda Grace and Janis Lawrence-Harper assisted with the collection of data and information. I also wish to thank the many women in each organization who patiently and willingly took the time to answer my questions and to provide supporting documentation.

Notes

1. There are some who would question the veracity of this statement given the women's sport governing bodies in the United States such as the National Section on Women's Athletics (NSWA) of the American Physical Education Association which was formed in 1932. In 1957 it became the Division for Girls' and Women's Sport (DGWS) of the American Alliance for Health, Physical Education and Recreation. There was also the Association for Intercollegiate Athletics for Women (AIAW) which began in 1972 as a division of AAHPER and in 1979 became an autonomous governing body for women's intercollegiate sport until it ceased to exist in 1984 since women's programs are now controlled by the former men's organization, the NCAA. Also, established prior to many of these organizations is the International Association of Physical Education and Sports for Girls and Women. Founded in 1952 primarily through the efforts of the American physical educator Dorothy Ainsworth, the IAPESGW continues to be recognized throughout the world as an organization that brings together women of many different countries working in the field of physical education and sport. However, I argue that all of these organizations were founded prior to the modern women's movement, in most cases were *sport* governing bodies, and have never defined themselves as feminist in any way.

2. There are of course other national women's sport advocacy organizations. For example, the Women's Sports Foundation Japan was founded in 1981. I have been able to obtain some materials from this group such as newsletters and newspaper articles, all of which are in Japanese, and although I have had them translated, they provide only a minimal amount of information pertaining to the organization itself. There is also the Women's Sport and Fitness Foundation of Malaysia about which I know very little. At an international women and sport conference in England in May 1994, a new organization, the Association for African Women in Sport, was formed. There are also several well established "women's committees" which are affiliated with national sports bodies, and which function very much as women's sport advocacy groups. For example, the Women's Committee of the Norwegian Confederation of Sports (founded in 1985) has published

two informative booklets in English which outline the history, objectives, and work of the committee (Norwegian Confederation of Sports, 1990, 1994). There is also a similar group in Germany, called the Federal Committee for Women in Sport, which is one of seven committees in the German Sports Confederation. Finally, there is the Women and Sport Working Group of the European Sports Council (see Fasting, 1993).

3   Janis Lawrence-Harper developed this framework for her thesis. For more detail, see Lawrence-Harper (1993).

4   See Hall and Richardson (1982), especially pp. 84-97 for a summary of these initiatives.

5   For a more thorough discussion of these issues, see Hargreaves (1994): pp. 237-42; and the Sports Council (1993).

6   These statements have been summarized from a one-page sheet entitled "Women's Sports Foundation Philosophy" which was undated but found in the archives at the WSF marked 1974.

7   I am grateful to Jim McKay, a sport sociologist in Australia, for sending me numerous newspaper accounts of this controversy.

8   These claims have now been substantiated by considerable cross-cultural research. See, for example, Fasting (1987); Hall, Slack and Cullen (1990); Knoppers (1992); McKay (1992); Whitson and Macintosh (1989).

9   This material has been summarized from a recent Women's Sports Foundation *Fact Sheet*.

10   This material has been summarized from an undated CAAWS document entitled *CAAWS: A Quick Tour* which I received in May 1994.

11   The information here has been collated from several WSF UK documents including *Networking for Women's Sport* (1992), the latest membership brochure, and *The National Development Project Year One Report* (1994).

12   The information for this section has been gleaned from the latest newsletters of Womensport Australia as well as personal communication with some of the key players in the organization.

13   I know this because I have seen correspondence (dated March 1994) to this effect between the WSF and the WSF in the United Kingdom.

14   The detailed budget information provided by Forbes (1993) was very helpful here.

References

Briskin, L. (1991) 'Feminist practice: A new approach to evaluating feminist strategy', in J. Wine and J. Ristock (eds) *Women and social change: Feminist activism in Canada.* Toronto: James Lorimer, pp. 24–40.

Brighton Declaration on Women and Sport. (1994) Women, Sport and the Challenge of Change International Conference, Brighton, England, May 5–8.

Cahn, S. (1994) *Coming on strong: Gender and sexuality in twentieth-century women's sport.* New York: The Free Press.

Canadian Association for the Advancement of Women and Sport and Physical Activity (1993) *Towards gender equity for women in sport: A handbook for national sport organizations.* Gloucester, ON: CAAWS.

Fasting, K. (1987) 'The promotion of women's involvement in Norwegian sports organizations', in T. Slack and C.R. Hinings (eds) *The organization and administration of sport.* London: Sports Dynamics Publishers, pp. 83–99.

Fasting, K. (1993) *Women and sport: Monitoring progress towards equality: A European survey.* Oslo: Women's Committee, Norwegian Confederation of Sports.

Forbes, S.L. (1993) *Government and interest group relations: An Analysis of the Canadian Association for the Advancement of Women and Sport.* Unpublished master's thesis. Wilfred Laurier University, Waterloo, Ontario.

Hall, A., Slack, T., Smith, G., and Whitson, D. (1991) *Sport in Canadian society.* Toronto: McClelland and Stewart.

Hall, M.A. (in press) 'Women and sport: From liberal activism to radical cultural struggle', in L. Code and S. Burt (eds) *Changing methods: Feminists reflect on practice.* Toronto: Broadview Press.

Hall, M.A., Slack, T and Cullen, D. (1990) *The gender structure of National Sport Organizations. Sport Canada Occasional Papers,* 2, No.1.

Halpert, F.E. (1989) 'Fifteen years of the Women's Sports Foundation', *Headway* (Fall): pp. 6–9.

Hargreaves, J. (1994) *Sporting females: Critical issues in the history and sociology of women's sport.* London and New York: Routledge.

Kimberly, J.R. (1987) 'The study of organization: Toward a biographical perspective', in J.W. Lorsch (ed) *Handbook of organizational behaviour.* Englewood Cliffs, NJ: Prentice-Hall, pp. 223–237.

King, B.J. (1982) *Billie Jean* (with Frank Deford). New York: The Viking Press.

Knoppers, A. (1992) 'Explaining male dominance and sex segregation incoaching: Three approaches', *Quest, No. 44*: pp. 210–227.

Krebs, P. (1984) 'At the starting blocks: Women athletes' new agenda', *Off Our Backs*:Vol. 14, No. 1: pp. 1–4.

Lawrence-Harper, J. (1991) *The herstory of the Canadian Association for the Advancement of Women and Sport*. Report prepared for CAAWS, November.

Lawrence-Harper, J. (1993) *Change in a feminist organization: The Canadian Association for the Advancement of Women and Sport and Physical Activity 1981–1991*. Unpublished master's thesis. University of Alberta, Edmonton, Alberta.

Lenskyj, H. (1991a) 'Good sports: Feminists organizing on sport issues in the 1970s and 1980s', *Resources for Feminist Research/Documentation sur la recherche féministe, 20*(3/4), pp. 130–135.

Lenskyj, H. (1991b) 'Combatting homophobia in sport and physical education', *Sociology of Sport Journal* Vol. 8, No. 1: pp. 61–69.

Martin, P.Y. (1990) 'Rethinking feminist organizations', *Gender and society* Vol. 4, No. 2: pp. 182–206.

McKay, J. (1992) *Why so few? Women executives in Australian sport*. Report prepared for the Australian Sports Commission, December.

Norwegian Confederation of Sports. (1990) *Women in sport*. Women's Committee Program 1985–90.

Norwegian Confederation of Sports. (1994) *Developing equity for women in the Norwegian Conferation of Sports*. Women's Committee.

Popma, A. (ed.) (1980) *The female athlete: Proceedings of a national conference about women in sports and recreation*. Burnaby: Simon Fraser University.

Scott-Pawson, S. (1991) *The Canadian Association for the Advancement of Women and Sport (1981–1991): An organizational case analysis of a feminist organization*. Unpublished master's thesis. Queen's University, Kingston, Ontario.

Sports Council (1993) *Women and sport: Policy and frameworks for action*. London: The Sports Council.

Theberge, N. (1983) 'Feminism and sport: Linking the two through a new organization', *Canadian Woman Studies/les cahiers de la femme* Vol. 4, No. 3: pp. 79–81.

Vickers, J. (1992) 'The intellectual origins of the women's movement in Canada', in C. Backhouse and D.H. Flaherty (eds) *Challenging times: The women's movement in Canada and the United States*. Montreal and Kingston: McGill-Queen's University Press, pp. 39–60.

White, A., and Brackenridge, C. (1985) 'Who rules sport? Gender divisions in the power structure of British sports organizations', *International Review for the Sociology of Sport*, 20: pp. 96–107.

Whitson, D., and Macintosh, D. (1989) 'Gender and power: Explanations of gender inequalities in Canadian national sport organizations', *International Review for the Sociology of Sport* 24: pp. 132–150.

Wilson, C. (1994) 'Cricket's battle of the sexes', *Sunday Age*, Melbourne, Victoria (January 23): p. 13.

Women's Sport Foundation of Western Australia (Inc.) (1993) *Annual Report.*

Women's Sports Foundation (1994) *The National Development Project Year One Report.* London: The Women's Sports Foundation, February.

Womensport Australia (1993) *Newsletter*, August.

Womensport Australia (1994) *Newsletter*, July.

SUBJECT INDEX

AUTHOR INDEX

This is a listing of authors cited or referenced within the main body of the contributions to the volume. It excludes authors cited only in footnotes and authors listed in references but not cited.